A brief guide TO ideaS

ZONDERVAN™

GRAND RAPIDS, MICHIGAN 49530 USA

A Brief Guide to Ideas
Text copyright © 1997 by William Raeper and Linda Smith

Original edition published in English under the title *A Brief Guide to Ideas* by
Lion Publishing plc, Oxford, England. Copyright © Lion Publishing plc 1997.

Requests for information should be addressed to:

ZONDERVAN™

Grand Rapids, Michigan 49530

Library of Congress Cataloging-in-Publication Data

Raeper, William, 1959 –
    A brief guide to ideas / William Raeper & Linda Edwards.
        p. cm.
    Includes bibliographical references and index.
    ISBN: 0-310-22774-7 (pbk.)
    1. Philosophy — History. I. Edwards, Linda. II. Title.
B72.R34 2000
190-dc21   99–055144
                                           CIP

Printed in the United States of America

99 00 01 02 03 04 05 06 / ❖ DC / 10 9 8 7 6 5 4 3 2 1

To Phil Edwards and Quality
Linda Edwards

To the music line students on the island of Stord,
whose philosophy of life has been deeply influential.
William Raeper

Linda Edwards would like to thank Peter Manning,
South Hampstead High School, for his considerable help
in bringing order to the chaos of Post-Modernity, and
Dr. Andrew Wright, King's College, London, for casting
his philosophical mind over the revised draft text.

William Raeper would like to thank
Robin Cranmer for a couple of useful suggestions and
Sigrid-Johanne Dahl for her hospitality.

Publisher's Preface

Students study philosophy for a variety of reasons: to prepare for the vicissitudes of life; because it's a required course; to skip third-hour gym class. Teachers are challenged to communicate the richness, meaning, and depth of philosophy in light of all these different motivations.

A Brief Guide to Ideas will appeal to any level of student participation. As its title says, the book is meant to be a concise treatment of the thinking that has helped shape society through the centuries. It is a kind of tour book, describing the milestones in the history of human thought along life's road. As such, it is the perfect supplemental text for any philosophy class.

Writing Style

Readers of the book will appreciate its clarity and accessibility. It does not become entrenched in philosophical jargon or technical discourse. The tone is conversational while avoiding forced or frivolous language.

Organization

The book is divided into sixteen relevant, practical, and progressive themes, each one grouping philosophies together to succinctly compare and contrast them. The three chapters under each heading consist of only a few pages each, thereby further contributing to the book's approachable writing style.

Study Questions

So as not to impede the flow of the content, study questions for each chapter are located in an appendix at the end of the book (see pages 367 – 81). These questions are designed to help students absorb what they've just read and put the concepts into their own thinking and words. Teachers can use these questions for quizzes, in-class discussions, or homework assignments.

Glossary

A glossary of philosophical terms is included to help students grasp or reinforce the main ideas of the more than forty philosophers presented (see pages 383 – 87). Teachers may want to use this glossary as the basis for vocabulary tests or other quizzes.

Index

Nearly four hundred key people, movements, and terms are alphabetically indexed to their page numbers, assisting both the student and teacher in quickly locating important philosophical viewpoints.

Goals

A Brief Guide to Ideas not only teaches how to think; it shows how to live. Its purpose is to be a starting-point in discovering life's thoughtful considerations.

Contents

Introduction

You might be wondering what philosophy is all about. Surely it is only for high-flying intellectuals who spend hours thinking?

Philosophy is not just about how to think; it is about how to live. Philosophy takes a closer look at the ideas behind how we live our lives. What we think is true affects our view of ourselves and how we treat other people and the world.

Each of us has a mixture of ideas in our heads about ourselves and the world. These ideas have come from somewhere. This book takes a look at different ideas – from different times, different people and different places. We have tried to show you why these ideas were thought of at all and what their importance is. In this way you can see yourself and your own ideas against a background and a history – as part of a whole history of philosophy which is still being written every time we think about something.

This book is being written primarily for the Western scene. We have therefore chosen to look at Christianity and Western philosophy, both of which have influenced and shaped Western society. Our book takes no account of Eastern philosophy or non-Christian religions. But even if you are a believer in another religion or of no religion at all, this study should be of use to you. Because if you live in the West, the ideas embedded in society have grown out of a 'Western' way of thinking.

Some of this thinking you may find difficult. It is. But we think it is worth the effort. Ideas are very important. Behind conversations, media, television, political opinions and educational policy there are often whole philosophies which go unnoticed because people have never learned to think about things in this way. If your mind can learn to travel over different territories of thought, it will be a source of interest and challenge to you all your life. And in the midst of so many opinions, beliefs, values and changes in our society today, you may be able to learn to recognize what is really being said – where the ideas come from and where they lead to. We hope the exercise of thinking philosophically and religiously will give you more choice in how to think about things.

Given the space and scope of the book we have not been able to cover all the important ideas in Western philosophy. For instance, there was no space to study Spinoza.

We hope this book will be of use. The big questions about life and meaning and reality and God are still being asked, and perhaps more than ever we need the capacity to think, and decide on what basis our lives should be lived.

Linda Edwards
William Raeper

PART 1

How and What Can We Know?

EPISTEMOLOGY

Knowledge and Reason

Plato and the Ancient Greeks

Philosophy is about ideas – ideas about the world, ideas about people and ideas about how to live. The common picture of a philosopher is of someone locked away with a pile of books, removed from everyday life. But philosophy is about everyday life. Philosophy and the Jewish-Christian tradition are at the foundations of Western culture and civilization. All of us carry ideas around which stem from the men and women who, throughout the centuries, have helped form the way we think. But what is philosophy, and how can it possibly matter to me? Many of us believe we are too 'practical' or 'commonsensical' to bother with ideas – but that is a philosophy in itself!

Two terms run through this book: 'philosophy', meaning 'love of wisdom'; and 'theology', meaning 'talking about God'.

Wisdom is a kind of knowledge. Philosophy is generally concerned with how we know things and what we can know. Philosophy asks questions such as:

* Is there a point to the universe?

* How should we live?

* Is there an order behind nature?

* Is there a morality for everyone or does morality change at different times and in different places?

Philosophical knowledge is not scientific knowledge. In fact, many modern philosophers would claim that philosophy is a skill, a way of thinking about the world. Philosophy is not 'what you know', but 'how you think'. The point of philosophy is to frame the right questions, not to find the right answers.

At school, students may move from classroom to classroom at the end of each lesson. They may study geography, history, maths and English. In any school timetable, the knowledge to be learned is divided up into different subjects. This was not always the case. When the Ancient Greeks began to think about the world they lived in, they called their search for knowledge 'philosophy'. The history of knowledge, then, is like a tree with one trunk and many branches.

Philosophy itself has divided into the areas of ethics, political philosophy, metaphysics, philosophy of religion, logic and language.

At university students of philosophy will find that the central part of their study is concerned with the nature and limits of human knowledge. This study, named after the Greek word for 'knowledge', *episteme*, is called 'epistemology'. Epistemology is at the very root of philosophy.

The beginning of Western philosophy

Western philosophy began 2,500 years ago in Ancient Greece at the beginning of the sixth century BC. The Ancient Greeks have had an incalculable influence on Western civilization and on how we think about the world.

The Greeks invented mathematics, science and philosophy. They were the first people to set down proper history and they thought about the world in an open-minded way, free from set ideas given by any religion. Their own religion, with its variety of human-like gods, had little to do with serious speculation about the universe. Alongside philosophy, the Greeks produced great literature with Homer's *Iliad* and *Odyssey*, great drama with the tragedies of Sophocles, Euripides and Aeschylus, and great architecture, the ruins of which still stand today.

Greece itself was divided into warring city states, among the most important of which were Athens and Sparta. These city states had differing forms of government: some were democracies, some were ruled by an aristocracy, and some were subject to a tyrant.

The Greeks stand at the very beginning of our search for knowledge about the world. How they thought still influences how we think. To some extent their questions are still our questions.

The earliest philosopher we know of from the sixth century BC is Thales. Thales believed that everything in the world was composed of water. Water heated becomes steam and is responsible for all the gases in the world. Water, a liquid, is responsible for everything that flows in the world. Water freezes to ice, which is solid, and is responsible for everything solid in the world.

Thales, therefore, accounted for the gaseous, liquid and solid characteristics of the earth. But why?

Philosophy began as a mixture of scientific, theological, magical and ethical questions about the world or 'cosmos'. The word 'cosmos', identified with the universe, means 'right (or good) order'. The earliest philosophers wanted to discover an ordered explanation for how the world was as it was. They wanted to find universal principles which would explain the whole of nature. In one sense, they were asking scientific questions. The thought of these early philosophers survives only in fragments or embedded in later writers' work.

The early Greek philosophers were obsessed with the problem of the One and the Many. They saw that the world, as it appears to our senses, is full of a variety of changing things. If everything is changing all the time, how is it then possible to find an underlying coherent order in the world? Finding such an order meant finding certain knowledge about the world, and that is why these philosophers sought it so eagerly. They wanted to discover a permanent reality behind the changing appearances of the physical world. For this reason, Thales claimed that the entire world was made out of one substance, water, just as Heraclitus (another early philosopher) believed that the basic matter of the universe was fire. The Greeks had very quickly identified the four elements of water, fire, earth and air.

Some important early Greek philosophers are:

HERACLITUS who believed that everything altered and changed all the time. He believed that the world was in flux, perpetually changing. It was impossible to step into the same river twice. The only permanent feature of the world was the fact that everything changed.

PARMENIDES who took the opposite view to Heraclitus. Parmenides argued that if the world was formed from some unchanging substance, then change was impossible. As a result, Parmenides denied time, variety and motion. The permanent element in the world could not be made of matter (which would change). The most that could be said about this basic matter was that it existed. The only truth that could be discovered about permanence, therefore, is that it is.

DEMOCRITUS who believed that the world was made out of single, indivisible units called 'atoms' (meaning 'that which has no part'). Each atom has a form and shape which cannot change, but these atoms are constantly moving and rearranging themselves. Democritus, therefore, advanced a clever theory which took into account both the changing and permanent aspects of the universe.

These early Greek philosophers are referred to as the 'Pre-Socratics' as they were born before Socrates. Socrates rebelled consciously against these philosophers and changed the nature of philosophy as it had been conducted up to that point.

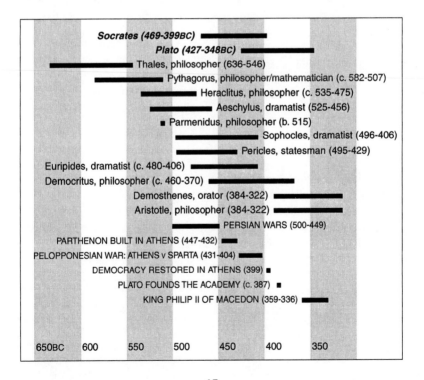

Socrates

Socrates (c. 469-399BC) was born and lived in Athens. Most of what we know about him comes from the writings of his brilliant pupil Plato (c. 427-348BC) who was the first Greek philosopher to leave writings of his own. Plato's writings are among the most important ever written and take the form of dialogues (like plays), usually with Socrates as the main character and philosopher.

In various dialogues, Plato, through the mouth of Socrates, tries to construct a theory of knowledge which covered:

* What knowledge was available.

* How we could obtain knowledge.

* Why this knowledge is true.

Socrates' driving force was truth. How much the Socrates we have in the dialogues is an invention of Plato is an open question. Underlying Plato's brilliant literary creation, however, there is undoubtedly a basis of historical truth.

Socrates' questions were ethical and not scientific. He did not speculate about the nature of the world, but about how human beings should live. This approach changed the direction of philosophy. In the *Apology* he states: 'God orders me to fulfil the philosopher's mission of searching into myself and other men'; and again, 'I have nothing to do with physical speculations'. Early Platonic dialogues (reckoned by scholars to be the closest to Socrates' actual teaching) are concerned with definitions of ethical terms. For example, the *Charmides* is concerned with temperance or moderation, the *Lysis* with friendship, and the *Laches* with courage.

Socrates is presented by Plato as the archetypal wise man. He is sharp and humorous. Socrates himself, however, constantly states that he is wiser than others only because he knows that he knows nothing. What is most important for him is the search for truth. Seeking, rather than finding, is the mark of the true philosopher, and Socrates' view has influenced philosophy throughout the ages.

Socrates also believed that if a person knew the right thing, then he or she would do it. Knowledge, therefore, is closely connected with goodness; evil is connected with ignorance. The connection between knowledge and goodness is characteristic of both Socrates and Plato. As Socrates said: 'No one does wrong willingly'.

Socrates was deeply concerned with the difference between opinion (what I *think* is correct) and certain knowledge (what I *know* is correct).

The method he used in his search was called *elenchos* or scrutiny. Socrates applied this method to practical decisions about how to live. So it was that Socrates came to have a profound influence on how philosophy was done: by 'enquiry', asking the right questions without necessarily believing that you will find the right answers; and by 'dialectic', the question and answer method used by Socrates as presented in Plato's dialogues. The importance of this method is that the questions lead to more questions and not to answers. For Socrates right thinking is more important than right conclusions.

In 399BC, after the restoration of democracy in Athens, Socrates was tried on a charge of disbelief in the gods and corrupting the young. He was condemned to death. The charge was: 'Socrates is an evil-doer and a curious person, searching into things under the earth and above the heavens; and making the worse appear the better cause, and teaching all this to others.'

The effect on Plato of his teacher's death was profound and he includes Socrates' death in several of his dialogues.

THE APOLOGY gives Socrates' defence at his trial.

THE CRITO lists Socrates' reasons for not trying to escape after he had been condemned.

THE PHAEDO recounts Socrates' last hours arguing for the immortality of the soul. Socrates took hemlock (a poison) and continued to talk with his friends gathered round him until the poison took effect. As he died, he was happy that in the next world he could go on asking questions, unable to be put to death again since he would now be immortal.

The death of Socrates was seen in later days as a martyrdom. A 'martyr' is someone who is killed unjustly for what he or she believes in. Socrates was seen by the Christian church almost as a pre-Christian Christian; because of his ideals and integrity, early Christian thinkers tried to adopt him as Christian. This is partly because Christianity wished to appear respectable to the ancient world by harmonizing with Greek thought, and partly because Socrates was an outstanding person. Socrates lived, of course, several hundred years before Christ.

In his second 'Apology', written c. AD150-160, Justin Martyr wrote of Socrates as a Christian before Christ. Justin claimed that Jesus had always existed in the world as the Word of God. The Word of God influenced the world for good, even before the 'incarnation', when Jesus became a man:

> 'Whatever things were rightly said by any man, belong to us Christians. For next to God we worship and love the Word, who is from the unbegotten and ineffable God, since he also became man for our sakes, that by sharing in our sufferings he might also bring us healing. For all those writers were able to see reality darkly, through the seed of the implanted Word within them.'

Plato

Socrates left no writings. His pupil Plato is, in many ways, the founder of philosophy as we know it. He wrote prolifically and magnificently.

Plato was born in 427BC in the early years of the Peloponnesian War. He was a well-to-do aristocrat. During his life he saw the end of the Athenian Empire and the founding of a new one under Philip of Macedon. Later, Philip of Macedon's son, Alexander the Great, conquered a great part of the known world. Plato devoted his life to philosophy and founded the Academy, a kind of informal university, which lasted for 1,000 years.

Plato was also influenced by the philosophers who came before him:

* Pythagoras gave Plato his belief in immortality, religion, mysticism and maths.

* Parmenides gave him the notion that reality is eternal, unchanging and timeless.

* Heraclitus gave him the conviction that there is nothing permanent in the physical world and that true knowledge cannot come through the senses.

* Socrates gave Plato his preoccupation with ethical problems and a desire to explain 'purpose' in the world. Both Socrates and Plato were concerned with knowledge of 'The Good'.

In his philosophy Plato attempted to find a resolution between the Heraclitan view of the universe, that the world of appearances is constantly changing, with the Parmenidean notion that reality is one and unchanging.

Both Socrates and Plato insisted that right opinion is not enough. Opinion is useless unless it is turned into secure knowledge by 'a reckoning of the reason'. This use of reason and the search for truth began what we call philosophy. Plato's solution was based not on physics, but on logic, metaphysics and ethics. His search for knowledge began a search which continues today and which involves us all.

Theories of Knowledge
Plato and Aristotle

What does it mean to 'know'?

* I know that 2 + 2 = 4.

* I know that Beethoven was a great musician.

* I know it's going to rain.

* I know that daffodils are yellow.

* I know Catherine very well.

* I know that God exists.

Most of us take for granted that we know things and that we can know things. But what is knowing and how can we be sure that what we know is true? If you look at the sentences above you will see that the word 'know' is used six times, but in six different ways. The word 'know' has several different meanings. So what does it really mean to 'know' something? How is 'knowing' different from having an 'opinion' or an 'impression'?

How we know and what we can know are questions philosophers have asked since the time of the Ancient Greeks. Those early Greek philosophers were faced with the problem of the 'One' and the 'Many' – trying to find a sure, underlying order in an uncertain, constantly changing world.

Even today, 'epistemology' the branch of philosophy which studies knowledge, asks:

* How do we know?

* How much can we know?

* How can we be sure that what we know is correct?

These are basic problems in philosophy. If we know that we can know basic things about the world, then science and philosophy are possible: we can think about the world and find out about the world. If we become convinced that it is impossible to know anything for certain, then knowledge becomes opinion rather than fact.

In Ancient Greece, Plato (c. 427-348BC) was a pupil of Socrates. In turn, Aristotle (384-322 BC), another highly important Greek philosopher, was a pupil of Plato. Both Plato and Aristotle formed theories concerning what we can know about the world. Their two contrasting theories are important foundations for the theory of knowledge as it has been studied since.

Plato and the theory of knowledge

Plato made two contributions to the theory of knowledge. One was that knowledge is recollecting what is in your head already, not perceiving new things. The other was his Theory of Forms, which we will consider below.

Plato was faced with two major problems when he came to consider what true knowledge is:

A PHILOSOPHICAL PROBLEM: he had to reconcile the problem of the One and the Many.

A HUMAN PROBLEM: he had to battle against the Sophists.

The Sophists were professional philosophers who lived in Athens at the time of Plato. Gorgias one of their number, had said: 'Nothing exists, and if it did, no one could know it, and if they knew it, they could not communicate it.' These Sophists were sceptics, believing there was no such thing as certain knowledge. Because of this, they treated philosophy as a skill to be sold to their students to enable them to be successful in life. Plato spoke out against the Sophists. He believed that truth, not worldly success, was the proper aim of philosophy.

In Plato's dialogue, the *Theaetetus*, Theaetetus says:

It seems to me that one who knows something is perceiving the thing that he knows, and, so far as I can see at present, knowledge is nothing but perception.

Plato profoundly disagreed with Theaetetus' notion of knowledge. Nowadays, empirical knowledge, knowledge from information which comes through the senses, is considered to be true and scientific. Plato's problem was that if the world is constantly changing, how can the world or the senses be relied on? He concluded that they cannot and that true knowledge had to come from elsewhere. He concluded that it was pre-existent.

In his dialogue, the *Meno*, Plato presents Socrates as setting a mathematical problem for a slave-boy to solve. The slave-boy has never been taught any mathematics, but he manages nevertheless to solve the problem. This is because he knows the answer already, even though he does not know that he knows. Socrates' claim is that we do not 'learn', we 'remember'. The knowledge exists in our minds all along. We possess this knowledge from before we are born.

Socrates says:

Either he has at some time acquired the knowledge which he now has, or he has always possessed it. If he always possessed it, he must always have known; if on the other hand he acquired it at some previous time, it cannot have been in this life, unless somebody taught him geometry.

For Plato the advantages of holding this view are that: education and experience do not matter: true knowledge is innate in us. And we do not have to rely on our senses for knowledge about the world. True knowledge consists of concepts (ideas already in our heads), not information (ideas that come to us through our senses).

Plato's Theory of Forms

Plato's Theory of Forms has influenced the development of philosophy and the Christian religion to such an extent that the entire history of Western culture has been permeated by it.

Plato believed that:

THE WORLD is divided into 'reality' and 'appearance' (the One and the Many).

OUR INFORMATION ABOUT THE WORLD is divided into 'knowledge' and 'opinion'. Knowledge is what we seek, but opinion is usually all that we have. In *The Republic*, Plato advances the view that opinion usually passes for knowledge. What is beautiful to one person is ugly to another, and what is just to one person is unjust to another.

Opinion, then, results from objects as presented to the senses. Two people may have differing opinions, for example, about a painting or about a friend. Objects in the natural world therefore have a contradictory nature: opinions clash about them and it is impossible to have true, universal knowledge about them.

Plato went on to claim that the person who is concerned with beautiful things has 'opinions' about them, but the person who is concerned with Beauty itself can possess 'true knowledge'.

And those whose hearts are fixed on the true being of each thing are to be called philosophers and not lovers of opinion? Yes, certainly.

In other words, Plato believed in:

* A visible world – the world of the senses, a world of opinions.

* An intelligible world – a world beyond the senses, a world of true knowledge.

Plato used a technical word for these ideas of Beauty, Truth and Justice: he called them 'Forms'. He conceived of them as having a real existence, independent of the mental world of people's minds or of the natural world. These Forms were to him objects or shapes, though Plato defined them rather than described them. The Forms are universal. There may be particular instances of beauty in the world – a painting or a flower – but these and all beautiful things share in the universal Form of Beauty.

Plato's interest in mathematics, proportions and harmonies led him to believe that these universal Forms were connected. The highest Form of all is the Form of the Good.

The highest form of knowledge is knowledge of the form of the good, from which things that are just and so on derive their usefulness and value.

> The good, then, is the end of all endeavour, the object on which every heart is set...

Knowing the Forms, for Plato, is a kind of mental seeing, and philosophy is a vision of truth.

Knowing leads to discovering the Form of the Good and, consequently, philosophy makes you a better person. The Good, in *The Republic*, is 'the greatest thing we have to learn'.

Plato's Theory of Forms is also important for classifying objects in the world and understanding their nature.

The word 'dog', for example, refers to a four-footed, barking animal with fur which is not a 'cat' and not a 'horse'. Yet, all dogs do not appear the same; their colour, size and breed are all different. All dogs in the world, however, share in some kind of 'dog-ness' (according to Plato) by which we recognize a dog when we see one. Plato believed there is an ideal dog or form of dog, just as there is a Form of Beauty or a Form of Justice. The ideal Dog is created by God and is the only real, true Dog; the other particular dogs in the world are instances of dog and only apparent.

Plato sums up his Theory of Forms in the 'Allegory of the Cave' in *The Republic*. The character of Socrates gives a picture of people sitting in a cave, chained, their heads turned away from the cave mouth and the sunlight, facing the wall at the back of the cave. There is a fire outside the cave. They can see the flickering shadows on the wall of the people passing outside and can hear their voices. 'The truth would be literally nothing but the shadows of the images.' These prisoners would take the shadows for reality. Socrates imagines if one prisoner were set free and were suddenly blinded by the light outside and confronted with reality. This would be distressing at first, but gradually the freed prisoner would be able to see things as they are, return to the cave, and teach the other prisoners the truth. Plato has Socrates explain the allegory:

> The prison-house is the world of sight, the light of the fire is the sun, and you will not misapprehend me if you interpret the journey upwards to be the ascent of the soul into the intellectual world according to my poor belief, which, at your desire I have expressed – whether rightly or wrongly God knows.

True knowledge, for Plato, meant abandoning the world of the senses and seeking by reason to discover the Forms or universals in one's own mind.

Grasping these Forms leads to grasping true knowledge and, finally, to grasping the Good.

Plato believed that only the Forms could be 'known'. Mathematics could be 'understood', but the changing, physical world of nature could never be truly 'known' and was not a fit subject for philosophical contemplation.

Mixed in with the theory of knowledge put forward by Plato in the *Meno* is some degree of mysticism. Plato's interest in mysticism and mathematics came from Pythagoras, one of the Pre-Socratics. The Pythagoreans were involved in mystery cults. They believed in reincarnation and the transmigration of souls (the same soul moving from body to body after death). These beliefs had a strong influence on Plato.

Aristotle

Aristotle, Plato's pupil, criticized Plato and put forward his own theory of what we could know about the world.

Aristotle was born, probably in 384BC, at Stagira in Thrace. His father was personal doctor to the King of Macedonia. At about eighteen years of age Aristotle arrived in Athens and became a pupil of Plato. He remained at Plato's Academy for nearly twenty years until Plato's death in 348BC. Aristotle travelled and married and in 342BC became tutor to Alexander the Great. Aristotle founded a school in the Lyceum at Athens, which became a rival to Plato's Academy. He fled when Alexander died.

Aristotle was one of the most prodigious thinkers of the ancient world. Unlike Plato, he took a keen interest in the natural world. He wrote on ethics, politics, botany, zoology, astronomy, history, mathematics and philosophy. Only one-fifth of his vast output survives. In contrast with the polished brilliance of Plato, Aristotle's style is terse and rugged.

From Aristotle's work comes the term 'metaphysics'. One theory to explain the term 'metaphysics' is that this word entered philosophical language when a book by Aristotle was found untitled among his papers. As this work came after *Physics* it was decided to call it *Meta-Physics* (*meta* is the Greek word for 'after').

'Metaphysics' involves searching beyond the world of the senses for an explanation of why the world is as it is, looking for the 'One' behind the 'Many'.

Aristotle's criticism of Plato

Aristotle severely criticized Plato's Theory of Forms.

If a 'particular' dog is merely a picture of an 'ideal' Dog, is there then a third dog – an ideal of the 'ideal' – behind the ideal? If so, is there one behind that, and one behind that? What is the sense in talking about an 'ideal' Dog at all?

While Forms of 'Beauty', 'Truth' and 'Dog' might appear plausible what about one-legged pirates, or blind white rabbits? Are there 'ideal' Forms of those? Aristotle argued that, pushed to its logical conclusion, Plato's Theory of Forms appears slightly ridiculous.

He began with a 'commonsensical' rather than an 'idealist' view. For Aristotle:

* Knowledge *is* perception: 'And for that reason, if we did not perceive anything, we would not learn or understand anything, and whenever we think of anything, we must at the same time think of an idea.'

* The natural world is the real world.

* Perception and sense-experience are the foundations of scientific knowledge.

For Plato, the reality of the world is in the Forms as apprehended by the intellect. For Aristotle, the reality of the world is in 'matter', the stuff the world is made of.

Like other Greek philosophers, Aristotle was fascinated by change. Plato could state that an acorn changes into an oak and retains its nature by sharing in the 'ideal' Oak. Aristotle had shut off that option. So he wondered, if an oak and an acorn appear to be two entirely different things, where is the continuity? Aristotle deals with the question of change in the *Physics*. He came to realize that material substances are, in fact, composite. A house is made of bricks and mortar, but it contains a structure – a 'house-ness' – that makes it not a garage or a shop. A statue is made of marble or bronze, but is cast into a certain shape. All substances, Aristotle decided, have two parts: material and structure – or 'matter' and 'form'. Matter and form belong to this world, not to a world beyond this world, like Plato's Forms. These two contrasting theories are basic to how we understand the world and gain knowledge from the world.

Form is the organizing principle which turns matter into recognizable objects. According to this belief, Aristotle was able to say that the 'soul' is the form of the body.

Objects change and their change has a purpose or goal. Objects have an actuality or a potentiality. Acorns turn into oaks; children turn into adults. This change Aristotle called 'teleological' as it had an 'end' (*telos*) in view. As objects are composed of matter, and matter is always subject to change, objects can never become perfect. Only God, who exists as 'form without matter', is perfect. Human beings, however, can draw close to perfection by contemplating pure form by means of pure thought.

Plato started with the intellect; Aristotle started with perceptions of the natural world. Plato's understanding was mathematical – dealing in concepts which can be worked out without relation to the natural world; Aristotle's understanding was scientific, based on perception, observation and investigation. Both these important thinkers developed ways of knowing about the world which are still important today.

Plato, Aristotle and Christianity

Plato's Theory of Forms has had an enormous influence on the development of Christianity. Early Christian thinkers used Plato's idea of a world beyond this one – an ideal world which gives value and meaning to our own – to develop ideas about the Christian heaven. His elevation of the soul and denial of the body and matter as inferior has been an important strain of Christian thought throughout the ages. In the *Timaeus*, Plato describes the demiurge or 'Logos' (the 'Word') through which the world is created and through which the ideal Forms are imposed on the ever-changing cosmos. Plato's Logos, as developed in later Greek philosophy, was identified by the early Christians with Jesus, the Word (or 'Logos') of God. Aristotle believed in an 'Unmoved (or Prime) Mover', a remote, changeless being who imparts change to the world. Change, Aristotle argued, results from love and the desire to attain the perfection of the Unmoved Mover. The Christian church came to adopt Aristotle's Unmoved Mover as the Christian God. As centuries passed, Aristotle's philosophy became the cornerstone of medieval theology.

Faith and Reason
Augustine

Imagine you take the same bus every day. As you rush to the bus stop in the morning, do you ever think for a moment that the bus will not take you where you want to go? Probably not. Because the bus takes you every day, you have reason to think that the bus will most likely do the same today. At the same time, you have to have faith that this particular bus will take you to the same place.

Faith is believing that something is true when we cannot be absolutely certain that it is true. All religions involve a measure of faith since religious truth is not a truth which can be 'proved' in the way that a mathematical equation can be 'proved', or a scientific experiment. However, faith is usually based on some evidence which is convincing to the believer.

Many people prefer 'reason' to 'faith' as reason seems sure and faith appears vague and cloudy. All of us, however, have to perform 'acts of faith' every day of our lives:

* When you step onto a bus it is an act of faith.

* When you share a secret with a friend, you have faith they will not let you down.

* When you marry someone it is an act of faith.

You may have reasons to back up your faith, but you still have to have faith. In everyday life, faith and reason go together.

Greek philosophy and Christian religion

The two major influences on the ground ideas of Western culture have been Greek philosophy and the Christian religion. Greek philosophy has stressed reason, while the Christian religion has stressed faith.

The first few centuries of the Christian era saw a sustained attempt by early Christian thinkers, the Church Fathers, to harmonize Greek philosophy with the Christian faith. They did this for several reasons:

GREEK PHILOSOPHY was part of the climate of the times. Plato's ideas were as much part of the ancient world as the ideas of evolution or progress are today. In order to develop a Christian theology, the Church Fathers had to turn to Greek philosophy to provide a philosophical language and framework within which they could explore their ideas.

THE CHRISTIAN CHURCH wished to appear intellectually respectable to the ancient world. By using the philosophical language of the time, these early Christians hoped to gain credibility and spread the Christian faith.

THE CHURCH FATHERS found that they had to answer philosophical questions which had no apparent answers in the Bible. For example, How was Jesus both God and man? What did God create the world out of, previously existing matter or nothing? The Church Fathers had to turn to Greek philosophy to help them with their speculations on these difficult questions.

The greatest of all the early Church Fathers was Augustine, known as Augustine of Hippo, a town in North Africa. He wrote in Latin, not Greek, and the amount of his surviving work exceeds that of any other ancient writer.

Augustine's importance as a writer and thinker is monumental. He was the greatest Christian theologian since the apostle Paul, and his ideas shaped the subsequent development of Christianity; his was the greatest influence on the Western, Latin-speaking, church. Augustine's thought dominated the Middle Ages, and both the Reformation and Counter-Reformation rooted their arguments in his teaching.

In addition, Augustine anticipated the *cogito ergo sum* of Descartes ('I think, therefore I am') and the subconscious of Freud. Thinkers such as

Anselm, Aquinas, Luther, Pascal and Kierkegaard all owe a great debt to Augustine. His books were among the favourites of modern philosopher Wittgenstein.

A great story of conversion

Augustine (AD354-430) was born at Tagaste, North Africa. His mother, Monica, was a Christian, but his father was a pagan. In Roman North Africa, Augustine inhabited a prosperous, cosmopolitan world which possessed a high literary culture. He became a law student at Carthage at the age of sixteen, but in 375 turned to philosophy as a result of reading Cicero's *Hortensius*. He converted to following the Manichean cult, and became Professor of Rhetoric at Rome in 383. From Rome, Augustine moved to Milan where he fell under the spell of the Christian bishop, Ambrose. For some time Augustine was drawn to neo-Platonism, but after a long, painful struggle he became a Christian in 386 and was baptized by Ambrose at Easter, 387. Augustine was intent on living a 'monastic' life, but in 391 he was forcibly ordained Bishop of Hippo (now Annaba in Algeria). He was bishop for thirty-four years, writing voluminously, combating heresies, and living in a community with other Christians.

We know more about Augustine the man than any other ancient writer. This is because he wrote the most famous and influential of all ancient autobiographies, the *Confessions* (begun in 391). This book gives a detailed portrait of Augustine's early life and the development of his intellect. Augustine emerges from his own pages as a worldly, profound, passionate man, driven in his search for truth. He was someone who battled constantly with his own emotions and weaknesses.

Augustine's writing appears modern, fresh, concise and compelling. His relentless search drove him to adopt a variety of intellectual positions at different times. Among the influences were:

CICERO (106-43BC). As a student, aged nineteen, Augustine read Cicero. Cicero wrote: 'The mere search for higher happiness, not merely its actual attainment, is a prize beyond all human wealth or honour or physical pleasure.' Cicero's writings set Augustine on the long search for truth.

MANICHEISM, a religion or cult which combined Christian and Zoroastrian elements. Augustine followed it for ten years. Manicheism came from Persia (modern Iran) and had two ultimate principles or gods – Light and Darkness. Manicheism was a dualistic religion. Basically, the human spirit or soul originates from the Light, while matter and the physical universe are evil and originate from the Darkness. This theory explained the origin of evil and denied human responsibility for evil actions. Augustine was particularly concerned with the problem of evil. Manichean negativity towards matter and the body left its mark on his subsequent theology. The Manichees followed strict moral rules and frowned on pleasure. Mani (c. 216-276), the founder of Manicheism, rejected the Old Testament, but acknowledged that truth was revealed in other religions.

ASTROLOGY. For some time Augustine was fascinated by astrology, though he became disillusioned with it.

SCEPTICISM. For a short time Augustine became a sceptic, believing that certain knowledge was impossible.

Ambrose and Augustine

When Augustine went to Milan in 384 to become Professor of Rhetoric, several new influences entered his life. First of all, he met Ambrose, Bishop of Milan. Augustine was impressed by Ambrose's wisdom and authority. Ambrose himself had been much influenced by the Platonist philosophers whom he called the 'aristocrats of thought'. Platonism and Christianity appeared to have much in common. Both were other-worldly. Christ had said 'My kingdom is not of this world'; Plato had said the same thing of his world of Forms. Both Greek philosophy and Christianity believed in immortality of the soul.

At first, Augustine was drawn to the Milanese 'neo-Platonists', who followed the teachings of Plotinus. At that time in Milan there was something of a renaissance in philosophy.

Plotinus (205-270) was born in Egypt, but taught in Rome. He adapted Plato's philosophy in certain important ways and his work was edited by his disciple Porphyry (c. 232-305). This philosophy became known as neo-

Platonism. Plotinus believed that creation emanated (or flowed) from the One (God) who was Good. There is, therefore, no radical distinction between God and his creation. Everything that exists must be good, or contain good, otherwise it could not exist at all. Plotinus' teaching was in contrast to the Manichees' and helped Augustine reconsider his metaphysical position. Plotinus also helped Augustine turn to philosophy again, and gave him a language for describing mystical experience. Neo-Platonic thought is woven right through Augustine's writing.

The Platonists had always felt they could offer a vision of God (or the Good) which could be attained by the unaided, rational 'ascent' of the mind to the world of Ideas or Forms. They found the Christian notions of God becoming man in Christ, the crucifixion, and the resurrection, simply barbarous. The idea expressed in John's Gospel that the 'Word became flesh' was impossible nonsense. Ultimate reality and ultimate truth could not be soiled by contact with the natural world of the senses.

Through Ambrose, Augustine turned from the writings of Plato to the writings of Paul in the New Testament: 'It was wonderful how these truths came home to me when I read the least of your apostles'. In Paul's letters, Augustine found a man who could describe his own experience – of weakness, of struggle with the body, of passion to do right. Paul wrote: 'So I find this law at work, When I want to do good, evil is right there with me.' Augustine came to realize that reason alone is not enough: he needed grace, help from God, in order to be a whole person and find authentic freedom.

At last, aged thirty-two, Augustine turned to Christ as the ultimate source of help, salvation and wisdom. He turned to the Bible as a source of authority and revelation. The conversions of the theologian Victorinus and St Antony, the desert father who lived as a monk, had already struck him deeply. Suddenly, Augustine found himself at a turning-point in his own life:

> I was asking myself these questions, weeping all the while with the most bitter sorrow in my heart, when all at once I heard the sing-song voice of a child in a nearby house. Whether it was the voice of a boy or a girl I cannot say, but again and again it repeated the refrain 'Take it and read, take it and read.' At this I looked up, thinking hard whether there was any kind of game in which children used to chant words like these, but I could not remember ever hearing them before. I stemmed my flood of tears and stood up, telling myself that this could only be a divine command to open my book of Scriptures and read the first

passage on which my eyes should fall... So I turned back to the place where Alypius was sitting, for when I stood up to move away I had to put down the book containing Paul's Epistles. I seized it and opened it, and in silence I read the first passage on which my eyes fell: 'Not in revelling and drunkenness, not in lust and wantonness, not in quarrels and rivalries. Rather, arm yourselves with the Lord Jesus Christ; spend no more thought on nature and nature's appetites.' I had no wish to read more and no need to do so. For in an instant, as I came to the end of the sentence, it was as though the light of confidence flooded into my heart and all the darkness and doubt was dispelled.'

Augustine's beliefs

Augustine was converted. He was changed. He believed that the truth he had failed to find by reason alone had been given, or revealed, to him by God's grace. He realized that a person could not be saved solely by his or her own power.

After his conversion, Augustine gave up his career, refused to marry, and renounced the world. He now believed that:

GOD IS SUPREMELY GOOD AND LOVING. God has created a world which is basically good, not basically bad (as the Manicheans believed). 'We move towards God,' Augustine wrote, 'not by walking but by loving.'

HUMANITY HAS FALLEN SHORT of God's intentions and needs to be restored and forgiven. Augustine developed the doctrine of 'original sin'. He believed all have sinned 'in Adam', the original man, and as a result all human beings are born sinful and in need of God's grace.

GOD HAS ACTED in human history culminating in Jesus, the 'incarnation', God become human. Believing in Jesus, having faith in him, and submitting to the church, is the only way to eternal life.

Philosophy, for Augustine, became 'the study of God and the human soul'. The way forward, Augustine asserted, is by faith: 'Vision will be granted to him who lives well, prays well, studies well.'

Augustine's belief that death is not the end relied, not on Platonic philosophy, but on personal faith in the risen Christ.

Augustine's *Confessions* is a fascinating book. In it, Augustine presents himself as the Prodigal Son and the Lost Sheep from Luke's Gospel. Lost and then found like the apostle Paul, he was someone who changed dramatically. He was like Everyman; Augustine's story is everyone's story.

The *Confessions* consists of thirteen books, nine autobiographical and four of theology. The last four show how Augustine understood his own story as a small picture of the creation, the fall into chaos, and the conversion to the love of God and return to order. His story is both personal and cosmic. Faith and reason are part and parcel of the universe.

Augustine was someone who struggled with himself all his life. His thought is not calm and abstract, but the result of an open-mindedness of the whole person to reality as a whole. His belief came out of deep, personal distress. Augustine saw the limits of reason (*cogito*, 'I think'), and grounded reason firmly in faith (*credo*, 'I believe'). Faith is grounded in the Bible's message. Biblical faith as guaranteed by the church is the only cure for scepticism.

Faith, for Augustine, was not blind faith, but rationally justifiable. In his work reason seeks to understand what faith believes. 'Know in order to believe' comes before 'Believe in order to understand'.

Augustine saw faith and reason, philosophy and theology, as all rooted in the one truth of God. Philosophy can be used to interpret the Bible; the Bible can be quoted to illustrate philosophy. Christ governs all reality. Although shaped by the classical world of Greece and Rome, Augustine became a critic of that classical culture and his Christianity set him at odds with the classical past. The Bible, not Plato, was the highest written authority, though Plato was useful and contained some truth. In Augustine, Plato's Forms, for instance, become thoughts in the mind of God.

Augustine wrote on a wide range of Christian issues. His use of the classical past, exposition of the Bible, and balance of faith and reason, were a major achievement and helped determine the development of Christianity for centuries to come.

PART

Who Am I?

THE QUESTION OF IDENTITY

The Nature of the Soul
Aristotle and Identity

Who are you exactly? That might seem a strange question, but have you ever suddenly caught sight of yourself in a mirror and wondered for a second who it is you are looking at? You can see a familiar face but just for a second you wonder who or what it is that makes you yourself apart from your body.

Once we start thinking about ourselves in this way all sorts of questions arise:

* Who am I exactly?

* How do I know who I am?

* How can I know I'm the same person today as I was yesterday?

* What is it in me that causes me to be alive?

* Do I have a soul which survives my body after death?

Plato and the person

In Platonic thought a person is part of the physical world in that he or she has a body through which sense-impressions can be received. But at the same time he or she has an immaterial mind which is capable of knowing eternal truths beyond the world. There is also a directing force, the soul, which Plato pictures as a chariot rider, which is guiding and being guided by two horses, mind and body.

The mind wants to travel into the heavenly realm of the ideas and to understand them; the body wants to be involved in worldly matters to do with the senses.

The human soul is caught between these two opposing forces. The soul is trying to steer but is trapped in the prison of the body. Therefore, according to Plato, people have no real freedom if their lives are concentrated on physical requirements. However, your soul can free itself from this bondage and direct your life, both your physical circumstances and your intellectual pursuits. But it is only after bodily existence that the soul rises upward to the eternal world of Ideas.

For Plato soul and body are two different things. The soul is immortal; it inhabits the body temporarily.

Aristotle and the soul

Aristotle's idea of the soul is very different from Plato's. In his account *On the Soul*, Aristotle gives a general account of what he believes a soul is. He follows the belief common to the Greeks that the soul is the principle of life: inquiry into the soul is enquiry into the different forms of life.

The basic form of life is found in plants, which feed themselves, grow, decay and reproduce. So the basic form of soul consists in the ability to do these things; all forms of life manifest this. The word 'soul' then, simply describes how something is alive in the world. A 'soul' is not necessarily separate from the body or eternal. On the contrary, a 'soul' is what gives a body life.

With animals there is the additional capacity for sense-perception, and in most of them the capacity for movement. For Aristotle oak trees and ostriches had *psyche* (or 'soul') as much as monkeys or men. The word 'soul' did not mean the same as 'mind'. Rather everything that lives has *psyche*, but human beings are at the top of creation. It is this hierarchical arrangement which makes it difficult to say that Aristotle had one single definition of the soul.

A soul is what makes a body work. These souls are not bits of special spiritual stuff which have been placed inside the living body. They are sets of powers, capabilities and faculties. For Aristotle, to have a soul is like having a skill; it is not a part of you which functions independently from any other part. He wrote: 'One should not ask if the soul and the body are one, any more than one should ask it of the wax and the shape, or in general of the matter of anything and that of which it is the matter.'

In Aristotle's thinking there is no problem about how soul and body can co-exist and work together. This idea of the soul makes any thought of personal survival after death impossible.

Plato had said that souls pre-existed birth and continued after the death of those bodies which they inhabited. Aristotle disagreed with this. Just as skills cannot exist apart from skilled people, so a soul is not the kind of thing that can survive the person. How could my skills, my character or my temper survive me?

A popular view at the time of Plato was that life begins when the soul enters the body. Aristotle argued that soul and body are inseparable: the soul cannot exist without a body any more than walking can happen without any legs. His works take the biological attitude towards life. The powers and principles of the soul are 'corporeal': to be alive ('animated') is to be a body with certain capacities.

Aristotle takes the idea of the soul out of the eternal and places it in the here and now. He reduces soul to the essence or form of body. He is seen as having a 'materialist' view of humankind because he rejects the Platonic idea of a spiritual soul. Soul does not somehow come in from the outside. The only thing that comes in from the outside according to Aristotle is 'thought' and 'intellect'. For Aristotle, the soul and the mind are not the same thing.

The immortality of the intellect

Thought gets a special status in Aristotle's thinking. It depends on the view that thinking does not involve any bodily activity. Yet in his general account of the soul he makes it clear that thinking is something done by 'natural organic bodies'. It is difficult to see how this can be consistent.

In Aristotle's philosophy, thought is an aspect of soul that is almost divine and immortal, but yet belief in personal immortality is impossible. It is important to remember that this is not a simple issue of materialism versus the spiritual/abstract view of immortality. In seeing the intellect as immortal, Aristotle provides a third way of seeing things:

* Who or what are we after death? Are we a 'soul' separated from the body? Is it just our 'thought' that continues?

* Who or what are we now? Are we a more developed version of plant and animal life? Or are we human because we have a soul, or spiritual element, in us?

* How does Aristotle's understanding of immortality compare with the Bible's?

The Bible has an integrated view of human nature. It never sees us as the sum total of different compartments – flesh, soul and spirit. The Bible writers were certainly people of their own time and used their own terms to describe humanity. Yet they believed most firmly in what we today call the 'psycho-somatic unity' of the person, the interdependence of body, mind and emotion. Not surprisingly the Greek view of 'soul' and 'body' affected the early church whose catch-phrase was *soma-sema*, 'the body a tomb'. To their mind the soul was released from its prison at death and set free. In the Bible, humankind is mortal but not purely animal. People are made in the image of God. They are open to the worlds both of flesh and spirit.

Mind and Body Divided
René Descartes' Dualism

We often use the word 'mind'.

* My mind is telling me not to, but I think I will anyway.

* I have a mind not to go after all.

* My mind says one thing but my body says another.

* His body is in a right mess but there's nothing wrong with his mind.

* Excuse me, my mind was elsewhere.

How do you think of yourself? As a body? As a mind? As both together?

The French philosopher René Descartes is well known for his dualist view that mind exists independent of matter. He believed in a split between body and mind.

Descartes and Rationalism

Descartes (1596-1650) was the first of the great rationalist philosophers. You can read about his life, his times and his ideas in Chapter 10. In everyday conversation, rationalism usually means the attempt to judge everything in the light of reason. This view disposes of the religious or the supernatural and concentrates on nature and clear material facts.

The philosophy of rationalism, however, is less atheistic. The rationalists of the seventeenth and eighteenth centuries were not necessarily atheists. Some of them were religious men, but the notion of God occupied a less important place in their thinking. What united them all was a belief in the rationality of the universe: that the universe works in a logical way and makes sense, and that the power of reason can understand it. Many of them were scientists who had made important discoveries in mathematics, especially geometry. Their reasoning rested on logic, and their philosophical techniques were taken from mathematics.

Descartes' dualism of mind and body rests on certain ideas.

* He argues that mind is a 'non-corporeal' (non-bodily) substance, which is distinct from material or bodily substance.

* Every substance has a property or a special character. So, for instance, the property of mind-substance is consciousness and the property of bodily or material-substance is length or breadth or depth.

If you read Chapter 10 you will understand Descartes' method of Doubt. Although Descartes could doubt that he had a body, there was one thing that it was impossible to doubt – the fact that he was doubting. This led to his famous saying, *Cogito ergo sum* ('I think, therefore I am'). This convinced him that mind can exist independently of matter. The ninth Principle of Part 1 of his *Principles of Philosophy* reads like this:

Next, I examined carefully what I was and I saw that I could suppose that I had no body and that there was no world or place where I was, but that I could not by the same token suppose that I did not exist. On the contrary, from the very fact that I was thinking to doubt the truth of other things, it followed very evidently and very certainly that I was existing. On the other hand, granted only that I had ceased to think, while all the rest of what I had imagined had been the case, I had no reason to believe that I had existed. From this I knew that I was a substance the whole essence or nature of which simply was to think; and which, to exist, needs no place and has no dependence on any material thing. Consequently I, that is to say my mind – what makes me what I am – am entirely distinct from the body; and, furthermore, the former is more easily known than the latter, while if the latter did not exist the former could be all that it is.

Criticisms of Descartes

Descartes has provided philosophers with a ready target for their criticism.

IF DESCARTES WANTS TO START WITH DOUBT, his initial starting-point should have been 'There are doubts', rather than showing that from this you can take the existence of a personal self for granted.

HE MAY PROVE TO HIS OWN SATISFACTION that mind and body can exist independently. But then he is faced with the problem of saying how the two distinct substances of body and mind interact to form what we call a person. How can a material substance affect a non-material substance?

During his own lifetime Descartes was aware of the many criticisms he received. He used to write letters to many influential people who all referred to him for discussion. This is an excerpt from a letter from Princess Elizabeth of Bohemia:

> I beg of you to tell me how the human soul can determine the movement of the animal spirits in the body so as to perform voluntary acts – being as it is merely a conscious substance. For the determination of movement seems always to come about from the moving body's being propelled... but you utterly exclude extension from your notion of soul, and contact seems to me incompatible with a thing's being immaterial.

Descartes rejected Aristotle's idea of the soul or mind as that which animates the body. His ideas were much more in the tradition of Plato. In his *Meditations on First Philosophy*, he wrote: 'My soul is not in my body as a pilot in a ship; I am most tightly bound to it...'

He is saying that the mind does not influence the body like a switch or a button which sets the body into motion. He insists on a much closer union in which the mind directly moves the body and directly experiences, rather than observes, the pleasures and the pains of the body.

The Cartesian view ('Cartesian' is the adjective describing Descartes' philosophy) of the nature of humankind falls within the Platonic school of thought. Like Platonic thought it promises immortality, and the word 'substance' is used in a similar way. But unlike Plato, Descartes begins with the immediate present subjective experience of one individual. He does not begin with a theory, he begins with me and how I think. This emphasis on the individual has not been welcomed by everyone.

Archbishop William Temple once asked himself the question 'Which was the most disastrous moment in European history?' His answer was the day that Descartes shut himself up in his stove (see Chapter 10). In giving this answer Temple was not criticizing Descartes for his view of God. What concerned him was the direction towards which Descartes turned European thought. Descartes represents a shift in direction. The direction he set was a retreat into individual self-consciousness as the one sure starting-point in philosophy.

The Cartesian version of the mind-body problem has been one of the most thought-about philosophical problems of the last three centuries. In the twentieth century J.B. Watson and B.F. Skinner have tried applying Behaviourist thought. Gilbert Ryle and Ludwig Wittgenstein have both applied themselves to it. Descartes' wider arguments inspired debate and opposition and admiration from the most eminent and influential people of his day: Thomas Hobbes, William Cavendish, Benedict Spinoza and many theologians.

Above all, Descartes inspired a confidence in the power of the intellect to understand the world and in the power of each individual to use reason in making judgments. In *Rules for the direction of the mind*, he wrote:

> We shall never be philosophers if we have read all the arguments of Plato and Aristotle but cannot form a solid judgment on matters set before us.

Survival after death

One critical aspect of the mind-body problem is the question of survival after death. If our selves really are divided, our souls and bodies connected but distinct, we can see how life after death is possible. The soul would be able to exist on its own and have a life without the help of the body. It can just leave the body at death instead of being destroyed with it. It may continue to exist on its own, or it may be attached to another body, or it may interact with other souls! Some believe one soul can take up residence in another body when it is born.

If dualism is not true and mental processes go on in the brain and are dependent on the brain's biological functioning, then when our bodies die life after death is not possible. Put another way: mental life after death would need a restoration of biological and physical life. We would need our bodies to come to life again.

You can see how people with this view have acted on occasions. People have paid huge sums of money to have their bodies (or even just their heads) frozen straight after death. The Christian belief in the 'resurrection of the body' is a non-dualist view: it is quite different from Greek ideas of the 'survival of the soul'.

Whether a person is a dualist or not, the question of how we feel about death is important. Is the prospect of our own death a bad thing, a good thing or neither? Of course how we feel about it depends on what death is. If life after death exists, then the future will be happy or terrible depending on the destiny of our souls. However, philosophically speaking, it is interesting to ask how we should feel if death is the end. Is it such an awful thing to go out of existence?

Death and the philosopher

Right through the ages, philosophers and writers have thought about death. 'Death, the most dreaded of evils, is therefore of no concern to us; for while we exist death is not present, and when death is present we no longer exist.' So wrote Epicurus, in a letter to Menoeceus in the third century BC. Or hear Antoine de Saint-Exupery in *Flight to Arras* (1942): 'Man imagines that it is death he fears; but what he fears is the unforeseen, the explosion. What man fears is himself, not death.' 'Death either destroys or unhusks us. If it means liberation, better things await us; blessings and curses are abolished' – so wrote Seneca, *Letters to Lucilius*, first century AD. Plato's *Apology* credits this to Socrates: 'Nobody knows, in fact, what death is, nor whether to man it is not perchance the greatest of all blessings; yet people fear it as if they surely knew it to be the worst of evils.' Tom Stoppard, in his 1967 play, *Rosencrantz and Guildenstern Are Dead* states the following: 'Death is not anything... death is not... It's the absence of presence, nothing more... the endless time of never coming back... a gap you can't see, and when the wind blows through it, it makes no sound.'

What Price the Soul?

Modern Debate on the Mind/Body Problem

Imagine that you are eating an ice-cream. You can feel the ice melting on your tongue. You can smell the flavour as you lift the cone to your mouth. Finally you taste the strawberry creamy ice. Now, what is happening inside your brain at this moment? Is the taste a physical event happening in one of your brain cells? If you were to look inside your brain, would you be able to detect your brain tasting the ice-cream?

Physical changes happen in our brains when we taste, eat and smell. But if you cut open someone's head, you could not detect enjoyment or find a memory. How, then, do these things really exist?

The question that arises is an important one: is your experience of the ice-cream inside your mind in such a way that it is separate or distinct from your brain? If so, then your experiences are not just physical states of your brain. Is it the case that 'you' are more than a body with all its chemical changes and physical processes and nervous system?

We have looked at one conclusion to this sort of question: the idea of a soul attached to your body and interacting with it. Descartes' dualism represents this view. Now we look at the view that people are nothing more than bodies, and that their mental states are actually physical states of their brains. The view that thinking is a purely physical activity of the brain is called 'materialism' (or 'Physicalism').

A materialist view of humanity

As understood in philosophy, the term 'materialist' is used of people who believe that whatever exists is either matter itself, or is dependent on matter for its existence. So all your experiences – tasting, hurting, loving, happiness – are mental states, but these mental states are simply states of the brain. They are material processes because they are located in the structure of the brain. A materialist might argue that although it might be strange that the experience of tasting ice-cream is nothing more than a physical event in your brain, it is actually no stranger than other scientific finds. It is only a matter of time and progress before scientists discover the biological nature of the mind.

The 'materialist' view of humankind and the universe has a history to it. Forms of materialism appear in the history of thought as far back as Democritus (c. 460-370BC). (Democritus was the subject of Karl Marx's doctoral thesis.) And Epicurus (341-270BC) described human experience in terms of arrangements of changeless atoms or indivisible material particles in empty space. These ideas have been revived from time to time. In the seventeenth century the new physics of Galileo and, later, Newton, saw a resurgence of this sort of thinking. Thomas Hobbes (1588-1679) wrote a very convincing account of such materialism, with the promise of a scientific world-view which would eventually explain everything.

More recently, Marxist thinking has replaced 'mechanistic materialism' with its own distinct 'dialectical materialism'. This sees matter not as a static thing on which change is imposed, but as something which contains in its own nature the 'contradictions' which supply the motive and the force for change.

A dualist, however, would have problems with the example of materialism given above. A dualist would say that there is a big difference between undertaking a scientific analysis of ice-cream and analyzing how the ice-cream feels and tastes to us.

A physical thing can be analyzed into small physical parts, but this is not the same with a mental process. Physical parts just do not add up to a mental whole. Mental activity is different.

How do you see this question?

DOES YOUR MENTAL LIFE GO ON IN YOUR SOUL? Or is your mental life merely a physical process in your brain?

OR IS THERE ANOTHER WAY OF LOOKING AT THIS? Perhaps your mental life goes on in your brain, but your experiences, thoughts, feelings and so on are not physical processes in your brain? What if your brain is not just a physical object? What if it has mental processes going on in it at the same time?

The view that the brain is the centre of consciousness but that its conscious states are not just physical is called 'dual-aspect theory'. In other words your body, and your brain as a part of your body, is not just physical. It is an object with physical and mental aspects.

Psychology and the mind-body problem

By the beginning of the nineteenth century, the metaphysical problem of the mind-body division was being thought about in two major ways:

* 'Mental philosophy' tried to explain the functions of men and women in terms of 'mental faculties' such as reason, will, memory and emotion.

* 'Empirical sciences' promoted the view that only experiments on observable 'matter' were valid.

In the field of psychology, various attempts were made to hold both fields of enquiry by studying humanity's inner being using the scientific method.

Wilhelm Wundt (1832-1920) started the first psychological laboratory in Leipzig. He ignored the debate on mental faculties and the human soul and concentrated on experience as the major subject of psychology. He conducted experiments on humans in which they would reveal their impressions of colour, the pitch of sound, bright lights and other sensory phenomena, so that he could check their experiences of these things against their actual value. This method of evaluating subjective assessment is called 'introspection'.

Introspectionism did not solve the body-soul problem. Indeed its methodology was heavily criticized by animal psychologists from Charles Darwin onwards, who said that introspection was not needed in order to study behaviour.

At the turn of the century three main attempts were made to help psychology study human nature: behaviourism, psychoanalysis and personalism. Here we look at Behaviourism.

Behaviourism

John Broadus Watson (1878-1958) was a professor at Johns Hopkins University in the United States and the founder of the Behaviourist school. He dismissed the study of consciousness, mental states, mind and so on. Instead he said that all psychology could be carried out in terms of stimulus and response. He wrote: 'The time seems to have come when psychology must discard all reference to consciousness.'

For Watson, all psychology was concerned with animal and human behaviour. His was a scientific view which looked only at how people act to explain what a human being is. He took no account of the soul. In the mid-1920s Watson came into the public eye for his radical views. He claimed that human behaviour could be controlled scientifically as witness this quotation from *Behaviourism* in 1925:

> Give me a dozen healthy infants, well formed... and I'll guarantee you to take any one at random and train him to become any type of specialist I might select.

Burrhus Frederic Skinner (1904-90) studied psychology at Harvard University. He had been impressed by the writing of Bertrand Russell, J.B. Watson and Ivan Pavlov, and like them he carried out hundreds of experiments on animals to establish his behaviouristic psychology.

Skinner's theory of human behaviour is primarily based on the concept of positive reinforcements. This means the more you praise and reward a person, the more they behave the way you want them to. In one experiment, whenever the pigeon raised its head, food was given. He regarded this 'operant conditioning' as improving the efficiency of the bird's behaviour. In time the pigeon learnt that this behaviour was productive.

There are various important points to Skinner's thinking:

HE ATTACKS HUMANITY'S INNER 'FREEDOM' to have internal states of knowing, will and destiny. Human beings are not autonomous or independent.

PEOPLE ARE COMPLETELY CONTROLLED by an environment. We are not the result of our religious views. Neither are we free to shape our own destiny. Skinner believed in the power of a totally controlling environment. Of freedom he wrote, in *Beyond Freedom and Dignity* (1973):

> Man's struggle for freedom is not due to a will to be free, but to certain behavioural processes characteristic of the human organism, the chief effect of which is the avoidance of or escape from so-called 'aversive' features of the environment.

The desire for freedom is seen as a response to negative reinforcement. For example, an overbearing mother may lead a young person to leave home. In contrast, Skinner argues that the experience of a sense of dignity arises from positive reinforcement. A rock musician who receives a standing ovation and a real feeling of worth will no doubt come back to perform an encore. Skinner looks at the behaviour of people as a product of evolution. He said that 'things are good (positively reinforcing) or bad (negatively reinforcing) because of the contingencies of survival under which the species evolved'.

'What is humanity?'

In his view of human nature, Skinner does at least accept that human consciousness exists. But he devalues human consciousness when he states that:

> BECAUSE CONSCIOUSNESS IS PRIVATE, it is foolish to say that it is any different from the world outside.

> HUMAN CONSCIOUSNESS IS A SOCIAL PRODUCT, which arises when people interact with each other. It does not exist when you are on your own. Skinner's idea of human nature is simple; a person is the behaviour they exhibit.

The picture which emerges from a scientific analysis is not of a body with a person inside, but of a body which is a person in the sense that it displays a complex repertoire of behaviour.

According to Skinner, a human being is a higher animal: 'Man is much more than a dog, but like a dog he is within range of a scientific analysis.'

But also, a human being is a machine: 'Man is a machine in the sense that he is a complex system behaving in lawful ways, but the complexity is extraordinary'. (These three quotations are all from *Beyond Freedom and Dignity*.)

Behaviourism has been strongly criticized:

IT REDUCES HUMANKIND TO A COLLECTION OF BEHAVIOURS and therefore dehumanizes us.

IT SUFFERS FROM A LACK OF REALITY in its assessment of people. The rich inner lives of men and women, which include imagination, creativity, faith in God, cannot be dismissed in terms of conditioning behaviour. How can you measure this?

THE MORE PERSUADED BEHAVIOURISTS ARE INCONSISTENT in that they use their own awareness to dismiss the self-awareness of those they observe. Thus human nature is reduced to suit the psychologist's assumptions.

Arthur Koestler, in *The Ghost in the Machine* (1976) criticized Behaviourism in this way:

Behaviourism is indeed a kind of flat-earth view of the mind. Or to change the metaphor: it has replaced the anthropomorphic fallacy – ascribing to animals human faculties and sentiments – with the opposite fallacy: denying to man faculties not found in lower animals. It has substituted for the erstwhile anthropomorphic view of the rat, a ratomorphic view of man.

Physical science has progressed by leaving the mind out of what it tries to understand. But the reasons against a purely physical theory of consciousness make it difficult to believe that a physical theory of the whole of reality is possible. If consciousness itself could be somehow identified with a form of physical state, then the way would be paved for a unified physical theory of mind and body. And who knows? Maybe a unified physical theory of the universe?

PART 3

Does God Exist?

PHILOSOPHY OF RELIGION

From Plato to Bertrand Russell

Arguments for the Existence of God

Trying to prove something is endlessly fascinating.

* Two and two is four, I'll prove it to you.

* Caroline fancies John, I'll prove it to you.

* I was not at home on the night of the fifteenth, I'll prove it to you.

* Water boils at 100 degrees centigrade, I'll prove it to you.

* God exists, I'll prove it to you.

Proving something true means showing certainty where before there was uncertainty. TV programmes or films about detectives usually hinge on proving something, which is part of their popularity. And in the history of science there has often been a race or a struggle to prove some great theory or new discovery, which has been exciting.

Some kinds of proof are easier to accept than others. Generally speaking, mathematical proof is taken as certain; you can show that two and two equal four. But scientific proof is taken as highly probable; you can show that an experiment has worked every time, but not that it will work every time in the future. In science there is always room for doubt, and you cannot say that something is absolutely true.

But what about philosophical proof? Is it possible to talk about 'philosophical proof' at all when philosophy deals with a variety of ways of thinking about the world? These ways of thinking have changed as cultures have changed and as our understanding of the world has changed. We may still wish to ask some of the same questions that the Ancient Greeks did or the early Christians did. It is unlikely, however, that we will accept their reasoning without some interpretation of our own, as our understanding of the world and the way we think about the world have changed.

The existence of God

For centuries philosophers and theologians were concerned with trying to prove the existence of God. Some of the greatest thinkers who have ever lived have pored at length over this question. For, as is obvious, proving God is vastly different from proving anything else.

If God exists, then God exists in a different way from, say, a tree or a flower. If God exists, he must exist beyond our senses as we cannot smell God, or touch him or hear him.

'Does God exist?' and 'How does God exist?' are two questions which have plagued philosophers and theologians from the time of the Ancient Greeks up to the present century. Proving God began with:

PLATO, who was the first to use the term *theologia*, which has come into modern use as 'theology'. In Plato's writings, the Form of the Good, the Ultimate Form in his world of Forms, has been identified with God.

ARISTOTLE, in whose thought the Unmoved Mover, that which causes all change and motion and desire for perfection in the universe, has been identified with God.

AUGUSTINE, who believed that there must be an Ultimate Truth which accounts for all the unchanging truths in the human mind. This Ultimate Truth, according to Augustine, has to be God.

Yet these definitions of God are philosophical definitions. Platonic and Aristotelian thought was incorporated into Christianity as a means of developing Christian theology. It is legitimate to ask, 'What kind of God were the Christian philosophers and theologians trying to prove?'

The simple answer is that they were trying to prove the existence of the Christian God. They believed that the Christian God was the only true God. These thinkers believed they had an understanding of the character of the Christian God through revelation found in the Bible; and through faith found in their own experience.

But these thinkers needed more than revelation and faith to make their claim for God's existence credible to the world at large; they needed to use reason – but reason in harmony with revelation and faith.

Revelation and faith provided the framework within which reason could do its work. They gave an understanding of God which reason sought to reach, or at least to reach partly, through its own merits.

The Christian God

The Christian understanding of God grew out of the Jewish understanding of God. The Hebrew Bible, which Christians call the Old Testament, declares in Deuteronomy:

> Hear, O Israel: The Lord our God is one Lord; and you shall love the Lord your God with all your heart, and with all your soul, and with all your mind.

According to such a statement, it follows that:

* This view of God is not 'polytheistic', believing in many gods, as was that of the Ancient Greeks. Jews and Christians, like Muslims, are 'monotheists', believing in one God.

* God is personal. He is not some distant, cosmic force. God declares repeatedly in the Old Testament, 'I am the God of your fathers, the God of Abraham, the God of Isaac, and the God of Jacob.'

This God is:

CREATOR, who made the world. The Bible begins with the words 'In the beginning God created the heavens and the earth'. Early Christians wished to claim that God had created the world *ex nihilo* ('out of nothing'). This was not so much for biblical reasons, as to show that God was first and foremost in the universe; that God and the creation were distinct; and that the entire creation is dependent on God for its existence.

LORD. God is Ruler and King of all, worthy of worship. Everything that exists stands in relation to God.

SELF-EXISTENT. God is not dependent on any other thing in order to be God. While we exist because God has created us, God exists just because he is. God is eternal, without beginning or end.

GOOD AND LOVING. God is good and has created a world that is basically good, though it has gone wrong through sin. God is pictured as a father. More specifically, in the New Testament, Jesus calls God 'Abba', which was the intimate family word children used of their father, a little like 'Daddy'. In the New Testament teaching about love, there is a strong distinction drawn between *eros*, love which desires because some object or person has caused that desire; and *agape* (pronounced 'a-ga-pey'), love which gives, and is universal and unconditional. 'Agape' loves something because it is, for the mere fact that it exists. It is the hallmark of the Christian God.

HOLY. Other, mysterious and terrifying. To be aware of God, for a worshipper, is to be aware of God's perfections and of human imperfections. As a result, human beings need forgiveness and cleansing.

This God, then, is the God whose existence the philosophers and theologians were trying to prove.

Anselm and the Ontological Argument

There have been many attempts to 'prove' God's existence. An important early proof which has intrigued thinkers since it was first put forward is the ontological argument ('ontological' means 'talking about being' – here the 'being' or 'existence' of God). This special argument was used by Anselm, a Benedictine monk who lived in the Middle Ages. Anselm sought to develop his theology within the faith of his monastic community and the turbulent politics of the world of his time.

Anselm (1033-1109) was born at Aosta, Piedmont, in modern Italy. He entered the Benedictine monastery of Bec, in Normandy, as a novice aged twenty-six. He later became prior and finally abbot of Bec, but ended his life as Archbishop of Canterbury (1093-1109).

Anselm clashed with several kings over the delicate relationship between church and State. As a result, he was forced to spend most of his time as Archbishop in exile on the continent.

Anselm was the first truly great theologian of the medieval period, and the founder of Scholasticism (the kind of philosophy taught in medieval universities). At a time when the church was gaining great power and influence, he brought theology back to a level which had been lost. During the centuries after Roman rule had crumbled in Britain – the 'Dark Ages' – monasteries had become the storehouses of learning and culture.

Because of this, faith and reason, philosophy and theology, had become united in the monks' lives and thought. In Anselm's time, many had come to believe that Christianity could be understood only by faith. In many ways, theology had been reduced to commentaries on the Bible. Anselm, however, allowed philosophy a distinct role within theology. While he believed that the content of the Christian faith could be given only by revelation (the meaning of the incarnation, for example, that Jesus is both God and human), reason seeks to understand what faith believes. This view of 'faith seeking understanding' is one Anselm received from Augustine.

Anselm sought to provide a 'proof' of God which would work by reason, but which would be in accordance with his Christian faith: 'The rational mind alone of all creatures is able to mount an investigation of the supreme being.'

After working on some early dialogues, Anselm wrote the *Monologion* in 1071. In this work Anselm offers a 'proof' for the existence of God. Briefly, Anselm asserts that as we can see degrees of goodness in the world, these forms of goodness must ultimately come from a Form of Goodness which we can call God.

Anselm's argument is Platonic. It rests on the assumption that the Ideal is more 'real' than the real, just as Plato believed that the Form of the Good was more real than particular instances of good in the world. Anselm's use of Plato as a way of understanding reality underpins his entire ontological argument.

This argument was put forward a year after the *Monologion* in the *Proslogion* (originally entitled 'Faith seeking Understanding'). In the *Proslogion* (which takes the form of a prayer to God), Anselm defines God as:

'that-than-which-a-greater-cannot-be-thought'. Once this definition is accepted – and it can be accepted by those who do not share the Christian faith – Anselm's argument develops:

> If then 'that-than-which-a-greater-cannot-be-thought' exists in the mind alone, this same that-than-which-a-greater-cannot-be-thought is 'that-than-which-a-greater-can-be-thought'. But this is obviously impossible. Therefore there is absolutely no doubt that 'something-than-which-a-greater-cannot-be-thought' exists both in the mind and in reality.

Anselm is claiming that:

* God is the greatest conceivable being.

* It is greater to exist in reality than just in thought.

* Therefore God exists.

Anselm's argument has caused consternation since it first appeared. One critic likened readers meeting it to 'when they see a conjurer extract a rabbit from an apparently empty hat. They cannot explain how the rabbit got there, but they are pretty certain that the conjurer introduced it somehow.' There has been strong disagreement ever since as to whether Anselm had expressed a vitally important philosophical truth, or whether he was just plain and obviously wrong.

Anselm's argument appeals to us, but we have to remember that when he was writing people had a very different view of the world. Nowadays the view that knowledge comes through experience is so powerful that it is almost impossible to think in any other way.

The issue is: 'Is there anything that must exist, just because we can think of it?'

Anselm's proof relies on pure thought and not experience – it is *a priori*, no previous knowledge of the world is required to understand it. His proof raises an important question about the nature of God. When we talk about God, is God's existence a predicate?

A house has walls, windows and a roof; these are things a house has to have in order to be a house. They are called 'predicates'. When thinking about God, then, is existence necessarily a predicate? Does God have to have existence in order to be God? Does the notion of God necessarily include the fact that God must exist?

To put it another way, certain statements contain their own definition: for example, 'a triangle has three angles'; 'a bachelor is an unmarried man'.

These statements are undeniably true. But, does 'God exists' apply in the same way? When we say 'God exists', is that exactly the same as saying 'a triangle has three sides' or 'a bachelor is an unmarried man'? Anselm thought that it was and he could think this because of the way in which Plato had influenced his understanding of reality. Plato viewed thought as being more real than objects in the physical, external world. On this basis, Anselm's argument works. Other philosophers since have not been so convinced. Many have accused Anselm of trying to define God into existence.

Fools and critics

Anselm considered that his argument was strong enough to persuade the 'fool' who, as Psalm 14:1 has it, 'says in his heart that there is no God'. Anselm's first critic was another monk called Gaunilo from Marmoutiers in France, who wrote *On Behalf of the Fool*. Gaunilo applied Anselm's argument to the most perfect island imaginable. He drew the conclusion that because he could imagine it, the island must exist. Yet, of course, there is no reason why such an island should exist.

Anselm's answer was that his argument applied only to God. An island is necessarily a dependent thing, part of creation. God, however, is independent, eternal and self-existent. An island is 'contingent' (it may or may not exist), while God is 'necessary' (God, by reason of being God, has to exist).

Since Gaunilo, Anselm has had his followers and his critics:

RENÉ DESCARTES (1596-1650) used a form of ontological argument. Descartes claimed that God's existence was necessary to the definition of God, just as three angles were necessary to the definition of a triangle. Like Anselm, Descartes was much influenced by Plato and believed that people were born with innate ideas.

BENEDICT SPINOZA (1632-77) used the ontological argument in his *Ethics*, though his definition of God was different from both the Christian and the Jewish ones. In the eleventh proposition of Book 1, Spinoza wrote: 'God, or substance, consisting of infinite attributes, of which each expresses eternal and infinite essentiality, necessarily exists.'

THOMAS AQUINAS (c. 1225-74) was one of many critics. He believed that Anselm made a mistake in claiming to know God's nature before his existence. Aquinas believed that the existence of God had to be established by other means and, after that, studying who God was would lead to the knowledge of God's nature found in Anselm's argument.

IMMANUEL KANT (1724-1804), following on from Scottish philosopher David Hume (1711-76), believed that 'existence' could not be part of the definition of any idea. For example, the idea of a dog – that it is furry and barks – is the same whether the dog exists or not. The extent to which we imagine God as the greatest conceivable being cannot be increased by imagining that God exists. Instead, Kant claimed, God stays firmly in the mind and no bridge can be built from the world of ideas to the world of reality.

BERTRAND RUSSELL (1872-1970) claimed that the word 'exist' was being used wrongly. To say 'cows exist' is to have an idea of a cow and then to find that an animal actually exists to which this description can be attached. This process does not work with 'unicorns exist' as there are no animals to which this description can be attached. The same is true of God. The phrase 'God exists' can be understood, but as there is no apparent reality to which this phrase can be attached, then it cannot be 'proved' using the ontological argument.

The ontological argument has been stubborn in its refusal to disappear. Many philosophers have written about it and all of them disagree about what they find mistaken in it. Anselm himself was aiming to show how reasonable faith is, rather than offer a strict proof of it. It is a testimony to his brilliance and ingenuity that the ontological argument continues to attract modern philosophers and continues to cause them to search into the meaning of the existence of God.

Influences on Anselm's thought

Anselm's philosophical background was made up of a variety of important influences. The Bible and the Church Fathers were among these, of course, particularly Augustine – Anselm held Augustine's view that 'I believe in order to understand'. Plato also was a strong influence; Anselm had a

Platonic rather than an Aristotelian outlook, though he had read Aristotle and used his logic. Anselm would have had access to Plato's works at second or third hand, as Greek was not studied in his time and much of Plato's work was unavailable. In the medieval world Plato was seen as a religious philosopher, author of the Theory of Forms. Neo-Platonism was also part of Anselm's mental picture: he used Plotinus to come to a knowledge of the Christian Trinity (the belief that God is three persons: God the Father, God the Son and God the Holy Spirit, and yet God remains one God). Neo-Platonism had its own 'trinity' of One, Mind and Soul. Boethius (c. 480-524) wrote the Consolation of Philosophy while under imprisonment by the Gothic King Theodoric. The 'Consolation' does not contain any explicitly Christian teaching, but relies on reason as a help in the face of disaster. Boethius saw reason and faith as two distinct ways of looking at the world. After the Bible, the 'Consolation' was, perhaps, the most read, translated and discussed book for several hundred years.

The Five Ways

Thomas Aquinas

To understand the Middle Ages is to grapple with a world very different from our own. If you lived in the Middle Ages you would believe that the sun went round the earth and that the earth was at the very centre of the universe. You would believe that the world had been created in six days, as written in the Book of Genesis in the Bible. You would believe that the 'Great Chain of Being', beginning with God, moved down through the angels to the lowest forms of plant and animal life, with human beings as the midpoint between the mortal and the divine. You would believe that the universe possessed a fixed order; everything had its place. Mathematics governed the circular movement of the heavenly bodies and learning was founded on the classical authors of Greece and Rome.

In the Middle Ages the major part of Europe, including Britain, France, Italy and Germany, used Latin as an international language. The two most powerful institutions were the Holy Roman Empire and the Roman Catholic Church. The church and the Christian faith enfolded every aspect of life.

This was the period which saw the rise of the universities. The University of Paris which had grown from the Cathedral School of Notre Dame, was approved by the Pope in 1215. Universities in Spain and Italy were just beginning, and Oxford and Cambridge received their first Chancellors. Students followed the same curriculum of the seven 'liberal arts': grammar, logic, rhetoric, arithmetic, geometry, music and astronomy. The most important centre by far for the study of philosophy and theology was the University of Paris.

Aristotle was *the* philosopher of the medieval period. Aquinas referred to him more times in his work than to the Bible. Aristotle's writings had been preserved by scholars from the first century to the sixth century AD. Interest in his works was revived in Byzantium in the eighth century, and they were translated into Latin and circulated in Europe in the twelfth. After initial suspicion from the church – his works had been passed on through suspect scholars and Muslim commentators – his science and philosophy went unchallenged in the West for four centuries.

Gradually there was a change: the centres of study moved more and more from the monasteries into the universities. The philosophy of this period was named 'Scholasticism', because it was taught by scholars in medieval universities. From this period on, philosophy found its natural 'home' in the university and became less and less exclusively associated with the church.

Thomas Aquinas

The greatest of the scholastics was St Thomas Aquinas (c. 1225-74), whose brand of philosophy is known as 'Thomism'. Aquinas' achievements were colossal. He made the works of Aristotle known and acceptable to the scholars of his day. By doing this he displaced Plato. He devised a vast metaphysical 'system' with a battery of technical terms. He put forward the famous 'five proofs' for the existence of God and dealt with the problem of religious language – how we can talk about God and mean something. Aquinas also defined the doctrine of 'transubstantiation', barely mentioned at the Lateran Council of 1215. Transubstantiation concerns the Christian service of communion, and holds that the bread and wine used in this ceremony in some way actually become the body and blood of Christ. Aquinas became the 'official' theologian of the Roman Catholic Church through a pronouncement by Pope Leo in 1879. If the great symbol of the Middle Ages is the cathedral – solid, resolute and enduring – then Aquinas' work is exactly typical of that time.

Thomas Aquinas was a saint, a mystic, a theologian and a metaphysician. He was born around 1225 near Naples, son of the Count of Aquina. Aquinas went to school under the Benedictines at the famous monastery of Monte Cassino and then attended the University of Naples. There, in 1244, he became a Dominican – a newly founded order of (poor) monks. His family was horrified and kidnapped him, but Thomas remained firm and had his own way.

Aquinas continued his studies at Paris, and at Cologne under Albert the Great. He was a large, slow man and the other students nicknamed him 'the dumb ox'. His brilliance, however, was never in question and Albert the Great declared: 'this dumb ox will fill the world with his bellowing.' Aquinas returned to Paris in 1254 where he became a full professor two years later. He taught in Paris and Italy until his death in 1274 on his way to the Council of Lyons. His work was condemned in Paris and Oxford and was not approved again until fifty years after his death. He was made a saint in 1323. While saying Mass in December 1273, Aquinas had an experience which may have been a vision or a nervous breakdown. He stopped writing. When urged to continue, he told his secretary 'I cannot, because all I have written now seems like straw.'

Aquinas' output was massive; his *Summa Theologica* alone contains more than two million words. His entire works were written within the space of twenty years.

Aquinas' two main works are:

Summa contra Gentiles or the 'Manual against the Heathen', written for those who do not believe in the Christian faith; and *Summa Theologica*, the 'Manual of Theology', written for Christians, especially for young monks studying theology.

Aquinas' Latin is dense but lucid. He shows concern for clear and accurate expression. Such care was a feature of the Middle Ages, and gives Aquinas' philosophy a modern cast at a time when concerns about philosophy and language have become closely linked once again.

When approaching Aquinas, it is important to remember that:

AQUINAS DISLIKED PLATO and rejected Anselm's ontological argument. He adapted Aristotle for the church's use with little alteration. He provided a new order of thought for a new age. Aquinas' philosophy started with the real world and not with ideas in the head.

AQUINAS WAS A CHRISTIAN and believed that studying philosophy would lead to the confirmation of Christian teaching. While he separated reason from revelation, Aquinas believed that there was nothing in revelation which could contradict reason. He believed that the Christian faith guarantees philosophy just as philosophy guarantees the Christian faith.

AQUINAS WAS A MEDIEVAL MAN. He believed, along with others of his time, that: reason is subordinate to faith; nature is subordinate to grace; philosophy is subordinate to theology; and the state is subordinate to the church.

Aquinas believed that correct philosophy can illuminate theology. He gave reason a special position, he believed that philosophy could find out some truths, though not all truths, regarding the Christian faith. In the work of Aquinas, therefore, reason and faith begin to separate. Aquinas believed that his system was like a 'two-storey house'. Aristotelian philosophy provided the foundations and first storey; Catholic theology perfected the house by adding the second storey and the roof.

Aquinas' emphasis on reason led to a gradual severing between 'natural' reason and 'supernatural' faith. He believed that reason could discover a limited number of truths about God, but doctrines such as the Trinity and the incarnation could only be understood through revelation. Reason travelled through the Middle Ages by way of the Renaissance and Reformation to the Enlightenment and the emergence of modern, autonomous humankind.

The five ways

Aquinas began by asking three questions: Is it self-evident there is a God? Can it be made evident? Is there a God? Aquinas was convinced that the existence of God was not self-evident. Human beings, after all, cannot describe God as they can describe an object in the world; they cannot touch, see, smell or hear God. He was also convinced, however, that reflecting on natural features of the world gave a great deal of evidence that God existed. His proofs began with what people experienced and observed every day. Unlike Anselm, Aquinas did not believe that understanding the term 'God' is enough to show that God exists. He rejected Anselm's *a priori* Platonic proof, which began in the mind, and concentrated on five *a posteriori* Aristotelian proofs, which began with the world.

Aquinas concluded:

> The awareness that God exists is not implanted in us by nature in any clear or specific way. Admittedly, man is aware of what by nature he

desires, and he desires by nature a happiness which is to be found only in God. But this is not, simply speaking, awareness that there is a God, any more than to be aware of someone approaching is to be aware of Peter, even should it be Peter approaching. Many, in fact, believe the ultimate good which will make us happy to be riches, or pleasure, or some such thing.

In other words, God is not obvious. So Aquinas rejected Platonism and thought it impossible to climb from truth to Truth and call that Ultimate Truth God.

Aquinas went on to set out five ways or 'proofs' of God. The word he used for proof is *demonstratio* which is a strong and conclusive term:

IN WAY 1, Aquinas concentrated on the fact of change in the world. 'Now anything in process of change is being changed by something else,' he wrote. Going back to Aristotle's Unmoved Mover, Aquinas concluded: 'If the hand does not move the stick, the stick will not move anything else. Hence one is bound to arrive at some first cause or change not itself being changed by anything, and this is what everybody understands by God.'

IN WAY 2, Aquinas concentrated on the fact that cause and effect exist in the world. 'Now if you eliminate a cause you also eliminate its effects, so that you cannot have a last cause, nor an intermediate one, unless you have a first.' Aquinas could not believe in an endless chain of causes and effects stretching back into eternity: 'One is therefore forced to suppose some first cause, to which everyone gives the name "God".'

WAY 3 takes up the idea of being and non-being in the world. Things exist, but they need not exist. Moreover, there was a time before they existed and there will be a time after they stop existing. 'Now everything cannot be like this, for a thing that need not be, once was not, and if everything need not be, once upon a time there was nothing...' Aquinas claimed that if everything in the world could or could not exist, then there must have been a time when nothing existed. Nothing can come from nothing: 'One is forced therefore to suppose something which must be, and owes this to no other thing than itself; indeed it itself is the cause that other things must be.' For Aquinas as for Anselm, objects in the world have contingent existence (they can or cannot exist), but only God has necessary existence (God must exist). If God did not exist then nothing could exist, for creation is dependent on God's necessary existence to exist at all.

WAY 4 concentrated on degrees of goodness and perfection in the world. 'For example, things are hotter and hotter the nearer they approach what is hottest. Something therefore is the truest and best and most noble of things, and hence the most fully in being; for Aristotle says that the truest things are the things most fully in being.' Aquinas went on to state: 'There is something therefore which causes in all other things their being, their goodness and whatever other perfection they have. And this we call "God".'

WAY 5 pointed to order and goals in nature. 'For their behaviour hardly ever varies, and will practically always turn out well; which shows that they truly tend to a goal, and do not merely hit it by accident. Nothing that lacks awareness tends to a goal, except under the direction of someone with awareness and understanding; the arrow, for example, requires an archer. Everything in nature, therefore, is directed to its goal by someone with understanding, and this we call "God".'

Aquinas' proofs link with each other and rely heavily on Aristotle's First Cause and Unmoved Mover. They also provided the foundation for the important Argument from Design formulated by William Paley (1743-1803) who said that the world was like a carefully constructed watch, and a 'watch' presupposes a 'watchmaker', God. Yet, while Aquinas' proofs are *a posteriori*, requiring human experience of the world, his apprehension of the nature of God (as opposed to God's existence) is *a priori* since we have no direct access to God through our senses.

Using mainly negative statements about the character of God, stating what God is not, Aquinas came in the end to believe that 'God's essence is his own existence'. Just as a fire's essence is heat, so God's essence is 'being'. God is and this 'is-ness' means that God is self-existent, self-sustaining, indivisible and eternal.

Aquinas developed an important notion of religious language. He defined three types of language: 'univocal', when two words are used in the same sense – John is big; Anne is big; 'equivocal', when two words are used in entirely different senses – the dog has a loud bark; the bark on the tree is brown; and 'analogical', when two words 'share' a sense – God is good; Peter is good. Peter cannot be 'good' in exactly the same way that God is 'good', as God's goodness must far surpass Peter's. Yet Peter's goodness does share, or point to, something of the truth of God's goodness. Analogy, therefore, allows theologians to talk about God (even partially) with meaning. Theologians since the Middle Ages have found Aquinas' notion of analogy useful and convincing.

Aquinas' proofs became standard in demonstrating the existence of God for several hundred years. Even today, some Christian thinkers believe it is possible to form a 'natural' theology which looks at the world and tries to deduce God. However, Aquinas' reasoning was strongly attacked in the eighteenth century.

David Hume (1711-76) attacked Aquinas' notion that cause and effect must come, ultimately, from a First Cause that could be called God. He believed that cause and effect in the world require no explanation; it is either an arbitrary fact of experience, or a function of the human mind as it shapes experience. Hume wondered why God had to be the First Cause anyway; why not another First Cause? Many thinkers have come to believe that Hume's criticism dealt a death-blow to Aquinas' proofs and put an end to any further attempts to construct a 'natural' theology.

Immanuel Kant (1724-1804) believed that cause and effect hold true for the world of sense experience, but only for the world of sense experience. As God exists (if God existed) beyond the world of sense experience, then it is impossible to 'jump' from reasoning about this world to reasoning about God. Reasoning about God, therefore, is reasoning beyond human capacity, and this is fruitless and doomed to failure.

The modern debate

Nowadays the modern debate regarding the existence of God has shifted. We no longer hold a medieval world-view. While Aquinas would have believed that his proofs were as scientific as they were theological, there is now a visible gap between theological language and scientific language which many thinkers are hard-pressed to bridge. Many modern theologians would think it unlikely that a 'scientific' demonstration of God's existence could be given. They would point to Aquinas' prior faith as the basis for his reasoning. In fact, many modern theologians have come to question what the terms 'God' and 'exists' actually mean. For, if God exists, how does God exist? The traditional notion of God as a personal, loving father and creator, active in the world, who wishes to love and save humankind, has been under threat.

Paul Tillich (1886-1965), one of the most influential of modern theologians, expressed his understanding of faith as 'ultimate concern'. Tillich's theology was existential and he claimed that as God cannot be said to exist in the way that anything else in the world exists, then God cannot really be said to exist at all. Tillich believed that the presentation of God in the Bible was a picture of ultimate human experience. Accordingly, he rejected the belief in a personal God. He stated instead that God was 'the ground of our being'.

Tillich's ideas were translated into popular form in John A.T. Robinson's book *Honest to God* (1963). Robinson, like Tillich, believed that the life of Christ contains an example for all to follow, and insights for all to share. What before was only possible, a truly good life had become actual in Christ. Christ lived in a way which cannot be trivialized and this, according to Tillich and Robinson, is the strength and truth of Christianity.

Aquinas' work remains as vast and complex and impressive as any medieval cathedral in any modern city. Yet, if the terms of the debate regarding the existence of God have changed, the fact of the debate has not. Human beings exist and the world exists, but whether God exists or not remains a question which each person has to face, a vital part of how we understand the place of human beings in the world.

The Argument from Religious Experience
The Bible and the Mystics

One well-known account of a religious experience from the Bible is the appearance of Jesus to 'Doubting' Thomas. The disciples of Jesus had experienced him as resurrected and believed in him; Jesus had risen from the dead. Thomas had not experienced and did not believe. Moreover, Thomas doubted the disciples' testimony. Presumably he knew the other disciples and trusted them, but because their story appeared to be impossible, he was not prepared to believe it. In other words, his philosophy prejudiced him against reality.

Arguments for the existence of God based on reason have a distinguished history, as do arguments from faith. But what about the argument from religious experience? What exactly is the argument from religious experience, and how is it to be counted in the debate concerning the existence of God?

The American philosopher, William James (1842-1910), who wrote the classic *The Varieties of Religious Experience* (1902), stated in 1908 that:

> I think it may be asserted that there ARE religious experiences of a specific nature… I think that they point with reasonable probability to the continuity of our consciousness with a wider, spiritual environment from which the ordinary prudential man is shut off.

The argument from religious experience states quite simply that God exists because people have experiences of God and can tell us about them.

The problem with the argument from religious experience is that there are many definitions of the term 'religious experience' in books and individual accounts, and even the word 'religion' is open to a variety of meanings.

What is safe to say is that a religious experience can be counted as such because this is the way it seems to the person who has experienced it.

A RELIGIOUS EXPERIENCE IS AN EXPERIENCE THROUGH THE SENSES of something beyond the everyday world of the senses.

A RELIGIOUS EXPERIENCE IS NOT THE SAME AS A PARANORMAL EXPERIENCE. Ghosts and poltergeists, telepathy and clairvoyance, cannot be identified as religious experiences. The effect and meaning of a religious experience in an individual's life is generally quite different from that of a paranormal experience. Religious experiences change people's lives. And the effect of a religious experience often lasts in a person's life – often leaving people feeling more able to cope afterwards, or that their life has new meaning.

Religious or paranormal? People seem generally aware as to what kind of experience they have had.

Religious experience in the Bible

The Bible contains a record of a variety of religious experiences.
One famous one is the prophet Isaiah's call (Isaiah 6):

> In the year that King Uzziah died, I saw the Lord seated on a throne, high and exalted, and the train of his robe filled the temple… 'Woe to me!' I cried. 'I am ruined! For I am a man of unclean lips, and I live among a people of unclean lips, and my eyes have seen the King, the Lord Almighty.'

Psalm 8 contains a more reflective one:

> When I consider your heavens, the work of your fingers, the moon and the stars, which you have set in place, what is man that you are mindful of him? the son of man that you care for him?

Joseph had a vision (Matthew 2:13):

> When they had gone, an angel of the Lord appeared
> dream. 'Get up,' he said, 'take the child and his mother
> Egypt.'

And so did Mary (Luke 1:26-28):

> In the sixth month, God sent the angel Gabriel to Nazareth, a town in
> Galilee, to a virgin pledged to be married to a man named Joseph, a
> descendant of David. The virgin's name was Mary. The angel went to
> her and said, 'Greetings, you who are highly favoured! The Lord is
> with you.'

The apostle Paul's experience threw him to the ground (Acts 9:3-5):

> As he neared Damascus on a journey, suddenly a light from heaven
> flashed around him. He fell to the ground and heard a voice say to
> him, 'Saul, Saul, why do you persecute me?'

These experiences fit the general types of religious experience which
individuals claim to have. They include perceiving God in nature; visions and
voices; dreams which contain an experience or some advice which has a
bearing on the waking world; mystical experiences; and religious
experiences which cannot be expressed in words.

Sometimes religious experiences are accompanied by sensations of heat,
or pain, or even floating. Sometimes they are described in terms of a 'holy
presence' or an 'ultimate reality' and do not speak in terms of encountering
God. Even researchers who admit the validity of religious experiences would
be hesitant to claim that they necessarily reveal the Christian God. In fact,
religious experiences cut across all religions, and both religious and non-
religious people claim to have religious experiences.

Some researchers would claim that such experiences are shaped by the
religious community of which the individual is a member. People often have
visions of the saints and deities found in their churches or temples. Some
researchers think that Protestants, Jews and Muslims, who do not use
images in worship, might tend to hear voices, while Roman Catholics and
Hindus might tend to see visions. It is certainly true that each religious
community possesses its own writings, culture and overall 'form' of religious
life which may give a shape or an interpretation to a particular individual's
experience. For example, a person may claim to have seen God as a 'king', a
real king in a vision, because that person's particular religious community
prefers to talk about or picture God as a king.

While certain types of people (such as prophets or mystics) may be more prone to religious experiences than others, it is a fact that many people, of all kinds, have them. If nothing else, religious experiences show that religion is a matter of living faith, not intellectual acceptance. The religious claim to 'know' God is knowledge by acquaintance, not knowledge merely by intellectual assent.

Criticisms of this argument

The argument from religious experience has been attacked from several directions. The most obvious problem with religious experience is that experience cannot be offered as intellectual proof or scientific evidence. Experience is what happens to someone, and experience is always open to a variety of interpretations.

In the end, we either believe a person's testimony or not. Some researchers would claim that if a person is trustworthy in other areas of life, then that is a good reason for taking a person's religious experience seriously on its own terms.

However, religious experiences have been derided as delusions, lies or hallucinations. Philosophers, psychologists, sociologists and anthropologists have tended to view religious experiences as purely human. They would claim that these experiences may have an emotional impact on people's lives, but they cannot be used as evidence to tell us anything about God.

These researchers would claim that religious experiences occur within the context of a particular religious language. This language gives shape to the experience and so the experience itself cannot be evaluated quite as it appears to the individual. Also, religious experiences are emotional events; they are private and can tell us nothing about God or an order of reality behind the everyday. Such experiences are ineffable, they cannot really be put into words. If they are, these words cannot be used as reliable evidence for what actually happened.

John Hick, in his book *Philosophy of Religion*, sums up a general theological view:

In short, any special event or experience which can be constituted as manifesting the divine can also be constituted in other ways, and accordingly cannot carry the weight of a proof of God's existence.

Christianity and religious experience

There are several kinds of religious experience which have a firm and honourable place within the religious tradition:

CONVERSION is a central one, which involves changing from one set of beliefs to another. Many people claim that they have been 'converted' by some experience to a particular religion. John Wesley, the founder of Methodism, recorded his conversion to Christianity in his journal for 24 May 1738:

> In the evening I went very unwillingly to a society in Aldersgate Street, where one was reading Luther's preface to the Epistle to the Romans. About a quarter before nine, while he was describing the change which God works in the heart through faith in Christ, I felt my heart strangely warmed. I felt I did trust in Christ, Christ alone, for salvation; and an assurance was given me, that he had taken away my sins, even mine, and saved me from the law of sin and death.

VOCATION is a term for the experience many people feel of being specially 'called' to a special task or job. This is not only true of religious people such as priests, nuns and missionaries, but of doctors and teachers, and others too.

HEALING can be a religious experience. Many people give testimony to remarkable or miraculous healings which they claim come from God or from some divine power.

THE 'SPIRIT' is a central feature: experiences such as overwhelming love, speaking in strange languages previously unknown to the speaker, prophecies, pictures, special 'words of knowledge' and other such manifestations are part of the everyday worship of some religious communities. These experiences apply to more than one religion. Within the Christian religion they have been associated with the Charismatic Movement ('charismatic' means 'receiving gifts from God'). This movement has gathered momentum over the last twenty-five years. The followers of the Charismatic Movement claim that these experiences are available to everyone, though different people receive different 'gifts' or experiences.

SOME IMPORTANT FIGURES IN THE GOD DEBATE

The Old Testament

The Mystics, God in experience

Plato (427-348BC), God is the Ultimate Form

Aristotle (384-322BC), God is the Unmoved Mover

Augustine of Hippo (AD354-430), God is the Ultimate Truth

Anselm (1033-1109), formulated the Ontological Argument

Thomas Aquinas (c. 1225-74), the 'five' ways

René Descartes (1596-1650), idea of perfection

Benedict Spinoza (1632-77), re-stated Ontological Argument

John Wesley (1703-91), need for experience of God

David Hume (1711-76), criticized Anselm and Aquinas

Immanuel Kant (1724-1804), cause and effect restricted to sense experience

William Paley (1743-1805), argument from design

Friedrich Schleiermacher (1768-1834), moved from philosophy to experience

Ludwig Feuerbach (1804-72), God is psychological projection

Charles Darwin (1809-82), does evolution preclude creator?

Karl Marx (1818-83), religion is opium of the people

Sigmund Freud (1856-1939), God is our own 'superego'

Bertrand Russell (1872-1970), heroic atheism

Martin Buber (1878-1965), relationship with God underlies all others

Paul Tillich (1886-1965), God is 'ground of our being'

400BC 200 0 200 400 600 800 1000 1200 1400 1600 1800

Mysticism has an honoured place within many religious traditions. It usually hovers on the fringes of orthodoxy. In Islam there are Sufis, in Judaism there is the Kaballah. Within Christianity mysticism begins in the Bible, but is first treated at length by the early Christian writers such as the Desert Fathers. Gregory of Nyssa (c. 300-395) wrote:

> The true vision and the true knowledge of what we seek consists precisely in not seeing, in an awareness that our goal transcends all knowledge and is everywhere cut off from us by the darkness of incomprehensibility.

Mystical experiences are often accompanied by a holy presence, a sense of 'oneness' with God or the universe, and an assurance.

These are often considered as the 'ultimate' religious experience, the closest a human being can come to meeting the divine reality and live. Insights gained through such experiences are, accordingly, 'ultimate' and never trivial. Mystics often claim that they have perceived what is universally and eternally true about the nature of human beings, the world, and their relationship to the divine.

Many famous mystics have written of their experiences throughout the ages: Teresa of Avila, Meister Eckhart, Jakob Boehme, Richard Rolle, and Dame Julian of Norwich, whose *Revelations of Divine Love* are still read eagerly today. The philosopher Blaise Pascal (1623-62) had a famous experience, and he recorded it on a piece of paper which was found sewn into his clothing after his death:

> From about half past ten in the evening to about half an hour
> after midnight.
> Fire.
> God of Abraham, God of Isaac, God of Jacob.
> Not the God of philosophers and scholars.
> Absolute Certainty: Beyond reason. Joy. Peace.
> Forgetfulness of the world and everything but God.
> The world has not known thee, but I have known
> thee. Joy! Joy! Joy! Tears of joy!

Whatever the validity of mystical experiences, their impact cannot be in doubt.

Two philosophers of religious experience

Another approach to religious experience has been to take experience as a foundation for constructing a theological outlook. Reason and faith have been the traditional bases on which to build a theology, but some religious thinkers have turned to the dimension of religious experience as a starting-point for talking about religion.

Friedrich Schleiermacher (1768-1834) was a professor of theology at the University of Berlin. Schleiermacher was the founder of the school of liberal theology. He lived at a time when Christian teaching was under attack from rational sceptics. Also at that time, Romanticism (with its emphasis on feeling and subjective experience) had a strong influence in Europe. Schleiermacher removed religion from theology and ethics, from knowledge and action, and claimed that religion was nothing but feeling and experience. This led to a new understanding of Christianity. Revelation became narrowed to the religious experience of each individual: 'Every intuition and every original feeling proceeds from revelation... If nothing original has yet been generated in you, when it does come it will be a revelation to you also.'

The essence of religion, according to Schleiermacher, did not lie in knowing or doing, but in 'the consciousness of being absolutely dependent or, which is the same thing, of being in relation with God.' In Schleiermacher, the Bible is treated as a record of religious experience, rather than a revelation from God or a record of his objective acts in history. Schleiermacher, in his thinking, separated religion from reason and faith from history. By putting religion beyond the attacks of the rationalists, many would claim that Schleiermacher also sacrificed Christianity's ability to communicate intellectually with the modern world.

Martin Buber (1878-1965) was a Jewish philosopher and theologian, born in Vienna. He lectured on Jewish religion and ethics in Frankfurt-am-Main in Germany from 1925 until the rise of Nazi power forced him to leave in 1933. Eventually he settled in Israel where he became a professor at the Hebrew University. Buber's most famous book is *I and Thou* (1923). In this book, Buber describes two basic attitudes to the world:

* I-Thou, which shows a mutual relationship existing between subject and object.

* I-It, which shows that some control or objectification exists between subject and object. Here 'I' is active and 'It' is passive; I-It is inferior to I-Thou.

Buber's notion of God is as the eternal Thou and relationship with God is the only I-Thou relationship which can be sustained indefinitely by humankind. In other words, I-Thou with God reveals the whole of existence as standing in relationship to God and this leads a human being into a special religious experience of the world. Buber wrote:

> For those who enter into the absolute relationship, nothing particular retains any importance – neither things nor beings, neither earth nor heaven – but everything is included in the relationship. For entering into the pure relationship does not involve ignoring everything but seeing everything in the You, not renouncing the world but placing it upon its proper ground.

In the context of Western culture and civilization, Christianity has made stringent efforts to appear credible and convincing to changing eras of thought. At the same time, Christianity has had to remind each new age that it is a living faith whose followers claim to experience God first hand. Although Buber was Jewish, it is not surprising that his work has appealed strongly to Christian theologians. If the argument from religious experience is not a proof of God's existence, perhaps the fact that ordinary and reasonable people claim such experiences to be true should at least make us re-examine our view of the world and how we believe reality is constructed.

Finally, if there is no such thing as a conclusive proof for the existence of God, it should not be forgotten that there is also no conclusive proof that God does not exist. The question of God's existence remains open; the question still has to be faced. What the argument from religious experience shows is that this is a question not just for our minds, but for our whole being.

Types of belief and unbelief

There are a variety of positions which people have taken up on this whole question of the existence of God:

'Atheists' deny that God exists. An atheist would claim that rational argument points away from the likelihood of there being a God.

'Agnostics' believe that it is impossible to believe one way or the other (in Latin *agnosco* means 'I do not know'). Agnostics think that there is not enough evidence to establish the existence of God or the fact that God does not exist. There are those, sometimes called 'fideists', who believe that religious knowledge cannot be based in any way on reason, but only on faith. On this view, the power of human reason cannot stretch as far as reasoning about God. Others focus on 'revelation': knowledge of God comes, not through using reason, but through revelation. People who believe in revelation claim that God has to reveal himself, and that philosophers are missing the point by relying on reason. Revelation usually comes through a particular text, like the Bible – or through a special experience.

'Pantheists' believe that the universe is God and God is the universe. There is no distinction between God and creation; God is everywhere, in everything, and is everything. The most famous example of pantheism is found in the work of Benedict Spinoza (1632-77).

'Deists' believe that God created the world and set it going. Now, however, God is removed from the world and plays no active part in it. Deists do not believe in prayer or in a personal relationship with God. Deism grew out of scientific advances in the seventeenth century and sought to account for the universe as mechanical and self-contained – like a clock. God was pictured as a 'watchmaker', but a watchmaker who had retired.

Routes to Knowledge

RATIONALISM AND EMPIRICISM

Knowing Through the Mind

René Descartes

Imagine watching television. Suddenly there comes a newsflash. Scientists have just discovered that the moon is made of green cheese. Green cheese! What is more, the earth is pyramid-shaped and balanced on the back of a gigantic turtle... What would you think?

This information would be a lot to take in. You might think it ridiculous, a joke – how could it be true? If it were true you would have to change the whole way you thought about the world. Suddenly, nothing would seem sure any more. You would begin to doubt.

René Descartes (1596-1650) lived at a time when beliefs about the world were changing. During his life, beliefs based on Aristotle were giving way to the new discoveries of science. Many people did not know what to think and had become sceptics – doubting if it were possible to prove that anything was absolutely and certainly true. As the rise of science seemed to conflict with a sure belief in God, the church was bitter in its attacks on developing scientific ways of thinking. There was religious conflict – Catholic against Protestant, church against science; and scientific conflict – Aristotle's views against Copernicus, Kepler and Galileo.

Nicolas Copernicus (1473-1543) was born in Poland. He was the founder of modern astronomy, and showed that the earth was a sphere which circled the sun. His work was condemned by the church because it showed humankind was not at the centre of the universe. Johannes Kepler

(1571-1630) was a German astronomer who showed that the orbits of the planets were not perfectly circular as had been previously thought. Galileo Galilei (1564-1642) founded modern mechanics and maintained, along with Copernicus, that the earth went round the sun. For this he was forced by the church in 1633 to reject his own views and was placed under house arrest for the remainder of his life. Galileo argued, among other things, for a separation of science and theology.

Descartes was born in 1596 at La Haye, near Tours in North-west France. His father was a lawyer. He was educated at the famous Jesuit College at La Flèche, where he received a traditional Aristotelian schooling, but also studied some of the modern advances in science. In his own mind, Descartes was first and foremost a scientist, but he is remembered as a philosopher.

Descartes became a soldier in Holland, but left the army in 1621 to devote himself to science and philosophy. On 10 November 1619, while at Ulm in Germany, he shut himself away in a stove-heated room; there he had a daytime vision and three dreams which he believed were a revelation from God about his life's work. This was to be the unfolding of a wonderful new science. He went back to France, but moved again to Holland in 1629 and stayed there, more or less alone, for twenty years.

His *Discourse on Method* was published in 1637, and he began his *Meditations* in 1639, in which he set out his philosophy. His work was aimed at the public, not just at philosophers, and he wrote in French, not Latin.

Descartes' writing provoked harsh arguments with some Dutch theologians, and in 1648 he accepted an invitation from Queen Christina of Sweden to teach her philosophy. This decision was disastrous; Descartes was unhappy at court and the Swedish winter did not agree with him. He died in Stockholm in 1650.

Descartes' method

Descartes' work is post-medieval. It shows a break with Aristotle and the beginning of modern philosophy. At a time when religion was suspicious of science and science was sceptical of religion, Descartes wanted to show that you could have both. He wanted a science acceptable to religion. Even so, his work was dominated by scientific questions.

Descartes wanted to put knowledge to the test, in order to find a sure foundation on which to build the entire structure of human understanding. To advance in science he found that he had to make a detour into philosophy. For this, Descartes devised a method: a method of doubting. He learned the method from his Jesuit education; the doubting came from the age he lived in. Descartes wanted to peel away everything that could possibly be doubted in order to find something that could not be doubted at all. He wanted to find certain knowledge.

His method was:

* Only accept self-evident truths (as in mathematics).

* Divide difficulties into smaller parts to make it easier to solve them.

* Order your thoughts to start with the simplest and work up to the more complicated.

* Make sure you have taken everything into account.

He set about subjecting all his opinions to this test, though he laid aside religion and morality as a kind of 'temporary shelter' while the 'house' of his beliefs was being rebuilt.

I think, therefore I am

Descartes said that we all experience being deceived by our senses. Oars appear to bend in water and people spotted in the distance turn out to be trees. If our senses can give us such faulty information, how can we know that we are not being deceived all the time? In fact, if I can dream I am awake while I am asleep, how do I know that I am not dreaming all the time and that what I see and experience is an illusion?

But, thought Descartes, if everything is an illusion – can parts of that illusion still be true?

For whether I am awake or asleep, two and three together always make five, and the square can never have more than four sides, and it does not seem possible that truths so clear and apparent can be suspected of any falsity or uncertainty...

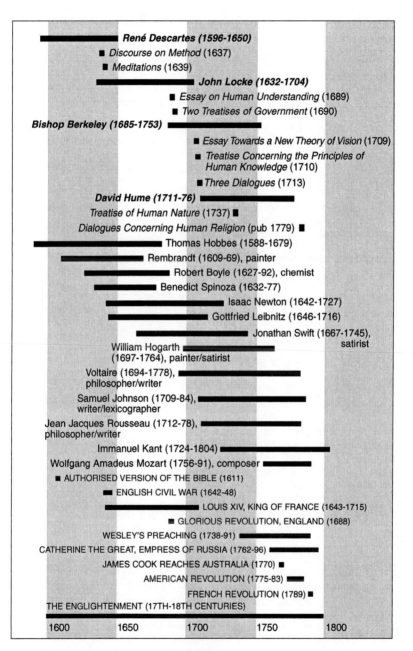

René Descartes (1596-1650)
■ Discourse on Method (1637)
■ Meditations (1639)
John Locke (1632-1704)
■ Essay on Human Understanding (1689)
■ Two Treatises of Government (1690)
Bishop Berkeley (1685-1753)
■ Essay Towards a New Theory of Vision (1709)
■ Treatise Concerning the Principles of Human Knowledge (1710)
■ Three Dialogues (1713)
David Hume (1711-76)
Treatise of Human Nature (1737) ■
Dialogues Concerning Human Religion (pub 1779) ■
Thomas Hobbes (1588-1679)
Rembrandt (1609-69), painter
Robert Boyle (1627-92), chemist
Benedict Spinoza (1632-77)
Isaac Newton (1642-1727)
Gottfried Leibnitz (1646-1716)
Jonathan Swift (1667-1745), satirist
William Hogarth (1697-1764), painter/satirist
Voltaire (1694-1778), philosopher/writer
Samuel Johnson (1709-84), writer/lexicographer
Jean Jacques Rousseau (1712-78), philosopher/writer
Immanuel Kant (1724-1804)
Wolfgang Amadeus Mozart (1756-91), composer
■ AUTHORISED VERSION OF THE BIBLE (1611)
■ ENGLISH CIVIL WAR (1642-48)
LOUIS XIV, KING OF FRANCE (1643-1715)
■ GLORIOUS REVOLUTION, ENGLAND (1688)
WESLEY'S PREACHING (1738-91)
CATHERINE THE GREAT, EMPRESS OF RUSSIA (1762-96)
JAMES COOK REACHES AUSTRALIA (1770) ■
AMERICAN REVOLUTION (1775-83) ■
FRENCH REVOLUTION (1789) ■
THE ENGLIGHTENMENT (17TH-18TH CENTURIES)

| 1600 | 1650 | 1700 | 1750 | 1800 |

This appears to be sure. But is it? Descartes goes on to doubt further: what if there is a deceiving demon loose in the world who can persuade me that even false mathematical knowledge is true? Then, I can know nothing – and I am in despair.

However, after casting doubt on sense information, scientific information and mathematical information, Descartes came to his famous conclusion:

> I resolved to pretend that nothing which had ever entered my mind was any more true than the illusions of my dreams. But immediately afterwards I became aware that, while I decided thus to think that everything was false, it followed necessarily that I who thought thus must be something; and observing that this truth, I think, therefore I am, was so certain and so evident that all the most extravagant suppositions of the sceptics were not capable of shaking it, I judged that I could accept it without scruple as the first principle of the philosophy I was seeking.

Even if the demon can lie to Descartes about everything else, he cannot lie about the fact that Descartes exists and is thinking:

* I think, therefore I am, or, perhaps a clearer translation, I am thinking, therefore I am.

* No one can deceive me into thinking I exist if I do not exist.

* I cannot think that my existence is false, because if I think this, then I am thinking and my existence must be a fact.

After establishing the existence of the self, can he go on to do anything more? Descartes goes on to establish the existence first of God, and then of the external world.

Descartes' view of God

Descartes' argument for God still uses reasoning that comes from Aristotle. He argues that his method is a method of doubting. As it is greater to know than to doubt, Descartes concludes that he is imperfect. He also concludes that he cannot be God, otherwise he would have created himself perfect – and he is not.

To know is greater than to doubt, and to be perfect is greater than to be imperfect. Descartes has an 'idea' of what a perfect being is like, but he is not perfect. The idea of perfection must come from somewhere. It must come from God, as Descartes is too imperfect to think of it himself. Therefore God exists.

Descartes uses Aristotelian reasoning. Aristotle believed in a chain of different kinds of reality. The cause of an idea has to belong to the same category as the thing it is an idea of. The idea of God has to be caused by an infinite substance, but there is only one infinite substance – God. Therefore God exists.

Descartes uses the ontological argument. God is perfect. It is more perfect to exist than not to exist. Therefore God exists. God's existence is in the definition of God. Just as a triangle has three angles, so God exists.

Descartes goes on to use God as an insurance and a guarantee for the existence of the external world. If God is perfect, then he is perfectly incapable of deceiving us. Therefore there can be no deceiving demon, as God would not wish us to be deceived.

> Every clear and distinct conception is certainly something, and therefore cannot come from nothing, but must necessarily come from God – God, I say, who is supremely perfect, and cannot be the cause of any error.

His argument proceeds in this way:

* My mind receives ideas and is passive. If my mind were only passive it would be inert, so there must be an active part which is separate from my mind.

* Ideas in my mind must be caused by active things – bodies, in other words. Therefore, I have a body, ideas in my mind come from bodies and so my body and objects in the world exist.

* The world appears to be there, and as God does not want us to be deceived we can trust that the world is there.

Even so, Descartes insists that only the mathematical properties of objects are certain: shape, size and so on. The sensible properties – colour, smell – are always open to doubt. Descartes drew a line, therefore, between the quantitative properties of an object and the qualitative properties. We can be sure about the first, but not about the second.

Descartes' philosophy has its own peculiar stamp. The soul is separate from the body. We are minds, or thinking things, attached to bodies. Because of this, the soul is immortal. His philosophy advocates a complete split between mind and body, and this is called 'dualism' (see Chapter 5).

Descartes believed that people were born with innate ideas. In this he is like Plato. We have an idea of God, but we never encounter God with our senses. We have an idea of a perfect circle, but we never encounter one in the world and so we are born with certain ideas in us which we can discover through reason: 'Certainly, the idea of God, or a supremely perfect being, is one which I found within me just as surely as the idea of any shape or number.'

These innate ideas give us:

* Knowledge of ourselves.

* Knowledge of God.

* Knowledge of mathematics.

Descartes' philosophy, therefore, is rationalistic, in that we can arrive at sure knowledge by reason and need not rely on our senses.

In Descartes' philosophy belief in God comes before belief in science. But his God is not necessarily the Christian God, concerned with salvation, rewards and punishments, and his soul is not necessarily the Christian soul.

Descartes wanted to be the Aristotle of the modern age. History has not granted him this, but his philosophy has opened the door to modern science and, in the modern age, reason still reigns supreme.

Knowing **11** through our Senses
John Locke and Bishop Berkeley

A telescope can see much further than the human eye. It can see beyond the planets and the stars we can see with the naked eye. The Hubble Space telescope was built and sent up above the atmosphere, above the dust and pollution, to observe the night sky from an even better position. By using scientific instruments we can learn more – much more than just standing at the end of the garden squinting up into space.

Scientific discoveries have shown us our limits and our shortcomings. We are not as accurate as the instruments we can create.

The Empirical philosophers of the seventeenth and eighteenth centuries were aware of this. They believed that all we knew came through our senses, but our senses were 'faulty' and did not always give us accurate information, so:

* What can we know?

* How well can we know it?

* What are the limits to what we can know?

These are the questions empirical philosophers asked. They asked them against a background of practical scientific enquiry. Two of the most famous empirical philosophers are John Locke (1632-1704) and Bishop George Berkeley (1685-1753). They are among the most famous of British philosophers and their ideas are still important today.

John Locke: knowledge through experience

John Locke had a Puritan background and a strong sense of duty. He went to Westminster School and Christ Church College, Oxford, and trained to be a doctor. His life changed dramatically in 1666 when he met Lord Ashley, later the Earl of Shaftesbury, an important political figure at the court of Charles II. Locke went to work for Shaftesbury and became involved in politics. In fact, his political writing is as important as his philosophy; his democratic ideas have had a great influence in Europe and America. Locke fled to Holland in 1683, afraid of being implicated in a plot against the king. He returned in 1688, the year of the Glorious Revolution, when William of Orange and Mary his Queen replaced the Roman Catholic James II.

In his political writing, Locke became a spokesman for the parliamentarian middle classes who had emerged from the English Civil War and the Restoration Settlement. His politics influenced his philosophy in his dislike of extreme conclusions. His Protestant world-view encouraged his philosophical world-view of a rational, self-conscious individual facing a Newtonian universe.

Locke published *An Essay Concerning Human Understanding* in 1689, and *Two Treatises of Government* in 1690. Fame came late to him, but these works did make him famous. He became a Commissioner of Trade and worked on new editions of the *Essay* until his death in 1704.

Locke's *Essay* sets out to give an 'Account of the Ways, whereby our Understandings come to attain those Notions of Things we have'.

Locke was in France from 1674 to 1679 and had studied the work of Descartes. He began by rejecting Descartes' doctrine of innate ideas. Locke did not believe that human beings were born with knowledge. He pointed out:

* Just because something is universally agreed, it is not necessarily true.

* Just because something is universally known, it is not necessarily innate.

Locke believed that all knowledge comes through experience. The mind is a blank sheet, written on by what comes to us through our senses:

> Let us then suppose the mind to be, as we say, white paper, void of all characters, without any ideas; how comes it to be furnished? Whence

comes it by that vast store, which the busy and boundless fancy of man has painted on it with an almost endless variety? Whence has it all the materials of reason and knowledge? To this I answer in one word, from experience: in that all our knowledge is founded, and from that it ultimately derives itself.

Locke wrote: 'All ideas come from sensation or reflection.' But what do these three nouns mean?

* An 'idea' is a 'mental image', a notion of experience. We perceive ideas, not the things themselves.

* 'Sensation' is perceiving through the senses.

* 'Reflection' comes after sensation. Reflection is any mental activity such as wishing, thinking, doubting and so on.

How do we know that all our knowledge comes through sensation and reflection? The problem is that there is no empirical way of being an empiricist.

And is all our thinking really 'empirical', derived from experience? Does our knowledge of the soul, of God, of mathematics really rely on sense-perception?

Plato and Descartes believed one thing; Locke believed another. The question is still open.

Isaac Newton (1642-1727), one of the most famous of British scientists, formulated the theory of gravity and made important contributions to mathematics and optics. His work profoundly influenced the empiricists to ask scientific questions in a scientific way. Robert Boyle (1627-1691) was the founder of modern chemistry. He divorced chemistry from the magic of alchemy, and conducted his work on an experimental basis – that is, a modern and scientific basis. It was the work of such scientists that enabled Locke to formulate a philosophical basis for a scientific description of the universe.

Locke's theory of knowledge

Locke divided ideas into simple and complex. A simple idea is 'in itself uncompounded'. We cannot produce it from nothing with our imaginations, but receive it passively. A complex idea is made up of simple ideas. We use our imagination to produce these actively.

When it comes to physical objects, Locke assigns these 'primary' and 'secondary' qualities. Primary qualities are mathematical ones such as shape, size and so on. Secondary qualities are 'sensible' ones such as colour, smell...

> The particular bulk, number, figure and motion of the parts of fire, or snow, are really in them, whether anyone's senses perceive them or no; and therefore they may be called real qualities, because they really exist in those bodies; but light, heat, whiteness or coldness, are no more really in them than sickness or pain is in manna.

What Locke is stating is that without ears there would be no sound, without eyes no colour, without noses no smell. He is following the scientists of his time in believing in a colourless, tasteless, soundless universe.

Locke goes on to claim that the properties we perceive must be held together in something. But what? He concludes that they must be held together in material substance; therefore matter exists.

We perceive the idea, but cannot know the thing and this is as far as Locke is able to go.

The implications of Locke's view are that we can never truly know the natural world. As a result, science is based on guesswork, not knowledge. Science can never be more than a belief, a kind of faith, and this view has persisted.

Locke believed in three kinds of knowledge:

* Intuitive knowledge, through which comes knowledge of the self.

* Demonstrative knowledge, through which comes knowledge of God.

* Sensitive knowledge, through which comes knowledge of the external world.

Only the first kind of knowledge, intuitive knowledge, is absolutely certain. The second, demonstrative knowledge, is sure in the way a mathematical proof was sure. Sensitive knowledge is problematic – at best good guesswork.

Even so, Locke said that while proof is one thing, ordinary commonsense is another, and sensitive knowledge is enough for the purposes of everyday life. He wished to demonstrate morals as well as science, but had to admit failure. He was aware that without God morals dwindle to a matter of taste, not duty. But, though he drew a fine line between faith and scepticism, Locke did believe his philosophy led to a knowledge of God.

Locke said that, given cause and effect, if something exists, something must have always existed, and this something is the cause of that which exists. What has always existed must be eternal, all-powerful and all-knowing – in other words, God. Locke's God, however, is a philosopher's God and not the Christian God. He admitted that the Christian God could only be known through revelation. Also, this God 'who sees men in the dark' is the only God capable of enforcing morals. Even so, Locke believed in subjecting revelation to reason and making reason the final arbiter, and he failed to find a Natural Law independent of revelation.

Bishop Berkeley: mind more important than matter

Bishop Berkeley (1685-1753) was a stout believer in God, who worried that the science and philosophy of his time were encouraging atheism.

If the thinkers of his day appeared to be pushing God out, Berkeley wanted to pull him back in. Berkeley was Irish; a fellow of Trinity College, Dublin. Three of his most important books, *An Essay Towards a New Theory of Vision* (1709), *A Treatise Concerning the Principles of Human Knowledge* (1710), and *Three Dialogues Between Hylas and Philonous* (1713) were all written by the time he reached his mid-twenties.

He went to America in 1728 to found a new college, but returned empty-handed in 1731, though he helped found Columbia University and the University of Pennsylvania. He mixed with the leading figures of his day in London, became Bishop of Clyne, Ireland, in 1731, and died in Oxford in 1753.

Berkeley took empiricism to some of its logical conclusions. As a Christian, he had a horror of materialism and so advocated 'immaterialism' instead. In his view, only the contents of our experience can be said to exist; he denied the existence of matter. Berkeley said that 'things' are a philosopher's invention; all people see are the 'ideas', and so only they can be said to exist. 'To be perceived', wrote Berkeley, 'is to exist.'

In his *Three Dialogues*, Philonous (mind) and Hylas (matter) debate the question. Philonous declares:

To me it is evident, for the reasons you allow of, that sensible things cannot exist otherwise than in a mind or spirit. Whence I conclude, not that they have no real existence, but that, seeing they depend not on my thought, and have an existence distinct from being perceived by me, there must be some other mind wherein they exist. As sure, therefore, as the sensible world really exists, so sure is there an infinite omnipresent spirit, who contains and supports it.

Put another way, if things are perceived there must be a perceiver. Therefore I have a notion of myself. But, as things continue to exist whether I perceive them or not, there must be a Perceiver. Therefore I have a notion of God.

Everything, therefore, is an idea in the mind of God.

Berkeley thought his ideas were sensible and commonsensical; his contemporaries thought them fantastic.

Ronald Knox summed up Berkeley's philosophy in a famous limerick:

> There was a young man who said,
> 'God, I find it exceedingly odd
> That this tree which I see
> Should continue to be
> When there's no one about in the Quad'.

Reply:

> 'Dear Sir: your astonishment's odd.
> I am always about in the Quad;
> And that's why the tree
> Will continue to be
> Since observed by Yours faithfully, God.'

Yet, if we have inherited the idea from Locke that matter is more important than mind, perhaps we should still look to Berkeley to argue that mind is more important than matter. And Berkeley's idea of the subject as perceiver is one which stubbornly refuses to go away even though many philosophers have tried to explain it away.

If Locke's legacy was the European Enlightenment, perhaps Berkeley's work has its own legacy and still has something important to say to us today.

The Limits of Knowing
David Hume

Every Olympic Games world records are broken – the 100-metres sprint, javelin throwing, weightlifting… But will there ever come a time when the fastest human has run the fastest race, thrown the farthest javelin or lifted the heaviest weight? Will there come a limit to what the human body is capable of? And, if there is a limit to the human body, what of the limits to the human mind? Locke and Berkeley had shown that there were limits: people could not know for certain what they had always taken for granted.

Berkeley went so far as to abolish matter; David Hume went further and abolished minds.

The man and his philosophy

David Hume (1711-76) was born and died in Edinburgh. He led a quiet life, but had a revolutionary philosophy. His father was a lawyer and landowner; his mother was a strict Calvinist. Hume went to Edinburgh University in 1723 aged eleven and went on to study law; but he preferred philosophy. He travelled to France, where he wrote *A Treatise of Human Nature*. On returning to London to have it published in 1737, he was disappointed when it 'fell dead-born from the press'.

Hume had a chequered career: he became tutor to the lunatic Marquis of Annandale and secretary to General St Clair, whose military expedition against the French Canadians had to be diverted as the wind blew in the wrong direction. Hume was unsuccessful in his attempts to become

95

Professor of Philosophy at Edinburgh, but he was appointed librarian to the Faculty of Advocates. He wrote steadily for the next twelve years, drafting the *Dialogues Concerning Natural Religion*, *The Natural History of Religion* (1757), *Political Discourses* (1752) and his six-volume *History of England* which appeared between 1754 and 1762.

Hume's *History* brought him fame and success. In 1763 he was appointed secretary to the British ambassador in France where he became a great social success. He was briefly Under-Secretary of State before he retired to Edinburgh in 1769. There Hume continued to revise the *Dialogues*, which were published after his death in 1779.

Hume's philosophy completes the empirical movement. He began by taking a scientific method and applying it to the mental world rather than the physical world. Hume believed that understanding human nature would lead to an understanding of the nature of human knowledge. He showed how our natures determined our beliefs.

He was the supreme sceptic. A sceptic says we cannot know, and Hume's philosophy states clearly that we cannot know about either ourselves or the world. Hume was not dogmatic; he did not provide beliefs, but merely criticized existing beliefs. He criticized knowledge of the world, knowledge of the self and knowledge of God.

Hume's criticisms were so devastating that they completely undermined many of the basic, commonsense assumptions people need to lead their daily lives.

Knowledge of the world and of the self

Hume set about demolishing reason as a principle. Reason, he declared, was no more than a habit or a custom. If I apply my mind to the world and decide something is so, it is on the basis that it has always been so. But it need not necessarily be so and may not continue:

> If we believe that fire warms or water refreshes, 'tis only because it costs us too much pain to think otherwise.

In other words, we cannot help believing, but we must not think our belief is grounded in reason.

Hume's age was known as 'The Age of Reason'. Reason was an important idea which is perhaps why Hume needed to show the limits of reason: he enjoyed knocking down the great ideas of the day. This age was also known as 'The Age of Satire'. Satire is a comic, political form of writing which tries to make a point. Hume was influenced by the satirical writers of his time such as Pope, Dryden and Swift. In his *Treatise* Hume divides human understanding into:

* Impressions: what we receive through our senses.

* Ideas: memories or 'faint images' of impressions which we combine in thinking and reasoning.

As ideas are ultimately derived from impressions, our knowledge is limited. Our imagination might appear boundless, but even something as fabulous as a centaur is no more than a combination of the impressions 'man' and 'horse'. And so, 'All this creative power of the mind amounts to no more than the faculty of transposing, augmenting, or diminishing the materials afforded us by the senses and experience.'

Hume agrees with Locke and Berkeley that we can never really know what is going on outside of ourselves.

He went on to demolish the cherished belief in cause and effect which had proved necessary both to science and religion. In his view, causation was an idea, not an impression. If you see a match burst into flames or a rock shatter a window, what you see is a match and then a flame; a rock and then broken glass. We can never see the one actually cause the other. Because we see the two events occur together and because, in our experience, they always occur together, we assume that the one has caused the other. But, Hume argues, just because these two things have always happened together, it does not follow that they will always happen:

When we look about us towards external objects, and consider the operation of causes, we are never able in a single instance to discover any power or necessary connection, any quality, which binds the effect to the causes, and renders the one an infallible consequence of the other.

Therefore:

* We cannot deduce effects from an object.

* What usually happens does not necessarily always happen.

Hume offers a psychological, not a scientific, explanation for cause and effect and says that the best we can say is that we see conjoined events.

Hume's next target was Descartes' idea of the self. Hume claimed that the self was an idea and did not come from any direct impression. Berkeley claimed that there were no thoughts without a thinker, no perceptions without a perceiver, but Hume declared there were only thoughts and only perceptions.

If I look inside myself I find only thoughts and perceptions, so how can there be said to be a self which exists?

> I may venture to affirm of the rest of mankind, that they are nothing but a bundle or collection of different perceptions, which succeed each other with inconceivable rapidity, and are in perpetual flux and movement.

And if there is no self, it follows there is no soul and no immortality. Hume's 'scientific method' destroyed many of the assumptions science was built on. Hume had demolished much of the basis of thought:

* There is no cause and effect.

* There is no principle of reason.

* There is no certainty in induction (deciding what is true from the evidence).

* The existence of matter depends on our imaginations.

Science was built, it transpired, on faith and not on certainty. By shrugging and declaring that 'Nature is too strong for principle', Hume showed that such empirical conclusions had to be laid to one side, since life had to be lived on some such bases as the ones he had taken apart.

Hume, God and miracles

Hume never declared himself an atheist although history has treated him as one. The biographer James Boswell visited Hume just before his death, to discover what he felt about facing the end of his life. He found Hume cheery and in good spirits. He declared that the philosopher 'persisted in disbelieving a future state even when he had death before his eyes'.

In his *Enquiry Concerning Human Understanding* (1748), Hume attacked miracles. In *Dialogues Concerning Natural Religion*, which he worked on for the last twenty-five years of his life, he attacked the Argument from Design.

This argument, often associated with William Paley, stated that by looking at how the world is made, it can be seen that there was a Maker, and this Maker is God.

Hume excluded miracles. He defined a miracle as 'a violation of the laws of nature'. A miracle, by its definition, is unlikely. In fact, a miracle is so unlikely that the evidence against it must always be greater than the evidence for it. 'There must, therefore, be a uniform experience against every miraculous event, otherwise the event would not merit that appellation.' Thus nature appears to exclude miracles. Hume goes on to criticize people who make claims for miracles. Either miracles are 'observed chiefly to abound among ignorant and barbarous nations' who do not know any better, or the people who claim them are generally lying and not to be trusted. In fact:

> No testimony is sufficient to establish a miracle, unless the testimony
> be of such a kind that its falsehood would be more miraculous than
> the fact which it endeavours to establish.

Testimony must always succumb before the laws of nature and, as the laws of nature exclude the possibility of miracles, miracles do not exist.

The argument from design

In the *Dialogues Concerning Natural Religion*, Philo, Cleanthes and Demea debate the traditional Argument from Design as a way of establishing the existence of God. Hume's battery of arguments is relentless against the longstanding beliefs of the church:

IT IS POSSIBLE THAT MATTER IS SELF-ORDERING and not ordered by a Maker.

IT IS IMPOSSIBLE TO DRAW CONCLUSIONS about the whole from a part. We do not decide what a person is like from a single hair, or a tree from a single leaf. How then can we decide about God from looking just at the world?

SOMEONE WHO BELIEVES IN GOD projects human beliefs onto a non-human world. How can we say God is like us, when he must be so different from us?

WHY DO WE BELIEVE IN ONE GOD and not several? Hume states that the universe could be the work of an 'infant deity', an 'inferior deity' or 'the production of old age and dotage in some superannuated deity'. Perhaps God is not as powerful as he is usually claimed to be.

MAYBE GOD IS STUPID. 'If we survey a ship, what an exalted idea must we form of the ingenuity of the carpenter, who framed so complicated, useful and beautiful a machine? And what surprise must we entertain when we find him a stupid mechanic…'

THE WORLD IS MORE LIKE A VEGETABLE or an animal than a machine. Perhaps it grew naturally.

As Philo says, 'I have still asserted that we have no data to establish any system of cosmogony.' He comes to the conclusion 'And I cannot, for my part, think that so wild and unsettled a system of theology is, in any respect, preferable to none at all.'

Hume attempted to refute two other traditional arguments for the existence of God. First, cause and effect: if cause and effect do not exist, then there is no First Cause and, consequently, no God. And then the Ontological Argument: Hume wrote 'Whatever we conceive as existent, we can also conceive of as non-existent.' He maintained that it is impossible to establish the existence of God by reasoned argument.

Hume and the Supernatural

Hume defines miracles in such a way as they cannot possibly exist. But, because something is unlikely, does that necessarily mean it is not true? Are all people who claim to have seen or experienced a miracle necessarily untrustworthy? Hume's arguments against 'design' are really saying, 'It's not obvious.' Before Hume, philosophers had had a different idea of how reality worked, and were able to 'prove' the existence of God through their theories. By the time Hume was born, the understanding of the world had changed. Hume did not say God did not exist, but he did show that the traditional arguments for convincing people that God exists no longer applied.

Hume is, perhaps, the most influential British philosopher who ever lived. His arguments have never been successfully refuted. He showed that it is absurd to be logical to the limit, but by going to extremes, he showed where the limits are. We know from Hume that we cannot know, but, like Hume himself, we must live as though we can.

PART

5

Why Do We Exist?

EXISTENTIALISM

Faith: The Highest Way of Living

Søren Kierkegaard

Have you ever wondered why you exist at all? Probably you have, and probably you have gone on to ask what the point of life actually is, and whether life has any meaning. You may also have asked other questions and had other feelings about yourself: you may have felt isolated, for instance, as one standing out from the crowd, different from others. You may have felt that no one understands you; and yet you may long for a life that is different from everybody else's.

These questions and feelings are 'existential'. They are problems that have been addressed by philosophers who, as the word suggests, have been concerned with the problems of human existence – not the existence of objects or plants or animals, but the special human existence that you or I have.

A philosophy of rebellion

The three major existential philosophers are Søren Kierkegaard (1813-55), Martin Heidegger (1889-1976) and Jean-Paul Sartre (1905-80). Kierkegaard was Danish, Heidegger German and Sartre French, and it is true to say that existentialism has been more influential in the rest of Europe than in Britain.

Unlike other philosophies, existentialism has never been a school or a movement. Rather, there is a 'family resemblance' between existential thinkers in terms of the questions they asked and how they viewed the place of humanity in the universe.

Fundamentally, existentialism is a philosophy of rebellion, focusing on the individual and the problems of existence. In some ways existentialism can be seen as a Romantic revolt against the ideals of the European Enlightenment with its emphasis on systems and rationality.

The word 'exist' literally means 'to stand out against' and existential philosophers have stressed how individual human beings 'stand out' against the world, against society, and against institutions and ways of thought.

* Kierkegaard criticized the Danish State church of his day.

* Heidegger believed that most of Western philosophy had been off the mark.

* Sartre wanted to start anew after the destruction of the Second World War with a new view of people and their possibilities.

All three were rebels; all three stood out; all three were concerned with 'existence' in one way or another.

Existentialism, then, is primarily a subjective philosophy: one seen from an individual point of view. It is a philosophy which concerns me and how I live. Because of this, existentialism has had an enormous effect on literature; writers such as Dostoevsky, Kafka, Beckett, Camus – and Sartre – have all been seen as having an 'existential' quality to their work.

Existential philosophers would claim that they are concerned with the real questions that face humankind. Their aim is to expose the illusions of everyday life and call human beings to a serious view of their responsibilities.

Many existentialists, for example, believe that there are no moral laws written into the structure of the universe. People have to choose what they want to do and how they want to be. They are free.

Certain key words recur frequently in their writing:

* Freedom.

* Individuality.

* Responsibility.

* Choice.

As an awareness of human existence necessarily includes an awareness of death, existentialists have also written about:

* Guilt.

* Alienation.

* Despair.

* Death.

They have been aware of the tragic elements in human existence and concentrated on these, which other philosophers have passed over.

In *The Death of Ivan Ilyich*, Leo Tolstoy expressed a deeply 'existential' feeling:

> It occurred to him that what had appeared perfectly impossible before, namely that he had not spent his life as he should have done, might after all be true. It occurred to him that his scarcely perceptible attempts to struggle against what was considered good by the most highly placed people, those scarcely noticeable impulses which he had immediately suppressed, might have been the real thing, and all the rest false. And his professional duties and the whole arrangement of his life and of his family, and all his social and official interests, might all have been false. He tried to defend all those things to himself and suddenly felt the weakness of what he was defending. There was nothing to defend.

Individual faith

The father of existentialism is generally considered to be Søren Kierkegaard. He lived in Copenhagen in the nineteenth century, the youngest of seven children, most of whom died. He had an isolated and unhappy childhood, and was deeply affected by the guilt and religious gloom of his father.

Two events changed Kierkegaard's life. One was his father's death in 1838. Then, by September 1840, he was engaged to Regine Olsen, but he broke off the engagement. This was a kind of sacrifice. Kierkegaard felt he was too sinful to marry, but also had a sense of mission about what he had to do in the world. He withdrew from the seminary where he was studying for pastoral ministry and began to write, living off the money left to him by his father.

'To produce,' he said later, 'was my life.' For the next ten years he produced a steady stream of books, mostly written under pseudonyms, and exhausted himself with the intensity of his work. Kierkegaard's writing was thrilling, emotional and literary, not at all the carefully reasoned arguments of traditional philosophers.

In his own day Kierkegaard's work received little attention. Early in October 1855, he collapsed suddenly and died a few weeks later. Despite his attacks on conventional Christianity, his funeral took place in Copenhagen Cathedral at his family's request.

'Truth,' Kierkegaard wrote, 'is subjectivity.' He looked to his own experiences as a drama out of which to fashion his philosophy. He was adamant that personal existence could not be confined in a system or reduced to the merely rational. 'A logical system is possible, an existential system is impossible.' Kierkegaard hated empirical systems and the idea of objectivity. Above all, he hated the philosophy of Hegel, the dominant philosophy of the time, which put everything into a system.

Kierkegaard saw the task of his philosophy as converting people to the subjective; he stressed the importance of faith. He did not want to add to knowledge like a scientist or a schoolteacher, but to illuminate a new way of living for people.

From his own life, Kierkegaard separated out three different modes of existence:

* Aesthetic: the 'immediate' way of living.

* Ethical: Hegel believed people found an ethical existence as part of society, part of the crowd; Kierkegaard said you had to stand out from the crowd.

* Religious: the highest way of living, involving faith.

Faith is Kierkegaard's great theme. Faith, for him, is a miracle that changes a person's whole way of living. In *Fear and Trembling*, Kierkegaard retells the story from the Bible where God asks Abraham to sacrifice his only son. This Kierkegaard calls the 'teleological suspension of the ethical', where normal moral laws are laid to one side because of a higher call of faith – a call from God.

The paradox that God became human – that timeless God entered into time and acted in history – is at the heart of the Christian faith. Kierkegaard believed that 'Faith begins where thinking leaves off'. The incarnation was an offence to human reason, showing that faith and reason cannot be reconciled. Knowing God is not like knowing an object in the world and so, to know God, human beings have to go beyond the rational through a 'leap of faith' into believing something objectively uncertain.

God can only be known in an intense, personal way; the truth of God, then, is an intensely personal truth. There is no such thing as evidence; there is only faith.

Twentieth-century legacy

Kierkegaard conducted his philosophy solely in relation to Christianity, believing that Christianity is the truth. He believed that human nature is such that an individual can only be free from despair and fulfil his or her fundamental hopes by embracing the Christian message. Throughout his life he stressed the call of Christianity on an individual's life, and criticized the worldliness and hypocrisy of the institutional church.

Kierkegaard's work was neglected during his lifetime and for some time after his death. Eventually German translations appeared, but he only rose to prominence as a result of his association with the existential movement in the 1930s and 40s when his books also appeared in English for the first time. His writing has had an influence on many writers, as well as on Heidegger, Sartre and other existential philosophers who were atheists. But his notions of faith and existential knowledge have also helped shape twentieth-century theology.

Karl Barth, Rudolf Bultmann, Paul Tillich and Dietrich Bonhoeffer all owe an enormous debt to Kierkegaard. Their emphasis on the central importance of faith has accompanied a stripping away of the miracle accounts and what these thinkers saw as the 'mythical' or 'legendary' aspects of the Christian gospels, to dig down to the existential heart of the gospel message.

Perhaps, in some ways, Kierkegaard's philosophy has had an effect he would not have intended or liked. But his intense vision of human existence,

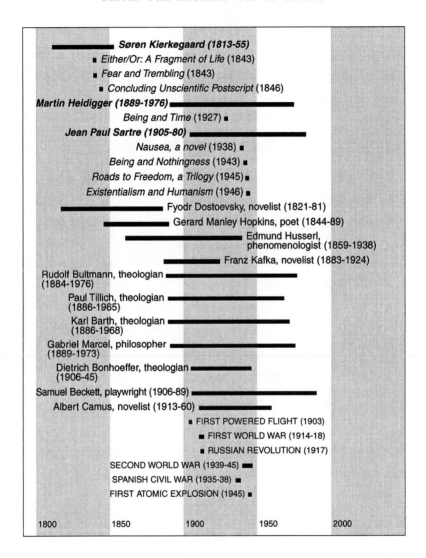

Søren Kierkegaard (1813-55)
Either/Or: A Fragment of Life (1843)
Fear and Trembling (1843)
Concluding Unscientific Postscript (1846)
Martin Heidigger (1889-1976)
Being and Time (1927)
Jean Paul Sartre (1905-80)
Nausea, a novel (1938)
Being and Nothingness (1943)
Roads to Freedom, a Trilogy (1945)
Existentialism and Humanism (1946)
Fyodr Dostoevsky, novelist (1821-81)
Gerard Manley Hopkins, poet (1844-89)
Edmund Husserl, phenomenologist (1859-1938)
Franz Kafka, novelist (1883-1924)
Rudolf Bultmann, theologian (1884-1976)
Paul Tillich, theologian (1886-1965)
Karl Barth, theologian (1886-1968)
Gabriel Marcel, philosopher (1889-1973)
Dietrich Bonhoeffer, theologian (1906-45)
Samuel Beckett, playwright (1906-89)
Albert Camus, novelist (1913-60)
FIRST POWERED FLIGHT (1903)
FIRST WORLD WAR (1914-18)
RUSSIAN REVOLUTION (1917)
SECOND WORLD WAR (1939-45)
SPANISH CIVIL WAR (1935-38)
FIRST ATOMIC EXPLOSION (1945)
1800   1850   1900   1950   2000

his striking literary imagination and his call to faith are still clear and powerful today. They call human beings to come face to face with the fact and meaning of their own existence.

The Nature of Being

Martin Heidegger

Martin Heidegger (1889-1976) began his philosophy with a simple, basic question. 'Why is there anything at all, and not just nothing?'

As a boy, Heidegger found himself overwhelmed with the sheer wonder of 'being'; he wanted to know why a thing 'is'. He became particularly obsessed with the 'is-ness' of things, the special quality that makes an object a 'being' and which he believed Western philosophers from the time of the Ancient Greeks had ignored.

This 'is-ness' Heidegger came to believe was part of 'Being'. 'Being' was 'in' everything in the world without actually 'being' the world.

Because Heidegger wished to examine the nature of Being in the world as a whole, and not just in humankind, he rejected the term 'existentialist'. He was interested in human existence only as a gate to understanding Existence as a whole.

A quiet life

Heidegger was born in 1889 in Messkirch, in the Black Forest region of Baden-Wurttemberg in Germany. He studied under the phenomenologist Edmund Husserl (1859-1938) at Freiburg, and became his assistant. After a spell at the University of Marburg (1923-28), Heidegger succeeded Husserl in the chair of philosophy at Freiburg. Unlike Kierkegaard, he was a system-builder and professional philosopher. He published his most important work *Being and Time*, in 1927.

Unfortunately, Heidegger had a brief involvement with Nazism in 1933 after Hitler came to power. Although he withdrew from politics within a year the damage was done, and his total silence on any political issue after the war condemned him in the eyes of many people. He taught at Freiburg until 1944, when he was suspended from teaching by the Allies until 1951. He retired in 1959 and died in 1976, being buried in the same churchyard he had passed every day as a boy on his way to school.

What is remarkable about Heidegger's life is that so little is remarkable about it: he hardly travelled at all and rarely went abroad. It is as though his whole existence was consumed by abstract thought.

Unlike Kierkegaard, Heidegger was not a Christian or a theist. Because of this, there is a greater emphasis on human freedom, on having to choose how to live and to search for purely human values. Heidegger also stresses 'dread' and 'death'. Because there is no God, human beings face nothing, their own extinction; this casts questions about their own existence into an urgent light.

Being and Time

Heidegger had an unusual and individual approach to philosophy. He simply believed that most philosophers had passed over the most important question of all to his mind: the question of 'Being'. From Plato and Aristotle onwards, Heidegger claimed, there had been a 'forgetting of Being'. It was the task of Heidegger's book *Being and Time* to call people back to face the full meaning of Being. In this way Heidegger saw himself as a kind of prophet, and his work as a kind of mission.

While Heidegger's notion of Being has proved alluring to many theologians, he never made any supernatural claim for it – certainly not that Being equals God.

Heidegger's work is hard to read and understand and many philosophers have dismissed his question of Being as irrelevant nonsense. They maintain that he is playing with words. His retort to this criticism was that Being resisted understanding and that a new language was called for to make the nature of Being clear.

Heidegger coined many new words and was convinced that German and Greek (the two languages he used) were the most suitable for this purpose.

He also believed that the words he used were not just signs, but things in themselves, as full of existence and Being as anything else.

Heidegger believed that human beings must be especially concerned with the question of Being because they are naturally concerned with their own existence. Because people are, they are open to Being, can listen and respond to it. Heidegger turns Descartes' famous saying on its head. Instead of 'I think, therefore I am,' he preferred, 'I am, therefore I think.'

Heidegger used special terms to convey his meaning:

* 'Facticity' is the fact of human existence: here we are in the world.

* 'There-ness' (*dasein*) is what dread (*angst*) and death make us aware of. We do not just exist, we know we exist, and so we exist in a special way. According to Heidegger, human beings are always transcending – going beyond the limits of their present situation – to try to become what they are not yet.

* *Geworfenheit* literally means 'thrown-ness'. People feel 'thrown' into existence, and this leaves them with an uncanny feeling. They are ill-at-ease in the world, not quite at home.

While Heidegger's philosophy might seem at first sight to concentrate almost wholly on the individual, he went on to describe objects in the world as 'instruments' lying to hand for human use. Part of the existence of objects is to have a use, and this use is provided by the fact that human beings exist. As instruments are used to make things for others, human existence has an aspect of care. Heidegger's philosophy, therefore, is not wholly individual, but on the contrary, considers it absolutely essential to be bound up with other people.

Authentic and inauthentic being

Like Kierkegaard, Heidegger pointed out the dangers of belonging to the crowd. As the importance of Being had been forgotten, Heidegger stated that the crowd often becomes the soul of a person's life, setting limits to that person's possibilities. He wrote, 'Everyone is the other, and no one is himself.'

Heidegger wrote about:

* Inauthentic Being, as part of the crowd.

* Authentic Being, being yourself.

To live authentically means coming to an understanding of Being. An inadequate understanding of Being means an inadequate understanding of oneself. Everyone has to seek their own relation to Being through thinking about their own death; and this is the only true way to live.

Being and Time made Heidegger famous and, despite his unhappiness with the 'existential' label, the book has been received as the greatest work to come out of the whole existential movement. But some problems remain. Heidegger never finished his philosophical task; the book due to follow *Being and Time* set to penetrate the very heart and nature of Being, never appeared.

More importantly, Heidegger used terms from his work such as 'being', 'truth', 'people' and 'leader' to marry his philosophy to Nazi ideology. Even though he did this for only a short time, arguments have raged over the matter ever since.

However, *Being and Time* has remained an enormously influential book, and Heidegger's continuing status as a major philosopher seems assured.

The being of things

Heidegger wrote a thesis on Duns Scotus (c. 1266-1308), a medieval scholastic theologian who stressed the 'this-ness' or 'being' of things. The English poet Gerard Manley Hopkins was also interested in Duns Scotus' ideas and wrote poetry bringing out the individual being of things in the world. He wrote in an unusual language, designed to give the reader a physical sensation of the things themselves. His poem 'Pied Beauty' illustrates this:

> Glory be to God for dappled things,
> For skies of couple-colour as a brindled cow;
> For rose-moles all in stipple upon trout that swim
> Fresh-firecoal chestnut-falls; finches' wings;
> Landscape plotted and pieced-fold, fallow and plough
> And all in trades, their gear and tackle and trim.
>
> All things counter, original, spare, strange;
> Whatever is fickle, freckled (who knows how?)
> With swift, slow; sweet, sour; adazzle, dim;
> He fathers-forth whose beauty is past change:
> Praise Him.

Heidegger and twentieth-century theology

Heidegger has had a profound influence on certain aspects of theology in the twentieth century. He has been useful, for example, in providing existential theologians such as Rudolf Bultmann, with a language in which they can talk about God to the modern world. There are several examples of this also.

* Heidegger's focus on 'Being' has been adapted as a way of talking about God.

* His language makes it possible, some think, to form a new 'natural theology', by which a person can look at the world and so begin to talk about God.

* Looking at the Bible existentially, the Old Testament prophets and Jesus himself can be seen as standing out against the rules and rituals of their time and calling people to authentic existence.

Existential theologians claim that the events and miracle accounts in the Bible are picture language. This language has to be 'decoded', so that the real meaning of what is happening in the text can be uncovered. In their view the world of the Bible seems foreign to us because it speaks from a world so completely different from our own.

These theologians claim that Being becomes clothed in different symbols, in story form, and emerges in the world in the guise of different religions.

Many Christians are uncomfortable with the conclusions these scholars draw, and would prefer to stress that the miracles and resurrection of Jesus actually happened in an objective, historical sense. However, in their emphasis on being and faith existential theologians issue a call which is hard to ignore — to examine our own existence.

Free to Choose
Jean-Paul Sartre

Have you ever wanted to be completely free? Have you ever felt that your parents, your town and your background all close in and squeeze you into a shape that you aren't happy with? Would you like to be a different kind of person, to choose another kind of life?

Maybe you have heard people complain, or have complained yourself:

* 'I couldn't help it…'

* 'I'm stuck that way…'

* 'I'm only a teacher. I'll never be anything else…'

Jean-Paul Sartre said that we *can* help it. He said that people are not stuck. He believed that humankind is free and his work centres on the meaning of that freedom and its implications.

Philosopher for a time of upheaval

Jean-Paul Sartre (1905-80) was the most famous and influential of the modern existentialists. The range and insight of his work have made him known the world over. He was born in Paris and studied at the Sorbonne, where he came first in his year in philosophy. Like Heidegger, Sartre was influenced by the phenomenological philosophy of Edmund Husserl and studied under him in Germany. Like other existentialists Sartre was interested in 'being' and 'ethics' rather than 'logic' and 'epistemology'.

Sartre became a teacher, but after the Second World War he devoted his life to writing and to political causes. Along with other left-wing intellectuals, he co-founded and edited the magazine *Les Temps Modernes* ('Modern Times'). This magazine captured the mood of young people after the war who were searching for a new philosophy to live by.

Sartre became internationally known for novels such as *Nausea* (1938) and the trilogy *The Roads to Freedom* (1945), as well as for plays, including *The Flies* (1943) and *No Exit* (1944). Sartre was offered the Nobel Prize for literature, but turned it down.

After the Second World War, the old certainties seemed to be in ruins along with most of Europe. Sartre's existentialism, born out of crisis and political upheaval, seemed to point the way to a new, optimistic order.

By the end of the 1950s, he had become more involved with Marxism, and many people were disappointed that he had not found existential answers to his own existential questions. When he died, thousands followed his coffin as a tribute to one of the most influential European thinkers and writers of modern times.

Being and Nothingness

Sartre's most important philosophical work is *Being and Nothingness*, published in 1943.

In this work he pointed out two ways in which people can live:

* Authentically.

* With 'bad faith' (*mauvaise foi*, perhaps better translated 'self-deception').

'Bad faith' is a belief in the lack of freedom. Sartre said that most people believe there are laws, or ways of behaving, written into society. These laws are formed, perhaps by God, perhaps by human nature. But Sartre said: there is no God, and there is no such thing as human nature.

Therefore humankind is completely free to choose its own values and ways of living. Not to believe this means living in bad faith.

Sartre's famous phrase is that 'existence precedes essence'. To quote from *Existentialism and Humanism*:

What do we mean by saying that existence precedes essence? We mean that man first of all exists, encounters himself, surges up in the world – and defines himself afterwards.

Essence and existence

Edmund Husserl (1859-1938) pointed out that objects in our consciousness exist for us, no matter what other existence they may or may not have. Because of this we can examine them, using strict rules, without making any decisions about their own notional existence. Husserl's philosophy is called 'phenomenology' because it studies objects as they appear to us.

In his essay *Existentialism and Humanism* (1946), Sartre explains his argument about existence this way:

If someone makes a paper knife, they have an idea before it even exists of what the paper knife will do and what it will look like. In this case essence precedes existence (the idea comes before the fact).

Traditionally, this is how people think of God: as a Maker. God made us and so we know what we are like and what we are for. Because God exists, human nature exists and meaning is written into the universe.

But if God does not exist, then people find themselves in the situation where they exist but do not know what they are like or what they are for. In this case existence precedes essence (the fact comes before the idea). This means that when people look at themselves they experience 'nothingness', but must fill this nothingness with something.

People, then, are absolutely free to choose; they must choose because everyone has to live their life in some way. Determinism is the great illusion. We are free to choose our own destiny. Most people, however, do not realize they possess this freedom and so live in 'bad faith'. They spend their lives acting like fixed objects or robots. The goal of life is 'authenticity', which means choosing, and so Sartre's philosophy is a philosophy of action.

Sartre claims that action shows what people are really like, and that they are defined as the sum of their actions.

He determined two ways in which anything exists in the world:

* 'In-itself', which describes objects which have a complete and fixed being, and which have no relationship to themselves or to anything else.

* 'For-itself', the human way of existing – fluid, with a lack of fixed structure and open to the future. Possibility and imagination are two marks of 'for-itself' and show how human existence is marked off from other kinds of existing.

Sartre's freedom, however, has a price. He proposed that in a godless world humankind has to take the place of God. Unfortunately, this desire is always frustrated because people are limited by their bodies, their abilities and their situation. At the same time, because God does not exist, life has no ultimate meaning and is absurd. And choosing a set of values to live by means choosing 'bad faith'. Values have no value because there is no God. Human beings are free to choose, but to believe there is any value in what is chosen is a delusion. In Sartre's words, 'Man is a useless passion.'

Many people have thought that Sartre's analysis of the human situation is too negative. He himself stated that his was a positive philosophy, and certainly his emphasis on freedom is exhilarating. But his description of the 'nausea' and absurdity of existence do seem pessimistic.

> My thought is me: that is why I can't stop. I exist by what I think... and I can't prevent myself from thinking. At this very moment – this is terrible – if I exist, it is because I hate existing. It is I, it is I who pull myself from the nothingness to which I aspire: hatred and disgust for existence are just so many ways of making me exist, of thrusting me into existence.

Gabriel Marcel (1889-1973) is the best-known representative of another kind of French existentialism. Against the pessimistic elements in Sartre, Marcel offered a 'metaphysic of hope', based on the belief that God exists. Marcel also confronted Sartre's individualism with a positive outlook on how human beings exist as part of a wider community.

The problem with Sartre's existentialism is that it does not give a clear indication of how an individual is to live with other people. What if my freedom conflicts with another's? Sartre's treatment of this question is not adequate. He claims that in choosing for me I am choosing for everybody. 'In fashioning myself, I fashion man.' What is good for me must be very good for all. But this view is subjective and many have found it unconvincing.

Sartre's book *Being and Nothingness* closes with the words: 'These questions... can be answered only on a moral level. I will devote my next work to them.' In fact, he abandoned this project seven years later and the fourth volume of *The Roads to Freedom*, which was to show authentic existence, never appeared. By the end of the 1950s he had become a modified Marxist. This showed, perhaps, that he was dissatisfied with extreme individualism as a guide to moral choice, and that analyses of the human condition were not enough.

Sartre reduced existentialism to an ideology and saw it going hand in hand with Marxism. He moved from seeing the struggle as against other individuals to the struggle against all – caused not by psychological friction but by economic scarcity. He came to believe that removing scarcity would result in removing conflict.

His writing on human freedom, human consciousness and human action has exercised a powerful hold over many people and his ideas will live on in his plays and novels as well as in his philosophical writings. Perhaps what he leaves along with his literature and philosophy is a mood: the mood of nausea and absurdity in the face of a godless existence. These feelings provoke deep questions which everyone has to make an attempt to answer for themselves.

PART 6

All in the Mind?

PSYCHOLOGY

God as Psychological Projection

Ludwig Feuerbach

Are you ever frightened at horror films? When a monster gropes on to the screen, do you hide and put a cushion over your ears? Maybe someone watching with you has said:

* 'Don't be stupid, it's only a film. It's not real!'

* 'It's only a film – images projected onto a screen.'

* 'It's only a film – ideas in the film-maker's mind made real and let loose to frighten us.'

It's only a film.

The same is true the other way round. Film-star heroes are just as much fantasies as film-star monsters. Stars' make-up, the way they are photographed, the characters they play – these are all fantasies springing from a writer's or a director's head. Literally, they are all projections.

If you stop to look, you can see that projections are part of our everyday life – in advertising, magazines, TV, the music world. We are surrounded by images of what we would like to be, or what we would hate to be, but these images are only images.

The idea of 'psychological projection' goes back beyond the history of film. It goes back to a German called Ludwig Feuerbach. He was fascinated by religion and wrote about God. What he said, and what many people still believe today, is that God is a projection from humankind. Instead of God making humankind, humankind made God.

For Feuerbach and his followers, examining the way people believe in God is fundamental to finding out how human nature works, because God is simply a fantasy projected out of people's minds.

Ludwig Feuerbach is not a well-known name today, but in the 1840s he was one of the most talked-about philosophers in Europe. Though his work is not much read nowadays, he had an enormous influence on Marx and Freud and on many other thinkers and theologians. Even if Feuerbach's name has been forgotten, his ideas still appear fresh and relevant.

Books and porcelain

Ludwig Andreas Feuerbach (1804-72) was born in Bavaria, Germany, into a gifted family of lawyers, academics and churchmen. As a young man he was very religious and went to Heidelberg University to study theology. He transferred to Berlin in 1824 and changed to philosophy.

Both Georg Hegel (1770-1831) and Friedrich Schleiermacher (1768-1834) were teaching at Berlin when Feuerbach was a student. Hegel's philosophy and Schleiermacher's theology stressed the dependence of human beings on God and their reliance on religious experience. Hegel's starting-point was an abstract idea; Schleiermacher's was human experience.

In 1830, Feuerbach published anonymously his *Thoughts on Death and Immortality*, which denied the existence of the immortal soul. This put paid to his career as an academic. In 1837 Feuerbach married Bertha Low, who had inherited a share of her father's porcelain factory. For the next twenty-three years they lived in her castle at Bruckberg, supported by the profits from the factory and the money made from his writing. *The Essence of Christianity*, published in 1841, was an enormous success. After the unsuccessful revolution of 1848, however, Feuerbach's reputation declined. 1848 was a year of revolutions across Europe. The American revolution of 1776 and the French revolution of 1789 had worried European governments as to their own safety. In Germany, for example, where religion was state religion, writing about religion automatically meant writing about politics. As a result, Feuerbach's work had a political character which is, perhaps, hard for us to understand. In the event, the 1848 revolutions amounted to little, and Feuerbach's influence faded quickly.

His income declined with his reputation; the porcelain factory foundered. Feuerbach continued to write, but without his earlier success. He suffered a stroke in 1870 and finally died in 1872. He was buried at Nuremberg and 20,000 people turned out to honour him at his funeral.

Feuerbach's whole approach is well summed up in this quotation from the preface to the first volume of his collected works (1846):

> The question as to the existence or non-existence of God, the opposition between theism and atheism, belongs to the sixteenth and seventeenth centuries but not to the nineteenth. I deny God. But that means for me that I deny the negation of man. In place of the illusory, fantastic, heavenly position of man which in actual life necessarily leads to the degradation of man, I substitute tangible, actual and consequently also the political and social position of mankind. The question concerning the existence or non-existence of God is not important but the question concerning the existence or non-existence of man is.

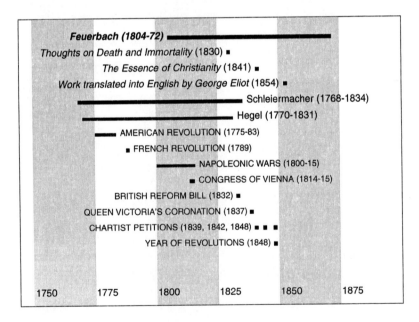

The Essence of Christianity

Feuerbach's best and greatest work was *The Essence of Christianity*, published in 1841. All his major ideas about religion are to be found in this book. Feuerbach was a humanist in that he believed humankind was the basis and starting-point of all philosophy. He believed that 'man is the measure of all things'. He also believed that religion was a fundamental expression of human beings' deepest wishes and feelings; he went as far as to say that 'religion is the dream of the human mind'.

For Feuerbach 'the secret of theology is anthropology'. By this he meant that by studying God a person would actually find out more about human beings. Christians have traditionally believed in the 'incarnation' of Christ: God becoming human. But in Feuerbach's thought the Human is, in fact, God.

The consequence of this was:

* There is no supernatural; only the natural exists.

* Religion is sociological, cultural and psychological.

Feuerbach was writing at a time when there was great enthusiasm for evolution and science. Ideas of progress were in the forefront, as was materialism. Materialism states that matter exists. Religious ideas such as the soul and the after-life are only fancies.

Sigmund Freud (1856-1939) saw religion as an illusion. Belief in God was no more than a result of human wishes. God was a kind of neurosis. Karl Marx (1818-83) claimed that religion was 'the opium of the people'. Marx believed that religion caused people to think of the after-life rather than this life, with the result that people were not encouraged to change things now. He also saw God as being produced out of human need. Both Freud and Marx relied heavily on Feuerbach's ideas when thinking and writing about religion.

In Feuerbach's time materialism had an optimistic outlook – people no longer needed to bow to a demanding God; they could concentrate on the here-and-now rather than the hereafter. In the light of this, Feuerbach wrote his famous dictum 'Man is what he eats.' He also wrote:

> God was my first thought; Reason my second; Man my third and last thought.

Religion, for Feuerbach, was grounded in dependence. Human beings felt helpless in an alien world and needed to invent God to comfort them. People were different from animals in that they possessed consciousness and animals did not. They also possessed memories and used past experiences to construct future hopes.

Feuerbach believed that the three attributes which make up human nature are Reason, Will and Love. These were projected onto an imagined God:

* Reason (God) became infinite knowledge; God is all-knowing.

* Will (God) became infinite will; God is absolutely moral.

* Love (God) became infinite love; God is love.

Feuerbach believed in two stages of human history:

* Humankind was at first dependent on nature. This led to polytheism (belief in many gods), and a desire for people's physical needs to be satisfied.

* Humans were later dependent on one another in a more developed society. This led to monotheism (belief in one God), and a desire for people's moral and spiritual needs to be satisfied.

Feuerbach believed that with social progress all religion would finally disappear. He also pointed out that religion alienates people from their own nature. What is good in human beings is ascribed to God, and people are emptied of their own good qualities. This is psychologically damaging as people cannot truly know themselves as long as they deny the best part of themselves and say it comes from God:

God and man are extremes: God is the absolutely positive, the essence of all realities, while man is the negative, the essence of all nothingness.

What Feuerbach wanted was:

* Love of people for each other and not love of God.

* People to have faith in themselves instead of belief in God.

* Complete involvement in this world instead of concern for the next.

Feuerbach's work was insightful and literary, not philosophically precise. His atheism is the basis of most modern arguments against the existence of God. As a psychological explanation for belief in God, Feuerbach's writing is very convincing. 'What man wishes to be, he makes his God.' Even those who do believe in God should perhaps learn some lessons from Feuerbach. The Christian tradition has often emphasized the spirit at the expense of the body. And its focus on God has sometimes been at the expense of human beings.

There are, however, some points on the other side:

RELIGION HAS NOT DISAPPEARED with social progress as Feuerbach predicted.

FEUERBACH'S METHOD NEED NOT LEAD TO ATHEISM. He was already an atheist before he put pen to paper. Feuerbach found out what he wanted to find out; he had decided beforehand.

DOES BEING ABLE TO TALK ABOUT GOD IN A HUMAN WAY mean that God is necessarily no more than a human product? Just because human beings have needs and wishes, does that mean that a God who meets those needs and wishes cannot exist? Perhaps we are made the way we are precisely because God does exist. The question has to be left open.

Is atheism, then, Feuerbach's own personal projection? Is not wanting God to exist as much a fantasy or a wish-fulfilment as wanting God to exist? In the end, does Feuerbach fall foul of his own philosophy?

Despite these considerations there can be no doubt that much of Feuerbach's psychological insight into the nature of religion is convincing. His work reads as freshly now as it did in the nineteenth century when he first wrote it. It was George Eliot (Marian Evans) (1819-90), a famous British novelist and author of *Adam Bede* and *Middlemarch*, who first translated Feuerbach into English in 1854. Like many people in the Victorian era, George Eliot found that she could no longer believe in God, but her loss of faith troubled her and Feuerbach's ideas appealed to her and others like her.

The Unconscious Mind
Sigmund Freud

Even if you have never met a psychiatrist, you probably have some idea of what one is and does. The patient talks; the psychiatrist listens. Through talking, the patient hopes (with the psychiatrist's help) to come to a deeper understanding of himself or herself. This method of therapy is called 'psychoanalysis'.

The emblem of psychoanalysis is the psychiatrist's couch on which the patient lies during sessions.

But where do these ideas and practices come from? Psychoanalysis – even the couch – comes from the life-work of one man, Sigmund Freud. Freud's work is highly influential and has helped shape the intellectual climate of modern times.

Excavator of the mind

Sigmund Freud (1856-1939) was born in Moravia (now a region of Czechoslovakia), but lived in Vienna between the ages of four and eighty-two. He graduated as a doctor in 1881, but did not feel drawn to practical work and continued his research. From 1882 he worked at the Vienna General Hospital, mainly in neuropathology (brain disorders). It was only after he went to Paris in 1885 that he became interested in hysteria and neurosis.

A further ten years in clinical work in Vienna saw the development of psychoanalysis as a method of treatment.

Until 1918, Vienna was the centre of the Austro-Hungarian Empire.

Around the turn of the twentieth century artists, writers and intellectuals thronged the city and made it famous throughout the world. There was also a large Jewish community in Vienna which was well-established, but suffered through prejudice and anti-semitism. Freud was Jewish (though not a believer), and felt something of an 'outsider' throughout his life.

Freud's interest moved from looking at neurotic symptoms to examining the workings of the human mind in general and then wider cultural questions. He had a happy marriage to Martha Bernays; his pet hates were religion and America. In 1938 the Nazis invaded Austria and Freud was forced to flee to London. He died there, in 1939, rather painfully from cancer of the mouth which he had suffered for fifteen years.

The development of anatomy and physiology in the second half of the nineteenth century had led to a kind of medical materialism, and it is important to sense the concerns of Freud's times in order to understand the nature of his ideas.

'Psychology' literally means 'talking about (or studying) the soul'. Descartes had divided people into souls and bodies, and the two were felt to be quite separate. Atheism, however, had led to materialism: the belief that only matter exists. Materialism, applied to medicine, proclaimed that only bodies exist. People have minds, but they do not have souls; so the mind is part of the body.

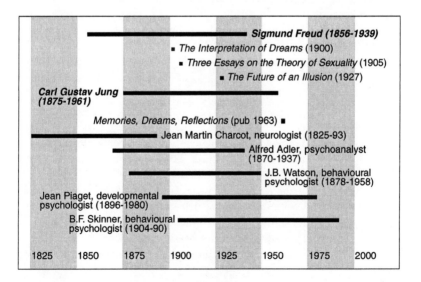

The relationship between mind and body was one of Freud's chief interests.

Being ill because you are depressed may seem obvious today, but this was not always so. Even now the connection between extreme mental problems and extreme physical symptoms may still not always be obvious.

Freud's work was clinical and theoretical: he practised medically and wrote for his entire working life. He likened his work to archaeology, digging up things in the human mind which had long been buried.

Freud's two major discoveries were

* the unconscious

* the Oedipus Complex.

Through these discoveries Freud believed he had come to a deep understanding of the structure of the human mind and the workings of human sexuality.

The unconscious

The turning-point in Freud's career was when he went to Paris in the winter of 1885-86 to observe Charcot's work with patients suffering from hysteria. Charcot had found that under hypnosis patients' symptoms disappeared. Equally, that under hypnosis healthy people could be made to show hysterical symptoms. It was obvious then that the cause of these patients' problems (some of them as extreme as paralysis) was not physical.

Freud was now set on a course of human discovery which was to change people's notions about themselves. His work was a kind of quest, and his ideas changed over the years.

Freud abandoned hypnosis and allowed his patients just to talk. He developed a method of 'free association' by which patients' problems could be located in the way in which they used words. The way words connected showed how the patient's mind worked, and revealed something about his problems.

One of Freud's famous case histories was the 'Rat Man'. The Rat Man decided that he was too fat and must lose weight. He stopped eating puddings, ran in the sun and climbed mountains until he was exhausted. Through 'free association' 'fat' (*dick* in German) was linked to his American cousin Richard, known as Dick. He was jealous of Dick who was showing too much interest in the girl the Rat Man was in love with. Getting rid of fat, therefore, meant getting rid of Dick. In going on a diet, the Rat Man was not punishing himself, he was punishing his cousin Richard.

Freud began by believing that neurotic symptoms were caused by buried memories, but he later came to believe that hysteria and its symptoms were a result of traumas, or emotional shocks, received in childhood. The patient forgot or repressed the shock, but the shock did not disappear. Its results surfaced unconsciously in obsessive habits or bodily symptoms. Through psychoanalysis these traumas could be found and dealt with. The goal of therapy, for Freud, was for a patient to be free to love and work again.

Freud believed that the unconscious shows itself in jokes, in errors, in slips of the tongue, but most importantly, in dreams: 'The interpretation of dreams is the royal road to a knowledge of the unconscious activities of the mind'.

For Freud, 'A dream is a (disguised) fulfilment of a (suppressed or repressed) wish.' In other words, dreams are a kind of code. If you can crack the code, you can find out what the problem is and set about curing it. For Freud, dreams were a combination of 'the residues of the day' (what had been happening) and repressed wishes (unconscious desires).

Freud came to see the structure of the human mind as made up of:

* The ego, the conscious self: the obvious, everyday personality.

* The id, the unconscious self: repressed desires and memories.

* The superego, the standard or morality of society forced onto a person from the outside, by which a person lives.

Freud believed that the ego emerges out of the id as personality develops. He also came to believe that human beings are driven by the two primary instincts of Love and Death and that these govern human behaviour at a fundamental level.

Freud's work took the form of famous 'case studies', whose symptoms and history he wrote about at great length. One of Freud's discoveries was that childhood traumas are often sexual in nature. At first he believed in a 'seduction theory', according to which children had been introduced to sexual experiences at an early age. Later he came to believe that infantile sexuality operates at an age before people believed children could be sexual at all. His view was very controversial as many people wished to believe in the 'innocent', non-sexual, nature of children.

Sexuality is basic to personality. For Freud, sexuality meant affection, love and sensuality in the widest sense. He called this sexual drive the 'libido'. Freud's theories also grew out of his own family experiences; after the death of his father, he came to an understanding of what he called the 'Oedipus Complex'.

The Oedipus Complex

Oedipus was a character in Greek mythology who, unknowingly, murdered his father and married his mother.

Freud believed that male children are first attached to their mothers and see their fathers as rivals for their mother's love. He later attempted to describe an 'Electra Complex' for girls, but this was not so developed. Feelings of fear and jealousy of a boy towards his father are mingled with a sense of guilt, as the child also has some feelings of love for his father. As a result of this early experience, the child's sexual feelings are repressed until puberty, when they surface again because of physical changes in the body.

Freud claimed that a man's goals in life are to:

* Detach himself from his mother.

* Reconcile himself to his father.

* Find someone to love who is not identical to his mother.

'These tasks,' Freud wrote, 'are set to everyone: and it is remarkable how seldom they are dealt with in an ideal manner.'

Freud showed how sexuality could shape the personality. He showed how problems could be caused in a person's development as a result of forgotten, unfortunate experiences.

In 1905 Freud summed up his conclusions on human sexuality in *Three Essays on the Theory of Sexuality* and regarded this and his *The Interpretation of Dreams* (1900) as his most important books.

Freud and religion

Freud came to apply psychoanalysis to literature, mythology, education and religion. He was an atheist with a publicly acknowledged distaste for religious ritual. In his main critical work on religion *The Future of an Illusion* (1927), Freud stated that religion is 'wish-fulfilment': the wish of helpless human beings for protection in an alien world; for justice in an unjust society; for an after-life; and for knowledge of the origin and meaning of the world.

He believed that religion is 'a universal obsessional neurosis', the origin of which lay in 'taboos' (a Polynesian word meaning things 'marked off' or 'prohibited'). At its roots, religious rituals are like neurotic, obsessive actions. In the ritual slaying and eating of the totem animal lay the Oedipal wish to kill and devour the father. For Freud, therefore, religion was mankind's Oedipus Complex.

He believed in a historical development leading through:

* Animism (investing objects or animals with religious qualities) to polytheism and then to monotheism.

* Magic through religion to science.

Nowadays Freud's ideas about the cultural origin and development of religion have largely been discredited.

He had no belief in religion, but he did have faith in science. He thought that religion would disappear and that science and rational thinking would bring about a better society.

Many of Freud's ideas were based on Feuerbach, but were reinforced by his new method of psychoanalysis. They have some clear weaknesses. A real God may correspond to a wish for God. Also, although religion may be an illusion or a neurosis, it need not be. And, while granted a child's attitude to her father may influence her attitude to God, this does not necessarily mean that God does not exist.

Like Feuerbach, Freud was an atheist before he began philosophizing about it, and the psychoanalytic method he established need not lead to atheism.

His work is still controversial, but it is also monumental. He stands as one of the great intellectual pioneers of the twentieth century.

The Collective Unconscious

Carl Gustav Jung

Sometimes when you go into an unusual place – a cathedral, perhaps, or a cave – it has a special atmosphere, an atmosphere of mystery. You can have the feeling that there is something here greater than the cathedral or the cave. This feeling is called 'numinous'; it is the feeling of something beyond, something outside, something supernatural.

Such numinous feelings are common in people's experience, probably more common than we would often like to admit. These feelings seem to be a matter, not just of individual psychology, but of collective psychology. It could be that a shared culture and history gives rise to a shared experience and outlook.

Such questions are not scientific or rational; they are about how human beings experience the world in a subjective way. They seem to pose questions which the laws governing our everyday lives cannot answer.

Carl Gustav Jung spent his life asking questions about human psychology and experience. He was a man who delved into mystery. His name is often linked to Freud's, although he and Freud developed a different outlook and came to different conclusions about what was important for human well-being.

The springs of myth

Carl Gustav Jung (1875-1961) grew up in the countryside of Switzerland. His father and eight of his uncles were clergymen and he spent his life pondering religious questions. Jung wanted to be an archaeologist, but went to study medicine at Basel University. He had a lifelong interest in the occult and parapsychology.

In 1900 Jung became an assistant at the Burgholzi mental hospital in Zurich, the city where he was to spend the rest of his life. He worked at the hospital until 1909 when he left to set up his own psychotherapeutic practice. From 1914 to 1918 Jung underwent a long period of self-analysis. This coincided with the First World War. Switzerland was a neutral and isolated country and he was cut off from international contacts. Afterwards, Jung continued his practice and wrote many books, travelling abroad. He led a modest life and his autobiography, *Memories, Dreams, Reflections* (1963), is a fascinating record of his inner rather than his outer experiences.

Jung was influenced by Freud and had read *The Interpretation of Dreams*. Yet the two men did not meet until 1907, when they talked for thirteen hours without stopping. Freud was twenty years older than Jung and became something of a substitute father to him. Jung's ideas moved away from Freud's, however, and the two men quarrelled and broke their friendship in 1913. The differences in approach are quite marked. Freud was interested in how people related to each other; Jung was more interested in the growth of the individual. Unlike Freud, Jung was not very much interested in childhood experiences, but in adult development. Freud concentrated on the body; Jung exalted the spirit. For him, the psychological was as real as the physical.

Jung's writing is suggestive and imaginative. It invites the reader to respond and find meaning in what he is writing. Jung is not a scientific or a clinical writer. Jung took Freud's discovery of the unconscious and expanded it. He believed there is:

* A personal unconscious, which contains the repressed desires, memories and wishes of the individual.

* A collective unconscious: this is the reservoir of the whole human memory out of which myth and religion springs. All human beings share in the collective unconscious and are connected with it in some way.

Archetypal symbols

Jung treated the different parts of his personality as though they were different people and even talked to them. He believed these figures exist universally in human consciousness and appear clothed in different forms in different times and at different places. These figures or symbols Jung called 'archetypes'. Archetypes occur in history, myth, literature and religion. They also surface in dreams. Jung believed that dreams are creative symbols which have a meaning. They can tell us about the past or about the future. Their meaning, however, is not merely sexual, as Freud thought. Dreams are not solely neuroses in code.

It is important to realize that an archetypal symbol cannot be explained rationally. When a person encounters one of these symbols he or she must respond emotionally and go on and on finding meaning in that symbol without ever exhausting it.

Jung identified four main archetypes:

THE ANIMA: the mysterious female part of the male psyche. She is creative and destructive, finding her way into mythology as a mermaid or a demon. She causes moods in men and can be projected onto real women to make them mysterious and attractive. She is the source of poetry and of death.

THE WISE MAN: he can appear as hero, king, saviour or medicine man. Merlin, in the story of King Arthur, is a good example of a wise man. Often people 'sleep on it' before coming to a decision, which shows that people do believe that wisdom comes to them mysteriously and unconsciously.

THE SHADOW: the dark, primitive, animal side of human nature. In Robert Louis Stevenson's story of Dr Jekyll and Mr Hyde, Mr Hyde is the shadow side (as his name 'hide' suggests). People often say 'I wasn't myself' or 'I don't know what came over me', when their shadow side gains control. Jung believed that people have to learn to live with their shadow side in order to lead healthy lives. He was positive in believing that there is no shadow without light.

THE CHILD: a symbol of wholeness, existing both in this world and the next. Jung believed that to lead a full life a person has to live connected to the conscious and unconscious parts of themselves. The joining of these two parts in a symbolic whole is called 'the self'.

Society represses parts of the personality pushing them down to the unconscious. Each person is forced to adopt a role and show a face, or mask, to the outside world. Jung called this the 'persona', named after the masks actors wore in ancient times.

A healthy, balanced life, according to Jung, is found in someone who can give expression to all these archetypes and who has learned to tolerate the opposites in their character. Reconciling opposites is a great theme in Jung's work.

It could well be argued that neither Freud nor Jung has much to offer women. Freud's 'Electra Complex' was not developed and seems only an imitation of his 'Oedipus Complex'. In Jung's psychology the male possesses the creative, suggestive anima, while the woman possesses the animus. The animus is aggressive and opinionated and seems rather secondary. It does appear that both Freud and Jung assumed traditional cultural roles for women and this influenced their psychological theory.

Personality types

Jung also classified people into types. He made 'introvert' and 'extrovert' household words, but he also wrote about other psychological qualities:

* Extroverts: outgoing, interested in facts.

* Introverts: quiet, interested in ideas.

* Sensing people, who accept things as they are and feel 'for the moment'.

* Intuitive people, who rely on hunches, inspiration and a 'sixth sense'.

* Feeling people, who give value and worth to people and things.

* Thinking people, who decide according to logic and analysis.

Jung believed that most people have one dominating type, although some people can show two or even three.

Jung came to see the 'mandala' as a symbol of the wholeness his patients were seeking. The mandala, taken from Eastern Buddhism, is a circle divided into four, used for meditation. In *Psychology and Religion*, Jung wrote that the mandala is:

An involuntary confession of a peculiar mental condition. There is no deity in the mandala, nor is there any submission or reconciliation to a deity. The place of the deity seems to be taken by the wholeness of man.

Jung found that many people in the second part of their lives are seeking wholeness and meaning. They are established and successful, but they want something more out of life. He realized that human beings are naturally religious and needed a myth or belief to live by. He believed that modern people are unhealthy because they can no longer believe in their myths, and need to develop personal myths.

Jung came to believe that people need meaning and significance in their lives. Unlike Freud, who saw human neuroses as stemming from sexuality, Jung believed that sexuality was only a symbol of a higher spirituality. Humankind needs 'God', or else we will turn to creating idols.

The quest for meaning, for spirituality, Jung called 'individuation'. As the word suggests, individuation is the journey towards becoming a full individual. It is the quest to find the 'God within' and the symbol of 'the self'.

When a person has undergone individuation, so Jung wrote in *The Secret of the Golden Flower*:

> It is as if a river that has run to waste in sluggish side-streams and marshes suddenly finds its way back to its proper bed, or as if a stone lying on a germinating seed is lifted away so that the shoot can begin its natural growth.

Jung spent many years studying alchemy, mythology and religious beliefs. Many people found his work too mystical and obscure to take seriously, and blamed him for using evidence to fit his own theories. There is no doubt, however, that he was a man of extraordinary insight and sensitivity.

Although his work is certainly religious, it is hard to say if he really believed in God in any traditional sense. Rather, he saw all experience – even so-called 'supernatural' experience – as somehow 'natural' and emanating from humankind. In his autobiography he wrote 'Life is – or has – meaning and meaninglessness. I cherish the anxious hope that meaning will preponderate and win the battle.'

How Should Society Be Organized?

POLITICS

The Republic
Plato

'It's not right!'; 'It's not fair!' How many times have you heard those words? But where do the ideas of 'fair' and 'right' come from?

These are ideas connected with justice. Justice is one of the most important human values, as it affects all our lives. Thinking about justice usually involves thinking about the kind of society we live in, or would like to live in, rather than simply relations between individuals.

Political philosophy handles the concept of justice and asks both metaphysical questions and ethical questions, such as:

* Is justice a God-given or eternal value that is absolutely true for all people at all times and in all places?

* Is justice a purely human value, embedded in our institutions to bring order and fairness to human societies? Can what is right for one group of people be wrong for another?

* What is the best form of government? What should be the limits of its power? What is the justification for any form of government?

Different societies in the world are organized in different ways: Democracies elect representatives who form a government for a limited period to take executive decisions (how to run the country). The principle of democracy is 'government by the people for the people'. Monarchies are kingdoms ruled by a king or queen in which the ruler has absolute power. In these societies, rule is handed on through one family. Dictatorships are societies in which one individual has seized power and governs absolutely, crushing all opposition. Theocracies are societies where government is based on religious rule. Officially the ruler of a theocracy is God. Ancient Israel was a theocracy. One of the most famous of modern theocracies was instituted by the Reformer John Calvin in Geneva from 1541.

Broadly speaking, classical philosophers tried to set out guidelines for an ideal society, while modern philosophers have tended to analyze existing societies and draw questions and conclusions from actual political situations.

The first philosopher we know of who drew up guidelines for an ideal society and asked 'What is justice?' was the Greek philosopher Plato who lived in Athens in the fourth and fifth centuries BC. He wrote *The Republic* in which he states that the central question any society has to face is 'Who should rule?'

In Plato's time, Greece was divided into a series of autonomous city states, constantly at war. The city states had a variety of political systems including democracy, aristocracy (government by a ruling class) and monarchy.

Plato wanted to see an end to war; he disliked the values of honour and glory that came with battle. He looked to see a society established in which people could live in peace and harmony, living full lives.

At the same time, Plato conducted his philosophy in opposition to the Sophists. The Sophists were a group of philosophers in Athens who sold their skills to their clients so as to make them successful rather than moral. Plato wanted harmony in the state and excellence in individuals and so he was opposed both to existing political systems and to the Sophists.

The magnificent myth

Plato thought that an ideal state would bring about an ideal life. He also believed that society was the individual writ large, and so what made a good person would make a good society.

He taught that there are three parts to a person's soul:

* The rational element, for reasoning and arguing.

* The spirited element, for courage and actions of the will;

* The appetites, for desires and passions, for food, drink and sex.

A person lives a good life when these three elements are balanced in harmony.

Because there are three parts to a person's soul, it follows there should be three classes to a society, also balanced in harmony:

* The rulers (or Guardians), who correspond to the rational element; they are to rule. These Guardians will be philosophers.

* The military, who correspond to the spirited element; they are to fight.

* The workers, who correspond to the appetitive element; they are to provide food and drink and the other essentials of life.

Plato's ideal society, therefore, is an aristocracy, or rule by a particular class. These three classes, he claimed, will continue largely unchanged through heredity, but special tests will promote some and demote others.

As this society is perfect it will never change, because once perfection is reached, change can only be for the worse.

Plato goes on to say that the people of his Republic will be taught a 'magnificent myth'. They will come to believe that when God created them he mixed gold with the rulers, silver with the military and bronze with the workers. In one or two generations, therefore, people will come to believe that they have a natural or god-given position in society. The purpose of this myth is to give stability to the state.

> Hence I was forced to say in praise of the correct philosophy that it affords a vantage-point from which we can discern in all cases what is just for communities and for individuals; and that accordingly the human race will not see better days until either the stock of those who rightly and genuinely follow philosophy acquire political authority, or else the class who have political control be led by some dispensation of providence to become real philosophers.

Justice and education

In the early part of *The Republic*, there is a discussion about whether justice is a skill in the way that medicine or navigation are skills.

If justice is a skill, as Plato thinks it is, then it follows that just as the best doctors have to be trained to heal people, so the best rulers have to be trained to rule people. Just as no one would dream of arguing against a doctor's expert diagnosis, so it would be ridiculous to argue against a ruler's expert rule.

Plato's central idea is that rule must be rule by the best. Bad rule leads to bad government, anarchy, tyranny and defeat; good rule leads to a stable society and happiness for everyone.

However, there are differing views as to where to find the true principles for justice. In the fifth century BC, Greek philosopher Protagoras proclaimed, 'Man is the measure of all things', thus putting forward a purely human basis for justice. In the Old Testament laws: 'If anyone injures his neighbour, whatever he has done must be done to him; fracture for fracture, eye for eye, tooth for tooth. As he has injured the other, so he is to be injured.' In the New Testament Jesus says: 'You have heard that it was said, "Love your neighbour and hate your enemy." But I tell you, love your enemies and pray for those who persecute you, that you may be sons of your father in heaven.' The Tao, composed by Lao-Tzu in China in the fourth century BC, sets out the Way, or natural justice, which is part of the nature of the whole universe.

In Plato's republic justice would be vested in the Guardians. They would have absolute power, and be above the law to the extent that they are makers of the law.

In *The Republic*, education is of primary importance. All children are to be taken away from their parents at birth and raised communally till they are eighteen. Women and children are held in common; marriages are to partners selected by the state. Just as animals are bred for the best quality, so too should children be, as the aim is to achieve the best.

First, children's characters will be formed, and then their minds. Their education will be physical and cultural, with some mathematics. They will be taken to see battles to make them brave in time of war. What they read and hear will be strictly censored so that they will have no bad examples to copy; everything taught to them will tend towards the highest excellence.

At thirty, people will be strictly tested, in order to choose new Guardians. Those chosen will study philosophy for five years and then will become civil servants working for the state for a further fifteen years. At the age of fifty these people will become Guardians, who will include both men and women.

These Guardians will live simply and communally without money and with only minimum private property. This is to discourage self-interest:

Guardians can be happy, but they are to rule for the good of the whole community and not for the good of their class.

The state must possess the four cardinal qualities of wisdom, courage, discipline and justice.

The conclusion Plato comes to is that 'justice consists in minding your own business and not interfering with other people.' In other words, justice is a harmony of the elements of society. Plato's view is an expression of the Greek belief that justice means finding your place in the natural order of things.

Plato's republic is a society opposed to any modern democracy. The problem that he poses is: if the best rule comes through being governed by the best people, is an authoritarian (but kind) state the best state possible?

Plato's confidence in his Guardians is founded on his own ideas about the good. To know Good is to become Good. Good exists as an objective fact and can be known through reason. Because people strive for what is best for themselves, they strive towards Good, and when they find it they find that this Good is good for everyone. Evil, for Plato, comes about through ignorance rather than malice.

But we need to raise some questions:

IN THE MODERN WORLD there are stark examples that 'power corrupts, but absolute power corrupts absolutely'. Infallible rulers may exist in philosophy, but unfortunately not in society.

THE GUARDIAN/WORKER RELATIONSHIP is like a parent/child relationship – a mature citizenry needs a measure of responsibility.

THERE IS NO CHANGE, no art, science or imagination in Plato's republic.

IN THE EARLIER PART OF *THE REPUBLIC* Thrasymachus claims that right is the 'interest of the stronger party'. Conflicts are often settled through force rather than reason. Thrasymachus is a relativist: if someone wins, then right is what they say it is. If justice does not exist in the universal, objective sense that Plato understood it, then perhaps Thrasymachus' argument gains more force.

Plato's *Republic* is one of the foundation stones of political philosophy. Many of his arguments still have to be taken seriously. This work has exerted a strong hold on people's imaginations throughout the centuries and is still an influence on our society today.

Plato's *Republic* was the first utopia. *Utopia* was a book about an ideal society written by Sir Thomas More in 1516. Modern writers have tended to be more pessimistic. Two famous 'dystopias' (the opposite of utopias) are *1984* by George Orwell, written in 1948, and *Brave New World* by Aldous Huxley, written in 1931. No one really knows what 'utopia' means, but it may mean 'no place'.

The Ultimate Political Pragmatist

Niccolo Machiavelli

'All's fair in love and war'; 'The end justifies the means'. Many people sympathize with such sayings, but fewer act on them; most people come to a sticking-point where they will not do something just because it benefits them. They are prevented by their morality, their principles or their religious faith.

Jean-Jacques Rousseau (1712-78) wrote *The Social Contract* in 1762. He was born in Geneva, but lived for many years in Paris. His key political idea was the 'general will' rather than the 'social contract'. He saw society as involving the subjection of every individual to the 'general will'. The 'general will' was the sole source of legitimate rule and was always directed towards the common good. Rousseau was for democracy and against the Divine Right of Kings (the idea that kings were appointed by God to govern). His ideas had an influence on the French Revolution.

Thomas Hobbes (1588-1679) wrote *Leviathan* in 1655. He had lived through the English Civil War in 1642 and fled to exile on the continent for eleven years. Not surprisingly, he hated chaos and believed that to bring order people should be compelled to obey the law and be punished if they did not. Hobbes believed in absolute monarchy. He believed the purpose of society was to escape the state of nature which was 'solitary, poor, nasty, brutish and short'. Society, in effect, is a compromise through which selfish individuals abide by laws; but as people are selfish these laws have to be enforced. 'Just' behaviour means obeying the law.

John Locke (1632-1704) wrote *Two Treatises of Government* in 1690. Locke's political theories lie behind modern Western democracies. Many of his ideas influenced the American and French revolutions in the eighteenth century. In his opinion, 'All men are created equal'; he held an opposite view to Hobbes. He believed Hobbes had confused a 'state of nature' with a 'state of war'. For Locke, the basis of government is law, not force. Laws are made by representatives of the people, on behalf of the people, and citizens have 'rights' immune from government interference. This belief was taken into the Bill of Rights in the American Constitution.

Christians take seriously what Jesus said: 'Give to Caesar what is Caesar's, and to God what is God's.' And Paul wrote: 'Everyone must submit himself to the governing authorities, for there is no authority except that which God has established.' Yet the question is often raised, should Christians obey God rather than other people? In many cases, Christians have faced the problem as to whether being a good Christian is the same as being a good citizen. In parts of the world this is still a pressing problem today.

Yet there are some people who appear unconcerned about principles of any kind and do what they want to get what they want. For these people pragmatism, not principle, is the guiding rule. Their behaviour is often described as 'machiavellian', after Niccolo Machiavelli, a political writer born in the renaissance Florence of the fifteenth century.

Machiavelli was the greatest political pragmatist of all time. His views were drawn wholly from his own observation and experience. They were shocking and remain shocking, to the extent that many people believed his work was inspired by the devil.

Fickle fortune

Machiavelli (1469-1527) was born and raised in Florence, Italy, where his father was a lawyer. He grew up in the golden age of Florentine culture and, in 1498, became secretary and Second Chancellor to the Florentine Republic. His post took him on missions to Louis XII, King of France, and Maximillian, the Holy Roman Emperor.

Machiavelli observed the rapid rise and fall of Cesare Borgia, Duke of Romagna, and the machinations of Pope Julius II.

In 1513, the Republic of Florence fell and the Medici family returned to rule. Machiavelli was excluded from public life, accused of conspiracy, tortured and imprisoned. After his release, he retired to his farm to live with his wife and six children and devote his time to writing. His most famous book, *The Prince*, was published in 1513 and dedicated to Lorenzo de Medici, ruler of Florence. Machiavelli hoped to flatter and impress his way back into public life, but his attempts were not successful.

Machiavelli lived in turbulent times. Rulers rose and fell; cities grew great and were then put to the sword. The political situation echoed Plato's time when the Greek city states had warred for prominence.

The renaissance Italians became almost obsessed with 'Fortune', which they pictured as a beautiful woman to be won and pleased. Fortune appeared to control events, but no one appeared to control her. These same scholars and statesmen asked questions such as 'Does our fate lie in the stars or in ourselves?' and 'Does God give us a destiny or do we make our own destiny?'

Machiavelli's book

The Prince is a book of advice to a prince on how to rule. Many such books existed in Machiavelli's day, but Machiavelli's was different in that he turned his face against contemporary morality. He was very honest about dishonesty, and his work has become a byword for cunning, deceit and bad faith in political affairs. His was an attack on the moral basis of political life.

Renaissance Humanism was based on Cicero and other Roman moralists. Cicero said that private interests should bow to the public good. He also urged his readers to fight against corruption and tyranny and reach out for the highest and noblest ambitions. Machiavelli's advice was not based on these principles.

In *The Prince* Machiavelli states that cities can be governed by republics or princes. He wrote that he would pay attention to princes, of whom some govern by heredity, while others seize power and govern.

Machiavelli addressed his advice to the second group. He maintained that new princedoms are held through 'virtue' or Fortune. Fortune is not to be trusted as it does not last forever. Therefore princes must govern well and make themselves secure for when their luck turns. 'New princes are in a precarious position,' he wrote. 'They are established by Fortune, but are without roots and can easily be blown away.'

As old rulers are more secure than new rulers, new rulers must come to appear like old rulers as quickly as possible. The methods by which this is achieved are set out with verve and wit in *The Prince*.

Such sayings as these are typical:

> The gulf between how one should live and how one does live is so wide that a man who neglects what is actually done for what should be done learns the way to self-destruction rather than self-preservation.

> There is nothing so self-defeating as generosity; in the art of practising it you lose the ability to do so, and you become either poor and despised or, seeking to escape poverty, rapacious and hated.

> It is far better to be feared than loved.

Machiavelli stated that the aim of a prince is to obtain glory and maintain his position. As such, it is not always rational to be moral: practising what most people preach as right will only lead to destruction. He was impressed by the fortunes of Cesare Borgia and learned from his fall. He was even more impressed that Pope Julius II made many promises to Borgia and, when his own position was secure, broke every one of them.

If the aim of a prince is to keep his power, he faces the problem of how not to appear wicked even when acting wickedly.

* People take things at face value.

* People judge by appearances.

He wrote that 'a prince who deceives always finds men who let themselves be deceived.' In fact, if a prince cannot always act like a man, then he must act like a beast. Like a fox – tricky; like a lion – savage.

However, a prince must enact good laws to secure his position and these must be enforced by a good army. Machiavelli was particularly insistent that a prince should raise his own troops and not make use of hired mercenaries as was then the custom. His advice can be summed up in this way: Do not act according to the dictates of morality, but according to the dictates of necessity.

Above all, a man must 'be wise enough to accommodate himself to the times'. And the man who possesses the greatest 'virtue' is most likely to attract Fortune's smile.

In Machiavelli's time, scholars argued for:

* An objective standard of justice, from the Classics.

* God's judgment, from the Bible.

Society acted in the belief that wrong action in this life would bring about punishment in the next. Machiavelli overturned contemporary morality and made no reference to the Bible or Christianity at all. He was resoundingly silent on the subject of God's judgment, and this drew much condemnation.

Machiavelli's Discourses

The Prince, however, is only one of Machiavelli's works. *Discourses on the First Decade of Livy* were written about the same time and put forward another political view.

The *Discourses* state that tyranny or imperial power hold cities back. Greatness lies in liberty and self-government. Because of this, republics are to be preferred to princes as the common good is always greater than an individual good. Cities, according to Machiavelli, need more than just one good ruler, because, when that ruler goes, good rule goes. Cities need someone who will impose his 'virtue' on the masses. This can be done by example, having an inspiring leader; or by coercion, forcing people to obey.

Institutionally speaking, any republic must encourage its citizens towards the common good:

* By religion, which will inspire and terrify people to the greater good.

* By laws, which will force people to serve the community.

'Virtue' has its origin in good education and good education has its origin in good laws.

Machiavelli concluded that 'pure' constitutional forms of monarchy, aristocracy and democracy are all inherently unstable because they set one group of interests over another. He believed the solution lies in a balanced constitution in which all parties have a stake in government and have to keep a watch on each other. As a result 'all the laws made in favour of liberty' will 'result from their discord'. This promotion of dissension horrified Machiavelli's contemporaries, but he went on to say that the price of liberty is eternal vigilance. People will always put self-interest before the common good and 'never do anything except by necessity'.

Machiavelli was finally admitted to the Medici court in 1520 and asked to write a history of Florence. Ironically, when the Medicis fell in 1527, Machiavelli was associated with their regime. He contracted an illness and died a few months later.

By turning virtues into vices and vices into virtues, Machiavelli shocked the world, but gained a grudging acknowledgment that his thought contained more than a grain of truth.

Class 21 Conflict

Karl Marx

The idea of 'progress' is firmly implanted in all of us. The world, we believe, should be getting better, not worse, and so we see history as a line along which we are travelling. In the past history has been seen as a circle or even as stationary. The idea of history as a line is only one possible way of seeing it.

But what is it that drives history along this line, and does this line have an end? Is there such a thing as a final, perfect society – the end of progress? If so, what will such a society be like? Will it be a dream or a nightmare?

Karl Marx believed that history involves progress towards a final, perfect society which will be a communist society. His ideas changed the world to the extent that, until recently, four out of ten people in the world lived in societies described as 'Marxist'. Controversially Marx has become a kind of 'religious' figure and his writings have obtained the status of religious books.

Marx's work has helped give birth to modern sociology, transformed the study of history and deeply affected philosophy, literature and the arts.

There are three elements to Marxist thought:

* Systematic philosophy.

* Economic theory.

* Ethics.

Marx wrote that 'the philosophers have only interpreted the world in various ways; the point is to change it'. His followers have taken him at his word.

Marx and his philosophy

Karl Marx (1818-83) was born in Trier, now in Germany, into a comfortable, middle-class home. His family were Jewish, but had converted to Protestantism. Marx became a student at Bonn and then Berlin where he gained a Doctorate in Philosophy. He did not become an academic, however, but turned to left-wing journalism until the government suppressed the paper he worked for. He married his childhood sweetheart and moved to Paris where, in 1843, he met Friedrich Engels and their lifelong collaboration began. After the failure of the 1848 revolutions across Europe, Marx and his family moved to London where he spent the rest of his life.

At first he was very poor, but money from Engels, weekly articles in the *New York Tribune* and his wife's legacy helped the family survive. The First International, the International Workingmen's Association, was founded in 1864, and the first volume of Marx's mammoth work, *Das Kapital*, appeared in 1867. Marx's reputation spread in the 1870s as *Das Kapital* was translated into French, Russian and English. He developed bronchitis and died in 1883, and the remaining volumes of *Das Kapital* were completed by Engels, a year before his own death in 1894.

As a student in Berlin, Marx found that philosophy was dominated by Hegel (1770-1831). Hegel believed that history is a metaphysical process leading to perfection. The Young Hegelians, who followed Hegel's philosophy, believed that this process or 'dialectic', is the history of human consciousness freeing itself from the illusions that prevent it from self-understanding and freedom.

Hegel's philosophy is important because it emphasizes certain ideas which other philosophers, including Marx, took up:

* History is a process.

* Events can be fitted into a system – history has a meaning and a goal.

* Change is progress.

* Optimism.

In a way, Hegel's system anticipated evolution, perhaps the greatest of nineteenth-century theories.

Marx incorporated much of Hegel's system into his own philosophy, but substituted 'economics' for 'metaphysics' and 'classes' for 'nations'. Instead of the history of 'Mind' or 'Spirit', history became the history of 'class conflict'.

'The history of all hitherto existing society,' according to the *Communist Manifesto*, 'is the history of class struggles.'

Marx called the historical process he had pinpointed 'dialectical materialism'. Its goal was a classless society. At first Marx believed that religion was the greatest illusion captivating humankind – he called it 'the opium of the people'. But later he came to believe that the greatest danger to human freedom lay in economics.

He believed that society moulds human nature rather than the other way round. Changing society, therefore, would mean changing human nature and society's problems and human problems would vanish as a result. He held this view because he was a materialist. He believed that only matter – bodies – exists. As a result, he did not believe that people have souls or spirits. Marx became an atheist while still young. He accepted that belief in God was merely 'wish-fulfilment', and that the work of Feuerbach (1804-72) had established atheism. Because of this, Marx was not interested in whether God exists or not, but only in religion as a social force. He saw religion as 'the opium of the people', bringing an illusion of happiness but no real happiness, and causing people to concentrate on the next life instead of this one. Marx wrote: 'The criticism of religion ends with the teaching that man is the highest being for man...' Getting rid of God meant being able to pay more attention to human beings. Yet just because people wish God to exist, does that mean that God does not exist? Marx's atheism was personal and preceded his philosophy. While Marx was illuminating in many ways as to how religion works in society, the question of whether God exists or not must remain open.

Marxist economics

Marx believed that society changes as its economic basis changes.

> Does it require deep intuition to comprehend that man's ideas, views and conceptions, in one word, man's consciousness, changes with every change in the conditions of his material existence, in his social relations in his social life?

Feudalism had given way to capitalism with the coming of the Industrial Revolution. Lords and serfs had been replaced by owners and workers. Inevitably, capitalism would give way to socialism as the final form of society. 'Consciousness does not determine life,' wrote Marx, 'but life determines consciousness.'

History was the history of class struggles; each society was ethically superior to the last. And with the disappearance of classes, conflict would disappear and history would end.

Marx identified three classes:

* Capitalists, who own or control the 'means of production'.

* Workers – those forced to depend on owners for work.

* The middle class – small businessmen, professional people and white-collar workers.

Marx believed the structure of these classes was determined by the 'means of production', that is, by pure economics.

He believed that labour is the 'essence of human life', but workers are 'alienated', cut off from their own humanity by having to produce objects owned and designed by others. In fact, workers suffer from self-alienation: industry, which should be making their life better, is making it worse because their work dehumanizes them. And they encounter a kind of fetishism, in that things are given value and not people. The products of labour are worshipped.

In capitalism, Marx maintains, workers receive a raw deal as a result of:

* The labour theory of value, by which workers exchange their labour for enough money to live.

* The theory of surplus value, by which capitalists sell products at a profit and so make more than they pay out.

* The concentration of capital: capital, according to Marx, is 'accumulated labour'. The worker receives the 'exchange value' of labour – wages for hours worked; but the 'use value' – the money from the products he or she makes – goes to the capitalist.

As capitalists want high prices and low wages, and workers want low prices and high wages, conflict is inevitable and Marx predicted revolution.

The weapon of criticism obviously cannot replace the criticism of weapons. Material force must be overthrown by material force.

The solution to the problem of capitalism is, quite simply, communism. Communism will abolish wages and private property, and usher in an equal, classless society. Everyone will be content. Armies will wither, exploitation will vanish and people will work for the good of all. Marx believed this revolution is inevitable. The basis of society will be, 'From each according to his ability, to each according to his needs.'

Marx was optimistic, and the ultimate aim of his ethics was human freedom. He felt that human beings had been devalued by the machine age and longed for a humane, free, equal society.

The Marxist utopia has not been realized – certainly not by the countries which have called themselves Marxist. Indeed, some scholars would claim that capitalist countries which have developed socialist features such as trade unions, social security and the welfare state have developed more humane societies.

Marx believed that in capitalist societies the rich would become richer and the poor poorer until there was a revolution. In fact, in many capitalist societies workers enjoy a higher standard of living than ever before.

Some criticisms

Marx showed how economic forces help determine a society's politics, religion and philosophy. He showed that these ideas do not have a magical, independent existence. And he gave useful insights into the 'consumer society', showing how capitalism often controls us when we should be controlling it. But some questions remain:

* How 'natural' is a 'pecking order'? The ruler and the ruled exist in nature, so can this division be seen purely as a creation of society?

* Surely people can struggle for what they believe is right and not just for their own class interests?

* Is human nature as fluid as Marx supposed? Are we entirely creations of society, or something more?

Marx paid attention to the struggle between classes, not within them. He was a great internationalist; 'The working men have no country,' he wrote. Perhaps he ignored the power of personality and the power of nationalism too easily.

Marx's work has marked millions. It has changed the world. But perhaps the changes have not always been the ones Marx expected.

PART

8

Is Man the Measure of All Things?

HUMANISM

The Rise of Humanism

Erasmus and the Renaissance

How would you describe the age in which you live? Is it an Age of Progress or an Age of Decay? An Age of Hope? Or Despair and Disillusionment? Is it Scientific or Post-Scientific?

Historians sometimes use the idea of an 'Age' to show a movement in the way people thought or acted. Hence such terms as The Age of Reason, or The Age of Revolution or The Dark Ages. Alternatively, an 'age' may simply delineate a period of time.

In Western Europe the first part of the middle ages, from about 500 to 1000, can be called The Dark Ages. It was a time when the Western half of the Roman empire began to crumble because of barbarian invasions, after Rome fell in 410. The West continued to be invaded by Norse and Danes from the north and from Islam via Spain in the south. In such instability, there was the danger that philosophy and the heritage of the past would be lost. There was some theological study, mainly through the monasteries, called 'monastic theology' for this reason.

In the year 1000, a crowd gathered in Rome on New Year's Eve to await the end of the world. The then Pope, Sylvester II, blessed the crowd and dispersed them. The end of the world had not come. Instead the eleventh century saw a revival of learning. During the Dark Ages many barbarian invaders had become nominal Christians. This stability meant there could be a revival of Western civilization. Theologians found themselves faced with the question of the relationship between faith (theology) and reason (philosophy).

How to harmonize reason and faith was a main issue in medieval thought. The philosophical approach to theology was called 'scholastic' theology or Scholasticism. This was an objective intellectual enquiry into knowledge rather than a devotional exercise linked with the spiritual life of the monastery.

By the year 1500 the Pope's influence over Western Christendom looked very secure; the church had amassed enormous wealth and influence. But it was soon to be shaken by the Protestant Reformation. A number of factors prepared the way for the Reformation. One of these was the rise of humanism.

The rise of humanism

The humanism of the sixteenth century is not to be confused with modern humanism which is agnostic or atheistic. In southern Europe there came a revival of interest in Greek and Roman classical life. This was the Renaissance.

The Renaissance, so the historian Jakob Burckhart put it in 1860, was the coming of age of man as a spiritual individual. From the middle of the fourteenth century groups of scholars, artists and writers in Italy and elsewhere used rich imagery to describe their experience of living in a new age. It was an age of reawakening, and 'rebirth', the meaning of the French word renaissance.

Many of the forms of classical culture were revived at this time:

IN SCULPTURE, Michaelangelo's Bacchus was such a fine imitation of classical style that it was believed for some while to be a genuine antique. Donatello went to Rome to study classical antiquity. By the year 1500 it was common for Italians of style to collect classical sculpture.

IN ARCHITECTURE, such men as Filippo Brunelleschi (1377-1446) and Donato Bramante (c. 1433-1514) journeyed to Rome to observe and measure classical buildings. The Colosseum, the Pantheon and the Theatre of Marcellus all provided models for a revival of the principles on which they were built.

IN LITERATURE AND LEARNING, Marsilio Ficino (1433-99) translated all the dialogues of Plato, along with other Greek works which included neo-Platonic writings. There was a revival of the use of classical Latin. Many commentators were highly critical of medieval Latin, which they saw as a travesty of the real thing. At the same time there was a revival of the principal literary forms of ancient Rome: the comedy, the epic and the tragedy.

Renaissance art

In the medieval past the focus of philosophical thinking had been on God and the world to come. Thomas Aquinas opened the way for the discussion of what has been called 'nature and grace'. In Aquinas' view the human will is fallen but the intellect is not. So in one realm, the intellect, humanity is autonomous. One result of this was the development of 'natural theology', which can be followed independently from our own reason and does not depend entirely on God's revelation through the scriptures. Aquinas prepared the way for the humanistic Renaissance. The focus shifted to humanity and our relation to the present material world; there was less stress on God and the past. It is possible to see this change in perspective through the art and painting of the day.

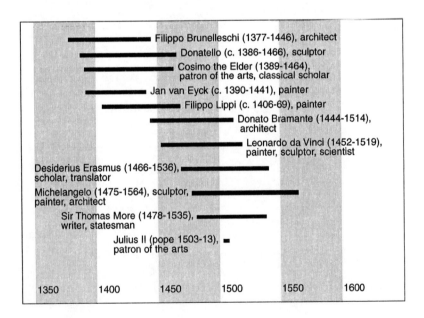

Filippo Brunelleschi (1377-1446), architect
Donatello (c. 1386-1466), sculptor
Cosimo the Elder (1389-1464), patron of the arts, classical scholar
Jan van Eyck (c. 1390-1441), painter
Filippo Lippi (c. 1406-69), painter
Donato Bramante (1444-1514), architect
Leonardo da Vinci (1452-1519), painter, sculptor, scientist
Desiderius Erasmus (1466-1536), scholar, translator
Michelangelo (1475-1564), sculptor, painter, architect
Sir Thomas More (1478-1535), writer, statesman
Julius II (pope 1503-13), patron of the arts

1350   1400   1450   1500   1550   1600

Cosimo the Elder, from Florence, died in 1464. He was one of the first to see the importance of Platonic philosophy. Thomas Aquinas had revived Aristotelian thought, and Cosimo began to promote neo-Platonism. Remember that Platonism is concerned with the heavenly (Universals, absolutes, God and Grace) and Aristotle with the earthly (Particulars, nature, creation and the natural world). The ancient philosophical question was asked of how to reconcile the One and the Many. If nature, the world of our senses, is full of variety and change, how is it possible to find an underlying coherent order in the world? How do we arrive at a permanent reality behind the changing appearance of the physical world?

Leonardo da Vinci (1452-1519) struggled with this problem. He saw that if you begin with autonomous independent reason then understanding comes through mathematics. But mathematics only deals with particulars, not with universals. Da Vinci was a man who realized the need for unity. It has been said that he died a disillusioned man because he would not let go of his hope for a unity of all knowledge. Da Vinci was living at a time when Universals were part of the past and had been overtaken in the rise of human reason, nature and Particulars.

In Northern Europe Jan Van Eyck (1390-1441) painted a tiny miniature. The scene is Jesus' baptism, but this takes up a very small area of the canvas. The miniature is dominated by nature: a river, a real castle, hills, houses. The landscape is all-important. In 1465 Filippo Lippi (1406-69) painted a picture of the Virgin Mary. In the near past, when the heavenly was all-important, artists had always painted Mary in a symbolic way, as a mark of their respect for the sacred. But Lippi's Madonna shows a shocking change. He paints a beautiful girl holding a baby against a landscape. She is no far-off symbol, but a very human young woman with a baby. But that is not all. The girl he painted was his mistress and everybody in Florence knew that. A few years before nobody would have dared to do such a thing.

Christian humanism

All this took place in Southern Europe. In the north, humanism was distinctly Christian. Its leader was Desiderius Erasmus (c. 1466-1536).

Erasmus was the illegitimate son of a Dutch priest. As a youth he was thoroughly schooled in classical ideas, and loathed Scholasticism. Late medieval theology was called Scholasticism because it was developed for teaching purposes by professional instructors in monastic schools and universities. Thomas Aquinas was its most influential figure.

According to Erasmus, the systems of the 'schoolmen' contributed nothing to human spiritual perfection. He interpreted the history of salvation as an educational process conducted by divine wisdom. He found parallels in Plato and Cicero. So this classical, non-Aristotelian wisdom, taught alongside the Bible, could be the way ahead for mankind.

As well as attacking the irrelevance of Scholasticism, Erasmus published satirical works against corruption in the church – the scandalous lives of the clergy and the state of the monasteries.

> Perhaps it would be better to pass silently over the theologians... They attack me with six hundred arguments and force me to retract what I hold, for if I refuse, they will immediately declare me a heretic... Those who are the closest to them in happiness are generally called 'the 'religious' or 'monks', both of which are deceiving names, since for the most part they stay as far away from religion as possible.

Erasmus was the most famous scholar of his time. He was a convinced Christian humanist, who believed that the best way to reform the church was to go back to the sources, the Hebrew and Greek Bible and the early Christian Fathers. He was whole-hearted in the task of making these sources available to a wide audience. Clergy and laity were to be educated in Christian philosophy.

Erasmus was a tireless writer:

IN 1509 he wrote *In Praise of Folly*. It is dedicated to his friend Thomas More, and was written in his house. This is one of the most popular of his works, a brilliant satire on monks and theologians. The quotation above, about corrupt theologians, gives the flavour.

IN 1516 he provided the first published edition of the Greek text of the New Testament, with his own translation in Latin. Erasmus wanted the Bible to be made available to everyone, not just to priests and theologians: 'I would to God that the ploughman would sing a text of the Scripture at his plough... To be brief, I wish that all communication of the Christian would be of the Scriptures'.

IN 1517 an anonymous work was published entitled *Julius Excluded from Heaven*. Erasmus denied authorship. The work was about former Pope Julius II who appears before the gates of heaven and is refused entry.

ERASMUS BECAME THE THEOLOGIAN OF THE 'CHRISTIAN HUMANITY' recorded in his *Handbook of a Christian Soldier* (1518).

When humanism is defined, as it used to be, in terms of the 'dignity of man', Erasmus can be seen as a true humanist because he believed in humanity's free will to respond to God. He fell out with Martin Luther, who was seen as anti-humanist because he believed that the fallen human will is in bondage, unable to do any good and therefore not 'free'. Luther had been educated in Scholastic theology, with little humanist influence.

Erasmus' impact on the history of ideas needs to be studied more carefully than here. More than any other single Renaissance figure, he represents the association between humanism and theology which was at its height in the first two decades of the sixteenth century.

Erasmus wanted peaceful reform of the church. His satirical writing had a profound effect in communicating his message against the corruption of Rome. His teaching was therefore condemned in 1527, and all his works were included on the Index of Forbidden Books in 1559. In this way he laid the foundations for the Protestant Reformation. No wonder it was said: 'Erasmus laid the egg which Luther hatched.'

Beyond Good and Evil
Friedrich Nietzsche

When you read Nietzsche you are immediately struck by the vital, exhilarating intellectual energy which comes off the page. His writings are notoriously and scathingly critical, full of strong forceful opinions on touchy subjects such as war, women and nationality. His style is full of value judgments where he pronounces 'yes' or 'no', acceptance or rejection, on almost every issue. He was a poet, thinker and philosopher. On the subject of whether God exists his answer was a resounding 'no'.

Prophet of power

Friedrich Nietzsche was born on 15 October 1844 at Rocken near Leipzig, of Lutheran parents. He was educated at the Schulpforta, and was a brilliant pupil. In 1864 he went to the university of Bonn, and then on to Leipzig. At the age of twenty-four he was appointed professor of classics at the University of Basel, without having written the qualifying thesis. Here he had the historian Jacob Burckhardt as a colleague and the composer Richard Wagner lived nearby.

Nietzsche became a full professor in 1870, but resigned nine years later because of ill-health. Illness threatened him throughout his life. Scholars disagree over the causes. Insanity ran in the family, or he may have contracted syphilis. Certainly, early in 1889 Nietzsche became insane. After this his sister Elizabeth looked after him until his death in 1900. By the time he died his reputation had been established. The popular image of him is as a person who advocated a passionate pursuit of power. He is often associated with Nazism and Hitlerism and there is little doubt that his ideas were open for exploitation by such movements.

Nietzsche's life spanned the second half of the nineteenth century. This period saw the sudden rise of Germany, united as a country under Prussian leadership in 1871, to a supreme place of power. Nietzsche was a child when the revolution of 1848 failed. Its ideals were replaced by Bismarck's policy of blood and aggression. German cities were decorated with monuments celebrating the new national achievements in arms and industry. There was a new pride in the cultural progress of the universities. Nietzsche was scathingly critical of this so called 'culture'. As he saw it, in gaining so much Germany had lost what really mattered. The country had become soulless and self-satisfied: rich in possessions but miserably poor within. Culture was 'decadent'.

The centre of Nietzsche's analysis was that Germany, with the whole of Europe, had turned against Christianity while lacking the courage to admit it. There is little doubt he saw himself as something of a prophet. He felt that he had a mission to his generation to rouse it from sleep and expose its false virtues.

The death of God

Nietzsche's starting-point was the non-existence of God. In this quotation from *The Joyful Wisdom* (1882) he gives powerful and poetic expression to his atheism:

> The most important of more recent events – that 'God is dead', that the belief in the Christian God has become unworthy of belief – already begins to cast its first shadows over Europe... In fact, we philosophers and 'free spirits' feel ourselves irradiated as by a new dawn by the report that 'the old God is dead'; our hearts overflow with gratitude, astonishment, presentiment and expectation. At last the horizon seems open once more, granting even that it is not bright; our ships can at last put out to sea in face of every danger; every

hazard is again permitted to the discerner; the sea, our sea, again lies open before us; perhaps never before did such an 'open sea' exist.

For Nietzsche, belief in God impoverishes human lives. Belief in a heaven after death reduces the dignity and the value of human existence now. He wrote in *Ecce Homo* (1888):

> The unmasking of Christian morality is an event without equal...
> Everything hitherto called 'truth' is recognized as the most harmful,
> malicious, most subterranean form of the lie; the holy pretext of
> 'improving' mankind as the cunning to suck out life itself and to make
> it anaemic. Morality as vampirism...

The 'death of God' means that humanity is no longer supported by divine wisdom. The supernatural has gone because there is no longer any place for it. For Nietzsche, as for many of his contemporaries, the idea of God as an objective reality was not compatible with modern scientific knowledge. But he realized, perhaps more than anyone, the frightening consequences of this.

Since God is dead then humanity must go on alone. Since God does not exist, then we must shape our own lives forcibly. Human beings cannot live without values but there is now no other source or direction for values other than humanity's own.

Nietzsche talked of 'the great seasickness' of the world without God. This phrase was picked up by Sartre in his novel *Nausea*. Walking in the park, Roquetin was overcome by the nausea of the meaninglessness of life. Samuel Beckett's play *Breath* is thirty seconds long. There are no actors or conversation; the whole script is the sigh of human life from a baby's cry to a man's last breath before he dies. The artist Francis Bacon said that humanity now realizes that we are an accident, completely futile beings who can attempt to beguile themselves only for a time. Art has become a game by which we distract ourselves.

Nietzsche is not against morals; he is passionately concerned for standards and direction, but old values have lost their force. His mission was to bring in the 'transvaluation of values'. He presented himself as a new Zarathustra (or Zoroaster) who, like the old Persian prophet of the same name, was a great moral teacher.

It is difficult to separate Nietzsche's writing from his own life. He had to make a continuous effort to overcome ill health. He had to take hold of life by force.

Saying 'Yes' to life

Nietzsche thought that the decadence he found in the culture of his day showed an acceptance of the forces that work for the destruction of life – the sickly instead of the healthy, the feminine instead of the masculine. His first book, *The Birth of Tragedy* (1872), was a highly original analysis of Greek tragedy and contains his famous discussion of the Apollonian and the Dionysian models.

The Dionysian urge is creative, dynamic and frenzied, even resulting in savage behaviour. The Apollonian is restrained and reasoned, with harmony. Nietzsche pointed out that in Greek tragedy the powerful Dionysian chaos is ordered by Apollonian qualities.

Dionysius was the Greek god of chaos, fruitfulness and ecstasy. Apollo was the sun-god, the god of ordered form and dreams. Nietzsche saw the birth of Tragedy as the union of these two fundamental impulses. The aim of Nietzsche's dialectic was to keep the interplay between these two fundamental modes of life and knowledge in balance.

In his later work the relation between the two changed. There was no longer an attempt to keep a balance: Dionysius was allowed to triumph over Apollo. Apollo came to be seen as a flight from life into a realm of ideal and therefore of illusion; whereas 'Dionysian pessimism' spoke of the hero who is strong and self-reliant and welcomes the savageness of life. Nietzsche spoke again and again of a form of life so rich and strong that it triumphs in the worst circumstances.

Nietzsche connected this affirmation of existence with the idea of 'eternal return': all things come round again and again, so that what is happening now has happened many times already and will happen many times again. Some critics would call this fatalism, or criticize Nietzsche for the lack of freedom in the idea. Where is human freedom if things return again and again? How do we get out? But Nietzsche's Dionysian man would not be daunted by a repetition of his suffering. He would welcome the thousand opportunities to conquer suffering so as to affirm life. To quote *Thus Spake Zarathustra* (1883-85):

> Oh! how should I not burn for Eternity, and for the marriage ring – the Ring of Recurrence? Never yet found I the woman by whom I would have children, save it be by this Woman that I love: for I love thee, O Eternity.

The will to power

Nietzsche attacked those traditional beliefs in a 'true' or more 'real' world which theologians and philosophers such as Plato or Kant had preferred to the world of everyday life. He was a strong opponent of metaphysics, as 'life-denying'.

According to Nietzsche, it is physiologically weak individuals or groups, such as priests, who use these ideologies to dominate the 'strong and healthy'.

What matters about a belief is not so much whether it is 'true' but whether it is 'life-affirming', capable of giving to those who seek it feelings of strength and freedom and power.

Like the existentialists, Nietzsche wrote that we make values rather than discover them. It is up to us to separate ourselves from the meaningless flux of things and exert a 'will to power' that accepts suffering as a way of gaining richer experience. This satisfies the yearnings of the heart rather than the dictates of reason.

The 'will to power' is a central concept in Nietzsche's work. He presented it as a principle to be seen in all of nature. It is that self or 'centre of power' which goes beyond its boundaries and asserts itself over another. The will to power is the means by which humanity, 'the weakest, cleverest being', becomes master of the earth. 'Will' is not the same as 'Life'. Life is open to chaos and must have a direction and purpose imposed on it. As he wrote in *The Will to Power* (1887-88):

> To stamp the character of Being on the process of becoming – that is the highest will to power.

Or again:

> I assess the power of will by how much resistance, pain and torment it can endure and turn to its advantage.

If human conduct is seen in the light of this single principle of the will to power, immediately its application stands out at every level. In every argument there is a striving for mastery, in the activities of the boss or the preacher or the politician, even in the sex-act: all these are unthinkable without the exercise of power.

The Superman

In the final phase of his work Nietzsche became the prophet of the Superman. This idea has frequently been misunderstood: it has nothing to do with racial superiority. The superman is the one who realizes the predicament human beings are in. He creates his own values and is able to fashion his own life. He triumphs over weakness and hates it in others.

> Who can attain to anything great if he does not feel in himself the force and will to inflict great pain? The ability to suffer is a small matter: in that line, weak women and even slaves often attain masterliness. But not to perish from internal distress and doubt when one inflicts great suffering and hears the cry of it – that is great, that belongs to greatness.

Nietzsche spoke of the common people as the dung that must be spread thick so that a single flower may grow. Only the noble, those in whom the Will to Power is strong, will transcend themselves. The Superman will be the Dionysian of the new type, with real vitality and strong power, self-confident and self-disciplined. This is the very opposite of Marx's view that the 'coming race' is the collective proletariat or ordinary people. Nietzsche is also opposed to Kierkegaard's 'individual before God' who never claims to be more than what anyone else has it in him to become.

Nietzsche's influence on European literature and philosophy has been great. Camus, Sartre, Spengler, Tillich and Buber are all among the philosophers who have been influenced by his thinking.

More than anyone else, Friedrich Nietzsche grasped the implications of what it is to believe that God is dead. In a world without God, humanity is not so much free as overwhelmingly responsible. For Nietzsche to be consistent, he had to become his own Superman. He felt the horror of having to be responsible for everything alive. Perhaps madness was a freedom from this overwhelming responsibility. *Thus Spoke Zarathustra* again:

> Alas, grant me madness... By being above the law I am the most outcast of outcasts.

Humanism in the Modern World

John Stuart Mill

It is not hard to see the common thread running through the following quotations.

President Kennedy said:

All man's problems were created by man, and can be solved by man.

Years before, poet Charles Swinburne wrote much the same:

Glory to Man in the highest! For Man is the master of things.

Sir Julian Huxley is very confident about the future:

Man is the latest dominant type of life on this earth, and the sole agent for its further evolution.

Or hear Shakespeare's Hamlet:

What a piece of work is man! how noble in reason! how infinite in faculties! in form and moving how express and admirable! in action how like an angel! in apprehension how like a god! the beauty of the world! the paragon of animals!

Last and most to the point is Gordon Childe:

Man makes himself.

Modern humanism is secular. It no longer accepts belief in God as a source of authority on how to live life. Humanity must solve its problems by itself.

Humanism believes this is the only life we have so it is important that it is good. It is based on agnosticism and atheism. Humanists regard human reason as the guiding force in life. They are secular, wanting to rid society of religious beliefs which, in their view, prevent human progress. Humanists are materialists, not believing in a spiritual world; and empiricist in their approach to knowledge, holding that knowledge comes through the senses. Unlike Christians, humanists see no particular value in having faith, being humble, obeying God's commandments or practising self-denial. Humanist morality is a code of human conduct, constructed by human beings for human benefit.

In different chapters of this book we have looked at some of the forerunners of modern humanism. Here we trace the progress of humanism as a philosophy.

The progress of humanism

The Golden Age of Greece (fifth century BC) was the time when the use of objective reason released science and philosophy from the stronghold of religion and superstition. Plato was an opponent of the humanist tradition. His philosophy held that human values of beauty, truth and goodness come

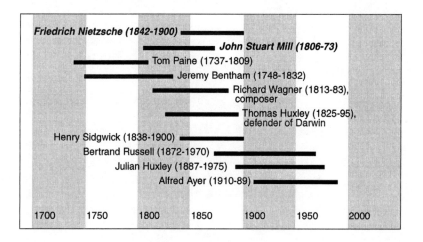

to us from the higher world. A humanist follows in the line of more 'down to earth' philosophers like Protagoras, Epicurus, and Aristotle.

During the Renaissance, from the fourteenth to the sixteenth centuries, the word 'humanist' was first coined. Human excellence was celebrated in an explosion of classical art, thought and literature. Early humanists saw no conflict between this and their Christian faith. Yet this is when the seeds of modern secular humanism are thought to have been sown. The Renaissance opened up what Vasari called 'the spirit of criticism', which gathered force and in the eighteenth century became the Enlightenment.

The Enlightenment, or Age of Reason, was an age when increasing scientific knowledge gave rise to strong criticism of Christian religious beliefs. The word 'empiricist' comes from the Greek word for experience. The empiricists claimed that all knowledge of reality comes from observational experience; they were sceptical about the existence of God. Yet eighteenth-century sceptics did not call themselves 'atheists'. Many of them called themselves 'Deists' meaning that they believed in an unknown (and probably impersonal) supreme being. The most famous English deist was Thomas Paine (1737-1809). Self-educated, he wrote three very important books: *Commonsense*, which contributed to the American War of Independence; *The Rights of Man*, a defence of the French Revolution; and *The Age of Reason*, a vehement criticism of the Bible. Paine said: 'It is the duty of man to obtain all the knowledge he can and make the best use of it.'

The scepticism of the eighteenth century, with no God to obey, made the question of morality a very real issue. Two ancient moral questions were crucial: 'Why be good?' and 'What is Good?' For Christian believers the answer is found in obeying God's commandments and the teachings of Christ. But for secular humanists there is no God. So why should humanists be good? An answer to this question was given by Utilitarians in the nineteenth century.

John Stuart Mill and Utilitarianism

John Stuart Mill was born in London in 1806. Educated at home by his father he was learning Greek, mathematics and history by the age of three. Before the age of eight he had read the whole of Herodotus' *Histories* in the original language.

His father had a vicious temper if John Stuart was slow. The boy had virtually no contact with the outside world except for his family, but he was allowed to meet his father's friends, who included philosophers, politicians and economists. One of these was the London philosopher, Jeremy Bentham.

In 1822 Mill's father considered sending him to Cambridge but decided against it and arranged for his son to work for the East India Company instead. Here he worked on boring clerical tasks but in the evenings met with different groups of thinkers. The most important of these was the Utilitarian Society, which met at Jeremy Bentham's house. Mill developed a philosophy of 'Utilitarianism'.

Mill's most important works are *On Liberty* (1859), a strong defence of the liberty of the individual; *A System of Logic* (1843), an empiricist approach to philosophical problems; *Dissertations and Discussions* (1859-75); *Representative Governments* (1861); and *Utilitarianism* (1863).

Originally Utilitarianism was very simple. Its three main proponents were Jeremy Bentham, Henry Sidgwick and John Stuart Mill who wrote:

The creed which accepts as the foundation of morals, Utility or the Greatest Happiness Principle, holds that actions are right in proportion as they tend to promote happiness, wrong as they tend to produce the reverse of happiness. By happiness is intended pleasure and the absence of pain; by unhappiness, pain, and the privation of pleasure.

On this view:

* Actions are judged by their consequences and the amount of pleasure that everybody obtains from those consequences.

* The aim is the greatest happiness of the greatest number.

In recent years Utilitarian theory has been subdivided into Act Utilitarianism and Rule Utilitarianism.

'Act Utilitarianism' holds that each individual action we take should be assessed on the results it alone produces. For example, if you give money to a charity you must try to estimate how much happiness that donation gives on that occasion.

'Rule Utilitarianism' is not concerned with individual acts but with the usefulness of a rule for action. For example, 'Everyone should give to charity'. The idea here is to do what is best for the greatest number even if on one particular occasion less happiness may result. The 'Act Utilitarian' says, 'What will be the result of my doing that?' The 'Rule Utilitarian' asks, 'What if everyone did that?'

There are three common criticisms of Utilitarianism:

* How can you assess the amounts of happiness likely to result from individual actions or general rules?

* It can be unfair, in that the happiness of the majority may require the sacrifice of an innocent party or an unjust system, such as slavery.

* Is it sufficient to say that morality is decided only by actions and never through intentions or motives?

Nietzsche believed that some people are inherently more important than others. Their happiness counts for more than that of the average person. He described Mill as a 'blockhead':

I abhor the man's vulgarity when he says, 'What is right for one man is right for another'. Such principles would fain establish the whole of human traffic upon mutual services, so that every action would appear to be a cash payment for something done to us. The hypothesis there is ignoble to the last degree; it is taken for granted that there is some sort of equivalence in value between my actions and thine.

Utilitarianism was really a return to the philosophy of Epicurus (341-270BC), who was concerned with the art of living. One of his sayings sums it up: 'Friendship goes dancing round the world proclaiming to us all to awake to the praises of a happy life.' He started from Aristotle's view that good conduct is what promotes human happiness. For Epicurus, the good life was pleasure and absence of pain; friendship and peace of mind. His followers included slaves and women, unheard of in that day. It is common to picture Epicurus as indulging in all sorts of bodily pleasures, but in fact he lived a disciplined life. When he had guests he provided modest food: cakes and water with a little cheese and wine for special occasions. He taught that peace of mind comes through 'moderation in all things'. The opposing ethical force were the Stoics, who believed men should not aim at pleasure but make themselves independent of the pleasures of life.

Humanism in the twentieth century

One of the greatest twentieth-century humanists was Bertrand Russell. As Earl Russell, he made important contributions in mathematics and logic, and was involved in education, liberal politics and international affairs. He was a philosopher, a proponent of 'logical positivism', but he believed that philosophers should have something to say about the society they lived in. So Russell was in at the beginning of the Campaign for Nuclear Disarmament in 1958, and even in his old age was out on the streets demonstrating against nuclear weapons. Thousands of young people followed his lead. At the age of ninety he was jailed for the second time because, like Socrates before him, he was shaking the establishment and 'corrupting the young'. From his early years he was an atheist, as he explained in *What I Believe* (1925).

> I believe that when I die I shall rot, and nothing of my ego will survive. I am not young, and I love life. But I should scorn to shiver with terror at the thought of annihilation. Happiness is none the less true happiness because it must come to an end, nor do thought and love lose their value because they are not everlasting. Many a man has borne himself proudly on the scaffold; surely the same pride should teach us to think truly about man's place in the world.

The British humanist movement was given a boost in 1955 when the BBC broadcast a series of lectures by Margaret Knight, a lecturer in educational psychology. They were entitled *Morals without Religion*, and caused a public outcry. It is hard to imagine such a reaction today. Knight said:

> In a climate of thought that is increasingly unfavourable to (Christian) beliefs, it is a mistake to try to impose them on children, and to make them the basis of moral training.

The mid-1960s saw humanism flourishing. Two outstanding intellectuals, Sir Julian Huxley and Professor Sir Alfred Ayer, were both presidents of the British Humanist Association. A confidence arose that the whole field of human development could be taken up within humanism. Huxley predicted that philosophical problems such as mind versus matter would be solved. He predicted that humanism would heal the split between the two sides in the cold war.

Of religion he said:

> Religion of some sort is probably necessary... Instead of worshipping supernatural rulers, it will sanctify the higher manifestations of human nature in art and love, in intellectual comprehension and aspiring adoration.

An alternative view of humanism is offered by theologian Hans Küng, in *On Being a Christian* (1974).

> Is the solution simply to invoke the human factor? Humanisms too are subject to rapid change. What remains of Renaissance humanism after man's great disillusionment through a series of humiliations? The first came when Copernicus showed that Man's earth was not the centre of the universe; the second when Marx showed how dependent man is on inhuman social conditions; the third when Darwin described man's origin from the subhuman world; and the fourth was Freud's explanation of man's intellectual consciousness as rooted in the instinctive unconscious... That is to say nothing of fascism and Nazism... fascinated by Nietzsche's superman... which cost mankind an unparalleled destruction of human values and millions of human lives. In view of this situation, after so many disappointments, a certain scepticism in regard to humanism is understandable.

PART 9

Who is Jesus?

THE PERSON OF CHRIST

Christology through the Ages

Jesus, the Son of God

It would be unusual to find anyone reading this book who seriously doubted the existence of Socrates or Plato. Why is that? No one today has met either of them – they lived 400 years before the Christian era. Perhaps it is easy to believe in Socrates because Plato wrote about him and his dialogues are still in print today. But why believe in Plato's existence? Because people have written about him, too, and they cannot all be wrong.

The historical existence of Jesus of Nazareth, like that of the Buddha and others, has been disputed. There was a famous dispute in the nineteenth century when Bruno Bauer explained Jesus away as 'an idea'. In 1910, Arthur Drew described Jesus as pure 'Christ myth'. These were both extreme views.

Since that time, no serious scholar has denied the historical existence of Jesus. But there has been a wealth of less serious literature about Jesus as a spaceman, an astral myth, secretly married – you name it. In this chapter we look at Jesus of Nazareth, locating him in history and reviewing how different people have understood him through the ages.

Jesus in history

Jesus of Nazareth belongs to history. He was born at a certain time in a certain place. The New Testament records Jesus being born during the reign of

Roman Emperor Augustus (27BC to AD14) and the Hasmonean rule of King Herod (27-4BC). His birth could not therefore have been later than 4BC.

He died about the year AD30, according to the Roman historian Tacitus as well as the gospels, while Pontius Pilate was governor of Judea, (AD26-36).

Jesus' birth and death are much like many other ancient events; the dates are known approximately but not with total accuracy.

Jesus was a Jew: a member of a small, poverty-stricken group living in an outpost of the Roman Empire. There are no official documents about him. If he was registered in any of the court files of the day, they have not survived. He lived a short life of about thirty-three years, of which his public life and teaching took only about three years (to judge by the three annual Jewish passover festivals recorded in John's gospel). It may have been less, since the synoptic writers, Matthew, Mark and Luke, mention only one passover.

There is no reason to believe Jesus ever travelled abroad, so his work was restricted to his own country. Even then he taught for most of the time in the obscure northern territory of Galilee and in Jerusalem.

Yet this man has influenced history so much that people have even started to date the years of the world from his birth. Throughout history the response to the teachings of Jesus has been enormous. In 1980 for example, according to the closely researched figures of David Barrett's *World Christian Encyclopedia*:

* Estimates range from one in three to one in four human beings being Christian.

* There were over 20,800 Christian denominations in the world's 223 countries.

* Christians were found in some 8,100 different ethno-linguistic peoples.

* Christian literature is now published in over 2,000 languages.

Unlike other people in this book, Jesus did not leave us with a single word written down. So we can't sit down and study his actual writings or philosophies. We depend on certain sources for our knowledge. There are contemporary Roman and Jewish sources, but these do not tell us much except that Jesus existed and that his followers were known. The main sources are the four gospels which were accepted as original testimony of the Christian faith.

The word 'gospel' means 'good news', so these are not biographies of Jesus. They do not provide the whole course of Jesus' life in its different stages and happenings. We know nothing of his early thinking or how his personality or his personal tastes developed. The gospel writers (or 'evangelists') all have some things in common and some differences in their presentation of Jesus. But it is clear that each of them is concerned to proclaim that Jesus of Nazareth is the promised Messiah, the Lord, the Son of God.

The gospels are not objective, scientific histories. They were written by people who believed in Jesus and whose lives had been profoundly affected by his life and teaching. For them Jesus was not just a dead hero but was alive and present with them. So the gospels are not just reports; they are proclamations to stir faith, committed testimonies, described by the Greek term *Kerygma* meaning proclamation, message, announcement. One powerful part of the message was that somehow this man was 'Immanuel', which means 'God with us'.

Christianity is bound to appear differently to different people, depending on what each one understands of Jesus. Who is he? We call the study of the 'person' of Jesus, 'Christology'. And we call the belief that Jesus was God made human, the 'incarnation'.

Christology: a brief sketch

What has the Christian church believed about Jesus through the centuries? Who is he? God? Human? or both?

The first Christians were Jews and so they shared the faith that 'the Lord our God is one Lord'. But by the time of the birth of the Christian church at Pentecost the early apostles had come to refer to Jesus as 'Lord'. The gospels show that gradually, because of Jesus' life and teaching and his resurrection from the dead, his early followers realized he was the Son of God, and the long-expected Messiah whom Jews expected to come and liberate them.

The early church used titles such as Redeemer, Saviour, Lord, Son of God, to describe Jesus. They had a high view of him. Perhaps one of the most exalted statements is in the prologue to John's gospel. Any educated Jew or Greek reading this at the time would have understood the supremacy of the language. This writer is claiming that Jesus is linked with the divine:

> In the beginning was the Word, and the Word was with God, and the Word was God. He was in the beginning with God; all things were made through him, and without him was not anything made that was made. In him was life, and the life was the light of men. The light shines in the darkness, and the darkness has not overcome it... And the Word became flesh and dwelt among us, full of grace and truth; we have beheld his glory, glory as of the only Son from the Father... For the law was given through Moses; grace and truth came through Jesus Christ.

Some of the early Church Fathers, writing in the second century, strongly argued that Jesus was both human and divine. Ignatius of Antioch (died c. 115) was concerned to argue that Jesus was a real man with flesh and blood. This was because the Docetists claimed that Jesus only appeared to be human, but he was really a divine visitor in human disguise – something of a first-century Jewish Superman. Other groups, such as the Ebionites (Jewish Christians), regarded Jesus as simply human but a supreme prophet. Others, like the Adoptionists, thought of Jesus as a very holy man who was 'adopted' to the position of God's Son at his baptism.

It was not until the fourth century that urgent questions arose about the divinity of Jesus Christ. Christians were accused of worshipping two Gods, the Father and Christ. One group, the Monarchians, responded to this accusation by making 'Father', 'Son' and 'Spirit' into different names for a single person. They said God uses different names for his different roles. In the third century, thinkers such as Tertullian and Origen had argued against the Monarchians by stressing that Father, Son (or Word) and Spirit were three 'persons' eternally distinct from each other.

Christology became a burning issue for the church. There were two main issues:

* The oneness of God: What is the relation between God the Father, the Son of God and the Spirit of God? This is known as the doctrine of the Trinity.

* The person of Christ: How can Jesus be thought of as both truly man and truly God yet remain one person? This debate concerns Christology.

These questions brought forth a crop of brilliant thinkers. Remember that what had started on Jewish soil had now spread far abroad in the Greek world. So the church of Jesus employed Greek terms and concepts to try and explain the mystery of the person of Christ.

Justin Martyr (second century) and the Apologists put forward the idea of Christ as the logos (the Word or Mind) of God. On this view Christ was the go-between in God's relationship with the world.

Arius (fourth century) taught that only the Father was true God. This denial of Christ's divinity was opposed by the councils of church leaders, including the famous theologian Athanasius, at Nicea in 325 and Constantinople in 381.

Athanasius was born at the end of the third century. He was bishop of Alexandria for forty-five years, and died in 373. All through his life he struggled against Arianism. Arius was condemned at Nicea, but the creed was not accepted by followers of Origen in the East. The Roman emperor wanted Christian unity and was prepared to be tolerant. Athanasius saw the divinity of Jesus Christ as the foundation of the Christian faith. He saw that only a divine Christ could save the world. This theme permeates his work,

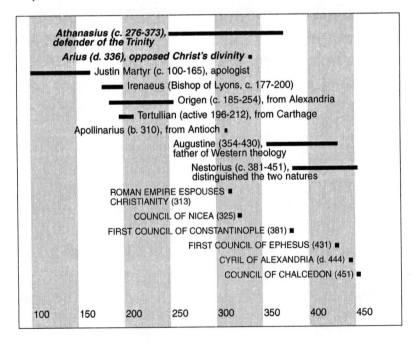

The Incarnation of the Word. Against those who said that the incarnation and crucifixion of God's Son is degrading, he argued that only the one through whom the world was created could restore it:

> We were the cause of his becoming flesh. For our salvation he loved us so much as to appear and be born in a human body... No one else but the Saviour himself, who in the beginning made everything out of nothing, could bring the corrupted to incorruption; no one else but the image of the Father could recreate men in God's image; no one else but our Lord Jesus Christ, who is Life itself, could make the mortal immortal.

The Council of Nicea

The controversy at Nicea was unique and decisive for the Christian faith. It was a bitter debate sparked off by Arius and his followers. The burning question was this: was Jesus fully divine and therefore really of the same kind as God himself? Or was he after all a creature, like the rest of humanity? Arian thought held that the Son must be a creature, and so must have had a beginning. Arius used a famous phrase, 'There was [a time] when He [the Son] was not'. Arian teaching can be found today in the Jehovah's Witnesses. The Church Council at Nicea saw the threat clearly. According to Arianism it was difficult to see in what sense Jesus could be called God or was indeed the Son of God. Arius replied that these were only courtesy titles: Jesus was called God in name only; he did not share in the nature of the Godhead. The theological battle at Nicea was for the status of the Son. Arianism was officially condemned. Every bishop present had to sign the creed drawn up:

> We believe in one God, the Father almighty, maker of all things, visible and invisible. And in one Lord Jesus Christ, the Son of God, begotten from the Father, only-begotten, that is, from the substance of the Father, God from God, light from light, true God from true God, begotten not made, of one substance with the Father, through whom all things came into being...

Apollinarius (later in the fourth century) taught that Jesus was controlled by a divine mind. So his flesh was human but his mind was divine. The church made it clear that Jesus had a human body and a human mind and soul.

In the fourth and fifth centuries two different approaches to the person of Christ developed, focused on two different centres:

IN ANTIOCH the theologians emphasized the importance of Christ's life as a full human being. This means that just like everyone else he had been tempted to sin and selfishness, but uniquely he had not given in. They said that Christ's human nature was distinct from his unity with the Son of God. Jesus had two natures. The problem with this was how to speak of a unity in Christ's person.

IN ALEXANDRIA the divine nature was the most important thing. Here the emphasis was on God coming down to rescue humanity. They held on to the unity of Christ's person but had to imply a fusion or mixture of his two natures into one. Their picture of Jesus tended to lean on the powerful, divine side and his human life was perhaps neglected.

The struggle between these views led to the Council of Chalcedon (AD451). The creed agreed by this council made sure that Jesus Christ was both fully God and fully man. In him two 'natures' were united in one 'person' but remained distinct:

Following the holy fathers, we confess with one voice that the one and only Son, our Lord Jesus Christ, is perfect in Godhead and perfect in manhood, truly God and truly man, that he has a rational soul and a body. He is of one substance with the Father as God, he is also of one substance with us as man. He is like us in all things except sin. He was begotten of his Father before the ages as God, but in these last days and for our salvation he was born of Mary the virgin, the 'God-bearer', as man. This one and the same Christ, Son, Lord, Only-begotten is made known in two natures, without confusion, without change, without division, without separation. The distinction of the natures is no way taken away by their union, but rather the distinctive properties of each nature are preserved... They are not separated or divided into two persons but they form one and the same Son, Lord Jesus Christ.

What was it about Jesus that caused people through the ages and even today to think that God was somehow on earth in the person of Jesus Christ?

In the next chapter we look at Jesus of Nazareth, and his teaching on the kingdom of God.

The Kingdom of God
Jesus of Nazareth

Jesus of Nazareth: What cause does he represent? What is central to his teaching? What did he think was the meaning of life? What laws or principles did he follow? What did he think of this world and reality?

When we study the person of Christ, in the way we did in the second half of the previous chapter, we find a problem. Much of our modern understanding of Jesus is based on dualistic Greek thought. But Christ was not born in Greece, nor was he Greek. He was Jewish.

For many scholars the pronouncements about Jesus at Nicea and Chalcedon, and the division of his nature into God and man are basically Greek. These ideas are not found in the New Testament message about Jesus.

In this chapter we are going to start out, not with a concept of Trinity, or of Son of God, but with the human Jesus of Nazareth. What was the message he gave to those first disciples as he sat on the shores and hills of Galilee? What is central to his teaching?

Modern theological scholarship is unanimous in the opinion that the central message of Jesus was the 'kingdom of God'. Mark, in his gospel, introduces the mission of Jesus in these words:

> Now after John [the Baptist] was arrested, Jesus came into Galilee, preaching the gospel of God, and saying, 'The time has come; the kingdom of God is near. Turn away from your sin and believe the good news.'

Matthew reviews the ministry of Jesus: 'He went about all Galilee, teaching in their synagogues and preaching the gospel of the kingdom.'

The kingdom, present and future

What does the term 'kingdom of God' mean? Various interpretations have prevailed. From the time of Augustine to the Reformation, the kingdom was in different ways identified with the church. Many Christian denominations do not hold this view today.

Some scholars have seen the kingdom of God in terms of personal religious experience: the rule of God in the individual soul. Others have thought Jesus saw the kingdom as being like the Jewish apocalypse – wholly in the future, 'eschatological' (relating to the end-time of world history).

'Apocalyptic' literally means 'the unveiling of what is covered or hidden'. This was a form of literature concerning the last days and the end of the world. It usually dealt in dreams, allegories and elaborate symbolism. In the Old Testament (the Jewish Bible) the second part of Daniel and of Zechariah are examples; in the New Testament, Revelation.

In Great Britain, C.H. Dodd has argued for what he calls 'realized eschatology'. On this view the kingdom of God is the transcendent order beyond time and space that has broken into history in the mission of Jesus. (This view is more Platonic than Jewish.)

In the Jewish scriptures the term 'kingdom of God' does not appear. But throughout the writings of the law and the prophets God is spoken of as king, both of Israel and of all the earth. God is king now, but other writings tell of a day when he will become king – that is, God will show his kingship in the world. The future kingdom is seen differently by different prophets. There are two main strands of thought in Judaism and the Old Testament:

THE KINGDOM WILL APPEAR AS A HISTORIC EVENT, and be ruled by a descendant of the great King David. He will be a Messiah, or deliverer. ('Christ' is Greek for 'Messiah'.) The kingdom will be on earth (see especially the opening of Isaiah chapter 9 for this). After the Jews were conquered and exiled by the Babylonians they lost hope in this view and in its place came the second view:

THE KINGDOM WILL BE WHEN GOD BREAKS INTO HISTORY in the person of a heavenly Son of Man, with a transcendental kingdom 'beyond history'.

In the light of oppression and exile Jewish 'apocalytic' writers tended to despair of history. Israel could only expect suffering in this age until God would act for his people by establishing his kingdom in the age to come.

Another group in Judaism concerned with establishing the kingdom of God were the Zealots. In the early part of the first century, revolt broke out in Israel against the occupying forces of Rome. The Zealots were radical Jews who did not plan to wait for God to act in bringing his kingdom, but who wanted to hasten it with force.

It is important, in interpreting Jesus' message about the kingdom of God, to remember this background. In his teaching, the kingdom of God could be seen as both present – God is king: he is ruling now – and future, the appearing of God's kingdom which would bring to an end this age and bring in the age to come.

When Jesus began his teaching, he would have had in mind the sort of beliefs we have mentioned so far. His teaching on the kingdom of God reflected both the eschatological kingdom to come and the present reality of the kingdom through his own ministry. These are some of its features:

* The coming of God's kingdom will mean the total destruction of evil – the devil and his angels.

* It will mean the forming of a new society without evil.

Jesus' teaching on the kingdom of God was different from mainstream Jewish thought. In Judaism the kingdom was seen in terms of the nation of Israel: non-Jews might be helped and converted, but the kingdom itself belonged to Israel. Jesus made every individual's response to himself and his message the determining factor for entering the kingdom; it was for the non-Jews, too.

The kingdom in prophecy

Also, Jesus saw his own work as fulfilling prophecies about the Messiah found in the Hebrew prophets. This is clear in Luke's gospel, chapter 4, where in the synagogue at Nazareth he reads a prophecy of Isaiah about the coming one sent by God to proclaim the year of the Lord. Jesus then added to the reading: 'Today this scripture has been fulfilled in your hearing.'

He opened the book and found the place where it was written, 'The Spirit of the Lord is upon me, because he has anointed me to preach good news to the poor. He has sent me to proclaim release to the captives and recovery of sight to the blind, to set at liberty those who are oppressed, to proclaim the acceptable year of the Lord.'

Elsewhere Jesus spoke of the present reality of the kingdom through what he himself was doing. This is found in the twelfth chapter of Matthew:

But if it is by the Spirit of God that I cast out demons, then the kingdom of God has come upon you.

Casting out demons was one of the signs that the kingdom of God had come.

In Judaism at that time, the 'kingdom of God' meant God's rule or sovereignty. For Jesus, the kingdom was not a place. It was within people and could be found among them. This from Luke:

Being asked by the Pharisees when the kingdom of God was coming, he answered them: 'The kingdom of God is not coming with signs to be observed; nor will they say, "Lo, here it is!" or "There!" for behold, the kingdom of God is in the midst of you.'

To summarize, the 'kingdom' has several stages:

 * It is the reign or rule of God.

 * It is the future act of God, when he will destroy his enemies and save his people.

 * It is the coming time of salvation when God's people will be gathered together to enjoy the blessings God has promised them.

In his teaching Jesus was not offering people new rules or principles to live by. In this sense he was not a philosopher. He did not defend any ethics based on natural law, as did the scholastics, neither did he propose any formal ethics based on duty, as did Kant in the Enlightenment. Jesus was not offering new rules to live by, he was offering new lives. And these new lives were to be lived in the kingdom of God.

Jesus' teaching on the kingdom of God is to be found in all four gospels. In John's gospel, it can be entered by new spiritual birth:

Jesus answered Nicodemus, 'Truly, truly, I say to you, unless one is born of water and the Spirit, he cannot enter the kingdom of God. That which is born of the flesh is flesh, and that which is born of the Spirit is spirit.'

In the kingdom, as the Lord's prayer tells us, God's name is sacred and his will is done on earth. Needs will be met, sin will be forgiven and guilt and evil overcome.

In the kingdom, according to Jesus' promises in the Beatitudes, the hungry are satisfied, those who weep are comforted, the weakest come into their inheritance and the poor enter the kingdom of God.

The kingdom is not to be narrowly defined, but is best seen in parables: it is like a ripe harvest, like a great banquet or celebration, like a seed growing secretly.

There are two great chapters in Matthew's gospel where powerful parables are collected round the theme of the kingdom. In chapter 13, we learn how the kingdom grows and is found: the parable of the sower, the wheat and the weeds, mustard seed, yeast, treasure, fish in a net... In chapter 25, the subject is judgment at the end of the age: the bridesmaids, the talents, the sheep and the goats. The kingdom of God is explained more by parables than by any other form of teaching.

The kingdom is to be received by those who are child-like. To receive it one must be as receptive as a child, who lacks self-consciousness and embarrassment and is content to accept what is given. To be willing to receive the kingdom is to enter it.

How will the kingdom come?

It is clear from the gospels that Jesus did not think the kingdom of God would come about through social change. Neither does the idea of the kingdom of God rest on a metaphysical view of God as being above or outside the world. God is not a timeless eternal reality as understood by certain forms of Greek philosophy. The kingdom is God's action in God's world now, and in Jesus' teaching God's kingdom is also a future reality, the hope for the future.

Jesus drew attention to the divine dimension of life: wherever a man or woman goes, in life or in death, God is there. On this view existing things in the world cannot define reality. They are unstable and changing. Humanity is therefore living in a critical situation without God. We are 'lost'. Since the reality of God is in the future, we need to commit ourselves to that reality.

The kingdom of God is a personal issue for each individual. And to live by its light requires a shift to the life of faith. If an individual has even the smallest amount of faith, even like a mustard seed, it will have powerful effect in their life. Jesus himself described the kingdom as a small seed growing in the earth:

> With what can we compare the kingdom of God, or what parable shall we use for it? It is like a grain of mustard seed, which, when sown upon the ground, is the smallest of all the seeds on earth; yet when it is sown it grows up and becomes the greatest of all shrubs, and puts forth large branches, so that the birds of the air can make nests in its shade.

Jesus existed for the whole person – not only for his intellectual life but also for physical, material well-being. The greatest miracle for the Christian church was Jesus' resurrection from the dead which represented the ultimate victory of the kingdom over death, disease and evil.

Revelation and Response

Some People of Faith

Have you ever had to change your way of thinking? To face up to some new truth? If you have ever had a sudden inspiration, what did you do? How did you respond?

Change does not come about only in our ideas or the way we think. For some people, change takes place in themselves and the way they view reality.

Blaise Pascal was a man whose life was a response to what had been revealed to him:

> God of Abraham, God of Isaac, God of Jacob, not of the philosophers and scholars. Certitude, certitude, feeling, joy, peace. God of Jesus Christ.

Blaise Pascal (1623-62) was one of the leading scientists of his day. Born at Clermont-Ferrand in France, he was educated by his father and proved brilliant in mathematics. Among his achievements was a theory for the barometer. He pioneered the theory of probability, and produced the first calculator. Through a religious group called the Jansenists, Pascal and his family were converted to a serious religious commitment.

The Jansenists were a religious movement inspired by Cornelius Jansen who was the Roman Catholic Bishop of Ypres. He was concerned about moral impurity in the church, and that the church was moving away from Augustine's teaching on grace (see Chapter 3). During Pascal's lifetime there was a bitter struggle between the Jansenists and the Jesuits. Pascal defended the Jansenists with a series of anonymous letters called *Provincial Letters*. These were superbly satirical against the Jesuits. Pascal presented the author as a puzzled local writing about events in Paris to a friend in the country. In them he attacks the low moral standards allowed by the Jesuit priesthood.

The mind and the heart

Pascal's greatest works come in his *Thoughts* or *Pensées*, issued in 1670, which were often written on odd scraps of paper. They were meant to be read by sceptics and rationalists.

One of his most famous 'thoughts' is called the wager. All of us have to stake our destiny on some world outlook. Pascal asks the questions: Is there a God or not? Is there such a thing as eternal life? He then says that reason cannot decide the issue, but even so people have to decide how to live. So we have to bet one way or the other. What are the odds? We wager with our short lives. We might win, in which case we gain eternal happiness. Or, if it turns out to be false and death after all is annihilation, what has been lost? All we really lose is a life of sin but we still gain a good character. He concludes that sane and prudent people must bet their lives on the claims of Christianity.

There are, of course, holes in Pascal's argument. He assumed there are only two alternative bets: become a Christian or not. As human beings are ignorant of the real facts, according to Pascal, there must be an infinite number of alternative choices in the variety of religious responses and experiences.

Pascal is interesting as a thinker, because as a scientist he allowed a very limited role for philosophy and reason when it came to matters of reality:

> Reason's last step is the recognition that there are an infinite number of things which are beyond it. It is merely feeble if it does not go as far as to realize that.

As a scientist Pascal concentrated on an objective, experimental approach over against the philosophical deductions of his predecessors. He stressed the importance of experience in faith, and his own faith sprang from his own personal discovery of God: 'The heart has its reasons which reason knows nothing of.'

Pascal did not encourage people to try and understand God rationally. He believed God is best understood as revealed in Jesus Christ.

When natural reason is relied on as the sole means of understanding, it makes humankind autonomous or independent. The individual becomes self-governing, and free to do what he or she wants with God. This view is very popular in the modern Western world; many of you reading this book may agree. But it is by no means the only view.

What if human wills are not 'free'? What if they are not capable of understanding God, or self, or reality? What if they are not autonomous?

A mind centred on God

Karl Barth (1886-1968), a twentieth-century theologian, transformed the human autonomy of the Enlightenment by saying that Jesus Christ is the only man with true autonomy. He is uniquely autonomous because he alone did not give in to human evil and the self-rule of sin. To show people their sinfulness by preaching the law (the Ten Commandments) to them, for example, is not enough. For Barth, the doctrine of sin cannot be understood except through Jesus Christ. Those who do not know Jesus have no true knowledge of sin. It is sin that isolates humanity from God. And it is God's grace, his love and forgiveness, and his humanity shown in Jesus Christ, which can overcome that isolation:

> In Jesus Christ there is no isolation of people from God or of God from people.

Barth put forward a God-centred view of reality in place of a human-centred view. His whole theology can be seen as an ongoing response to Feuerbach: it is an attempt to show that God is not made in mankind's image, as a psychological projection. To understand God, we must start with God, not mankind, and with that revelation in Jesus Christ as revealed in the Bible, the Word of God. This Word confronts us, overtakes us: it is the event of God speaking to us through Jesus Christ. This is God's revelation.

The scientist Pascal and the theologian Barth both found revelation and personal response crucial to a true understanding of the purpose and mission of Jesus of Nazareth. For neither of them was Jesus simply an important historical figure: he was God acting in their lives and radically changing them.

Some remarkable 'conversion stories' have been recorded. Take Saul, for example, later called Paul:

> It was on the road at midday that I saw a light much brighter than the sun, coming from the sky and shining round me and the men travelling with me. All of us fell to the ground, and I heard a voice say to me in Hebrew, 'Saul, Saul! Why are you persecuting me?'

This happened around AD35. Or John Wesley, founder of Methodism, in 1738.

> About a quarter before nine, while a speaker was describing the change which God works in the heart through faith in Christ, I felt my heart strangely warmed. I felt I did trust in Christ, Christ alone, for my salvation...

Anthony Bloom, head of the Russian Orthodox Church in Britain, wrote of an experience in 1930:

> While I was reading the beginning of Mark's gospel, before I reached the third chapter, I suddenly became aware that on the other side of my desk there was a presence. And the certainty was so strong that it was Christ standing there that it has never left me.

Noel Fellowes, wrongly imprisoned for manslaughter in 1978, wrote of the following experience:

> I found myself suddenly gripped in muscular spasm. I couldn't move. Fear gripped me. I could see, I could hear, but every muscle in my body was totally locked. Then what can only be described as heat fell upon me. After what seemed an eternity, but which was probably only a minute or so, I felt the hurt I had carried for so many years coming up out of the pit of my stomach, and I broke down... I knew with absolute certainty that I had met the living God.

Other Christians, such as C.S. Lewis, follow the argument for God's existence but are persuaded by revelation that the case for God is overwhelmingly strong.

Surprised by joy

C.S. Lewis (1898-1963) was a scholar, and a don at the universities of Oxford and Cambridge. He also wrote science fiction and children's books. He is famous for popular fiction, especially *Out of the Silent Planet* and the *Chronicles of Narnia*. C.S. Lewis came to the Christian faith reluctantly. In the end he discovered that there is no escape from the logic of Jesus' claims.

When Lewis was a boy his mother died. When she was dying he prayed that she would live, but she still died. So he abandoned any religious faith. He could not believe in a God who did not answer prayer. His schooldays were miserable. At boarding school he met with brutality and even at his second school, Malvern College, he was depressed and unhappy. When the First World War was over he went to Oxford University and eventually on to a fellowship at Magdalen College.

In his early Oxford days he struggled with his own inner questions of whether the Christian faith was true or not. In his book *Surprised by Joy* he described his situation as one who was trying desperately to prevent himself from becoming convinced that God exists. Yet the more he thought about it, the clearer it became to him that it was true. Years later, he was asked how he had come to the point of accepting God's existence and his claims on his life. Lewis cited two events in reply.

The first was a day in 1931 when he and his brother had visited Whipsnade Zoo.

> When we set out I did not believe that Jesus Christ is the Son of God. When we reached the zoo I did. Yet I had not exactly spent the journey in thought. Nor in great emotion. 'Emotional' is perhaps the last word we can apply to some of the most important events in our lives. It was more like when a man, after a long sleep, still lying motionless in bed, becomes aware that he is awake.

Another description of his conversion experience came in a letter to a friend:

> You must picture me alone in that room in Magdalen, night after night, feeling, whenever my mind lifted even for a second from my work, the steady, unrelenting approach of him whom I most earnestly desired not to meet. That which I so greatly feared had at last come upon me. In the Trinity Term of 1929 I gave in, and admitted that

God was God, knelt, and prayed; perhaps, that night, the most dejected and reluctant convert in all England.

C.S. Lewis went on to be a spiritual guide for many ordinary people. He broadcast live on radio every Wednesday evening during the Second World War from 1941 onwards. He has been called an apostle to the sceptics. He maintained that there were many people who wanted to believe in God and in Jesus Christ, but find it too difficult in the modern world because such belief seems no longer to make sense. He spent his gifts, his talents and his extraordinary mind trying to make the message available to a wide audience of people.

Lewis strongly attacked the view, still popular, that Jesus was a great moral teacher but not God.

I am trying to prevent anyone saying the really foolish thing that people often say about Jesus: 'I am ready to accept Jesus as a great moral teacher, but I do not accept his claim to be God.' This is the one thing we must not say. A man who was merely a man and said the sort of things Jesus said would not be a great moral teacher. He would either be a lunatic – on the level with the man who says he is a poached egg – or else he would be the devil of hell. You must make your choice. Either this man was, and is, the son of God; or else a madman, or something worse. You can shut him up for a fool, you can spit at him and kill him as a demon; you can fall at his feet and call him Lord and God. But let us not come with any patronizing nonsense about his being a great human teacher. He has not left that open to us. He did not intend to.

The cost of discipleship

For all sorts of different reasons and through all sorts of different revelations people respond to God in Jesus Christ and to his claim on their lives. Sometimes that response costs them heavily, even at the price of their lives. Dietrich Bonhoeffer was one such, now thought of as a 'secular' Christian.

Dietrich Bonhoeffer (1906-45) was born in Breslau, then in Germany but now in Poland. He studied theology at Tübingen and Berlin, and then became a Lutheran pastor. In 1931 he took a lectureship at Berlin

University. This coincided with Adolf Hitler's rise to power. Two days after Hitler became Chancellor, Bonhoeffer opposed the Nazi leadership on the radio, but was cut off before the end of the broadcast. Increasing restrictions were placed on him as the war progressed. In 1939 he joined the resistance movement and later the German Counter-Intelligence. In 1941 he was forbidden to publish. He was involved in a plot to assassinate Hitler and in April 1943, just after getting engaged to be married, he was arrested by the Gestapo. In September 1944 they had all the evidence they needed to accuse him. On 9 April 1945 he was hanged, along with Admiral Canaris and others who had plotted against Hitler. His last words were: 'This is the end; for me the beginning of life.'

While he was in prison, Bonhoeffer wrote to friends, and his *Letters and Papers from Prison* have become famous. They can be seen as a radical departure from the rest of his teaching though their meaning is a mystery that died with Bonhoeffer. In them Bonhoeffer proposed a 'religionless Christianity'. He argued that modern people have the same problem believing in God as he himself had believing in miracles. The old-fashioned rituals of the church do not speak to modern people. Therefore they must be done away with. This is partly what Bonhoeffer meant when he said Christianity should be 'religionless'. The challenge for the Christian is to be able to speak about God in a secular way. Bonhoeffer was brought up in a secular family and was aware of the secular world.

But Bonhoeffer saw that, from the time of the Renaissance and the rise of humanism, humanity had moved progressively towards independence from God. All areas of life – ethics, education, politics, science and art – had been freed from church influence. He was radical because he did not see this evolution from God's authority as negative but as right and good.

> God would have us know that we must live as men who manage our
> lives without him... before God and with God we live without God.
> God lets himself be pushed out of the world onto the cross.

Bonhoeffer asked hard questions about how the church can speak to a non-religious, secular society. Who is Christ really for us today? Should Christians use human weakness and crisis to bring people back to faith?

He is strong to criticize such behaviour. And he sees the 'religious' sort of Christianity as making a church of people preoccupied with themselves and their own salvation, seeing the rest of the world as a source of potential recruits to be rescued and brought into the religious circle.

Bonhoeffer worked at bringing God and the church right back into the secular twentieth-century world. He believed God was at the centre of life, not just at the edge. It is difficult to know how he would have continued his thinking. But his letters fight for the right of the secular, non-religious person to hear about Jesus Christ in their own language and in their own world:

> God is the beyond in the midst of our life. This is why the Christian must learn to live his Christianity and speak of God in a secular way. The church is not to be preoccupied with its own religious concerns, but to serve the world. It is to follow the pattern of Jesus, 'the man for others'.

What Place Has the Bible?

THE QUESTION OF INTERPRETATION

The Struggle for Understanding

The Early Christians

The Bible comes from the Greek word *biblos* which means simply 'book'. For Christians the Bible is not merely a book, but the book of books. Christians have lived by, and died for, the Bible through the centuries. The Bible is a book which has changed the world. Christians believe:

ALL THE BIBLE IS INSPIRED: God inspired the writers of the Bible to record timeless truths for each generation. These truths enable people to believe in God through faith.

SOME CHRISTIANS BELIEVE THE BIBLE IS SO INSPIRED THAT IT CONTAINS NO MISTAKES, that it is 'infallible'. Their claim is not that the entire Bible is literally true (though some believe this), but rather that the Bible is infallible in matters of faith and moral behaviour.

OTHER CHRISTIANS BELIEVE THE BIBLE HAS GROWN OUT OF HUMANKIND'S STRUGGLE TO UNDERSTAND GOD. As a result, these Christians are happy to reinterpret its message for each new generation. These Christians believe the Bible writings are shaped by the times in which they were written. Nowadays, therefore, its writings have to be translated afresh. Certain rules and attitudes which were appropriate in Bible times are not appropriate today.

The Bible is not one book, but sixty-six, a library of books. These include law, history, poetry, letters and prophecy; they were written over the space of a thousand years.

Decisions had to be made about which books went into the Bible and which books did not. There is, therefore:

* The Old Testament canon, the books of the Jewish Bible.

* The New Testament canon, the books written to explain Jesus Christ.

One of the tasks facing the early Christians was how to put the New Testament together. The church was not organized then as it is now. Within the Roman Empire the Christians were a persecuted minority. Members came from all social classes and were bound together by their faith in Jesus. They met to share a sacred meal, to sing psalms, listen to readings and pray together. Organization came quickly and every town or area soon had its own 'bishop', whose job was to be a pastor and guardian of the true faith. He was known as 'Father'. By the fourth century the title of 'Church Father' was applied to all the early Christian writers who were responsible for forming standard Christian belief.

Early Christians and the Bible

The early Christians used the Septuagint, the Old Testament translated into Greek. They also used the gospels, Paul's letters, other writings and an oral tradition about Jesus passed on from person to person and church to church.

Irenaeus, who became Bishop of Lyons in 177, was the first writer to mention a 'New Testament' alongside the Old Testament. He claimed that there were four gospels just as naturally as there were four winds. He wrote about the 'Rule of Faith' – an early 'creed' (or statement of faith) which set out true Christian belief. He asserted that this 'Rule of Faith' had apostolic authority.

The 'apostles' were the twelve leading disciples of Jesus (including Judas' substitute); later, Paul was added. Apostolic authority became a very important notion for the early church. Many believers had formed their own interpretations of Christianity, and there were many different books passing from hand to hand. Christianity had to remain true to its nature in the face of:

* Pagan syncretism, which believed all religions are the same.

* Magic.

* Astrology.

* Mystery cults which met secretly and had special, esoteric rites.

One of the early Church's greatest battles was against Gnosticism, with its controversial views about Jesus. Gnosticism was especially powerful between AD80 and 150. Gnosis is the Greek word for 'knowledge'. The Gnostics believed that they possessed special, secret knowledge. Their beliefs were a mixture of Christianity, Judaism, Platonism and later Zoroastrianism. Gnostics believed that the spirit is everything and the body is nothing. They rejected the Christian idea of the resurrection of the body in favour of the immortality of the soul. Their beliefs led them to deny the body by going without food or not marrying. Or sometimes their beliefs led them to deny that the body is important, so they could do as they liked. Gnostics rejected the Old Testament. They believed that the world was in the grip of evil, spiritual powers. After death the soul had a dangerous journey past these powers to heaven. Gnostics had to learn magic passwords and wear charms to force these evil, cosmic powers aside. They also believed that Jesus' disciples had learned a hidden teaching from him which had been passed on to only a few. For a time Gnosticism was a powerful challenge to Christianity, but Christianity gradually overcame it.

Two important questions which faced the early church were: How do we know what is true? And where is the source for believing what is true about Christianity?

Their answer was based on apostolic authority. If a book were written by an apostle, or by someone associated with the apostles, then it was to be believed. And if a belief had been handed down by the apostles, then it was true.

On this basis, the four gospels of Matthew, Mark, Luke and John were immediately admitted. Writings such as *The Shepherd of Hermas*, the first epistle of Clement to the Corinthians and the *Didache* (or 'Teaching of the Apostles') were excluded. They had been written too late, in the eyes of the early church, to be apostolic. Other 'gospels' such as *The Gospel of Philip* and *The Gospel of Peter*, were excluded for the same reasons. It is also fair to say that there is a vast difference in quality between these later writings and the gospels and other writings which did find their way into the New Testament.

The books from Hebrews to Revelation were disputed for some time, but eventually they were admitted.

What is astonishing is that the early church agreed so quickly on what should go into the canon and what should be left out.

Philosophy and the Bible

At first the Christian church spoke Greek, the language of the New Testament. The earliest of the Church Fathers to write in Latin was Tertullian (c. 160-220), a lawyer who tried to translate Christian theology into exact legal terms. The Christian church gradually divided into a Greek-speaking East and a Latin-speaking West. In the early centuries of the church, the three great Christian capitals were Rome, Alexandria and Constantinople. Rome and Constantinople remain important. (Constantinople is now Istanbul in modern Turkey.)

Rome became the capital of the Western, later 'Roman Catholic', Church; Constantinople became the capital of the Eastern 'Orthodox' Church. Certain philosophical differences lay behind the two churches:

> THE ROMAN CHURCH was influenced by Platonism. It believed in a great divide between God and his creation. The created order is made of matter and not divine.

> THE EASTERN CHURCH was influenced by neo-Platonism. It believed that the creation flows out of God. As a result, there is no great division between God and his creation. There is in a sense, divinity in all things. All things ultimately come from God and are not just created out of nothing by God. People are either on the road to God or from God. There is not the same need for conversion or salvation as the Roman Church believed, because there is no split between God and his creation.

In the East Christians believed (and still believe) that the Spirit 'proceeds' or 'has his being' from the Father through the Son. In the West, the belief grew that the Spirit proceeds from both the Father and the Son equally. In the West, therefore, the custom was to add the words 'and the Son' to the creed. Rome was cautious, but added these words officially in the eleventh century. This helped to ensure the final division between Rome and Constantinople in 1054.

Origen, father of Eastern Christianity

The great mind which inspired the theology of the Eastern church was Origen (c. 184-254). Origen was born in Alexandria of Christian parents. His father was killed for his faith. Origen became head of a Christian school which instructed believers. He quarrelled with the local bishop and moved to Palestine. In the Decian persecution (249-51) Origen was imprisoned and tortured. He died several years later as a result of his injuries.

A master of philosophy, Origen was called on to give his opinion on many difficult questions. For him the only written source of revelation was the Bible (not the Greek philosophers), and he devoted many hours a day to reading it. He wrote a great deal, worked to exhaustion and often went without sleep or food. Origen's theology was unusual and drew heavily on neo-Platonism. There was a movement against him in the fourth century and he was condemned as a heretic in the sixth century. Origen wanted to be orthodox and loyal to the church. He wrote:

WORKS ON THE BIBLE including an edition of the Old Testament with the text in Hebrew and Greek. He accepted the apostolic tradition, though sometimes he speculated beyond it. He also wrote commentaries, instructive works, and notes. Origen used allegory to look for a hidden spiritual meaning behind the history of the Old Testament. This was a method of reading the Old Testament which Christians later came to reject.

'FIRST PRINCIPLES', the first attempt to produce a systematic theology, or entire scheme of Christian belief. This work was divided into four books dealing with God, the world, freedom and the Bible.

'AGAINST CELSUS', Origen's answer to a pagan philosopher's writing against the Christians.

PRACTICAL BOOKS, dealing with the Christian life, such as *Prayer* and *Exhortation to Martyrdom*.

Origen believed that being saved means becoming like God. The Christian does this by fixing the mind on God. The human soul has to rise from the everyday world to the eternal world through Jesus, the Word of God. The Christian has to realize that Jesus was not just earthly and human, but the eternal Word of God. These ideas are more Greek or Gnostic than Christian.

He taught that the Persons of the Trinity are at different levels, the Father greater than the Son, and the Son greater than the Spirit. The Father alone is the 'true God'. The Son is God, but at a lower level.

Origen believed that God first created a world of spiritual beings. These beings worshipped God until they had become exhausted, then they fell. Depending on how far they fell they turned into angels, demons or humans. The humans lived in a material world specially created for them by God. They had forgotten their true nature and where they had come from. One being did not turn away from God – Jesus. Human beings are, in some way, divine and on their way back to God.

Origen's theology is demanding, but for all its unorthodoxies its main thrust has influenced the whole outlook of the Eastern church.

To sum up these first Christian centuries, Christians struggled with many different ways of reading the Bible and with many ways of understanding the person of Jesus. Eventually, the Church Fathers set out a biblical canon and beliefs which they declared to be orthodox. Even so, Origen in the East, differed in his understanding and interpretation from Athanasius and, later, Augustine in the West. However, what was decided as true then is still held to be true today by the Christian church. What the Church Fathers thought still influences what Christians believe. The Church Fathers' work still presents a challenge to theologians and Christian believers in the modern struggle for understanding.

The Reformation
Martin Luther and John Calvin

At the beginning of the sixteenth century a cry went up across Europe. This cry was for 'reform in head and members' of the Roman Catholic Church. The dispute was not about the truth of Roman Catholic teaching but about the way the church behaved. The result was a cauldron of change and reform, now called 'the Reformation'.

Church officials held powerful offices of state. Many were no more than rich politicians. Those supposed to promote the kingdom of God appeared to identify too closely with this world. The church demanded taxes and sold spiritual goods for money – pardons, masses, candles, ceremonies, bishoprics, even the Papacy itself. The Pope was the head of the Roman Catholic Church, but acted like a worldly prince. Many called the church corrupt. In 1502 the humanist thinker Erasmus said that an ordinary person would be insulted if he were called a clergyman, priest or monk.

The states of Europe wanted to limit the authority of the Pope; many complained that he had become a prince of state, not a spiritual leader. The reform demanded was administrative, legal and moral.

Between 1500 and 1517 the three popes were Alexander VI (Borgia), Julius II (whom Machiavelli so admired), and Leo X. Julius II rose at the head of a papal army. He saved the Papal States from collapse and laid the foundations of St Peter's Cathedral in Rome, as well as employing Michelangelo to paint the Sistine Chapel at the Vatican. Yet if the call had gone up for spiritual reformation, what had resulted was tyranny. Other mighty forces were at work and Europe was changing:

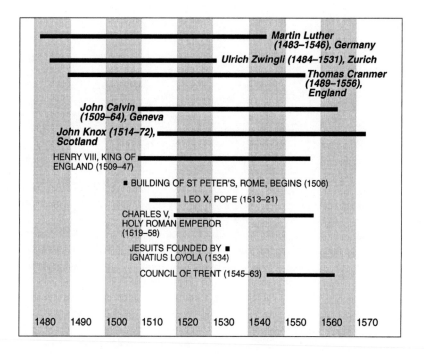

Martin Luther (1483–1546), Germany

Ulrich Zwingli (1484–1531), Zurich

Thomas Cranmer (1489–1556), England

John Calvin (1509–64), Geneva

John Knox (1514–72), Scotland

HENRY VIII, KING OF ENGLAND (1509–47)

BUILDING OF ST PETER'S, ROME, BEGINS (1506)

LEO X, POPE (1513–21)

CHARLES V, HOLY ROMAN EMPEROR (1519–58)

JESUITS FOUNDED BY IGNATIUS LOYOLA (1534)

COUNCIL OF TRENT (1545–63)

1480 1490 1500 1510 1520 1530 1540 1550 1560 1570

KINGS WERE INCREASING THEIR CONTROL OF THEIR KINGDOMS. In England, for example, Henry VII and Henry VIII were much more powerful than previous kings. Along with the emergence of these rulers came the idea of a nation: one people with one ruler. Monarchs began to resent paying money to Rome and having foreign powers interfering in their affairs.

EDUCATION WAS IMPROVING. Humanism had resulted in a return to classical studies. Education and the universities had improved. People were now more aware of what was wrong with the church and what needed to be changed. People began to use the freedom to think for themselves. Individualism, not blind obedience, was part of the new climate of the times.

Another vital factor in the Reformation was printing. For the first time books and pamphlets could be turned out at speed and distributed. Printing spread the Reformation message across Europe in a manner unthinkable only a generation before.

Reforming a corrupt church

The Reformation began with a spark which soon fanned into a flame. Pope Leo X was continually facing bankruptcy. By 1513 he owed at least 125,000 ducats, and he also needed to raise money quickly to pay for St Peter's. One method of raising funds was to sell indulgences. The Roman Catholic Church taught that souls went to a place called Purgatory after death. In that place souls were made fit (purged) for heaven. By buying an indulgence, ordinary people believed that they would spend a shorter time in purgatory, and also that the soul of someone already dead could be freed from purgatory and go straight to heaven. According to Tetzel 'As soon as the coin in the coffer rings, the soul from purgatory springs.'

The young Archbishop Albert of Mainz employed a Dominican monk called Tetzel to sell indulgences. Martin Luther, Professor of Holy Scripture at the University of Wittenberg, was unhappy with the practice of indulgences. He thought that when ordinary people bought them they saw no further need to change their behaviour. Luther was shown a copy of the Archbishop's instructions to Tetzel and was appalled. On 31 October 1517 he attached a placard to the door of the castle church at Wittenberg, which was inscribed with 'Ninety-five Theses upon Indulgences'. Even Luther himself did not realize that at that moment the Reformation had begun.

Set free by faith

Martin Luther (1483-1546) was born at Eisleben, Germany. He was training to be a lawyer when a brush with death turned him towards the monastery. Luther joined the Augustinian friars at Erfurt and studied theology. In due course he became a professor at Wittenberg. A stubborn man and a hard, persevering worker, Luther suffered from the belief that God was a judge condemning him. He believed that God loved everyone except him; he could never be saved. Luther was earnest; he prayed endlessly and went without food. He had a particular problem with Paul's letter to the Romans, chapter one, verse seventeen:

> For in the gospel a righteousness from God is revealed, a righteousness that is by faith from first to last, just as it is written: 'The righteous will live by faith.'

Luther wrote of that psychologically troubled time:

> I tried as hard as I could to keep the Rule. I used to be contrite, and
> make a list of my sins. I confessed them again and again. I
> scrupulously carried out the penances which were allotted to me. And
> yet my conscience kept nagging... I was trying to cure the doubts and
> scruples of the conscience with human remedies, the traditions of
> men. The more I tried these remedies, the more troubled and uneasy
> my conscience grew.

Luther turned to the writings of Augustine and gradually his outlook changed.
He adopted a simpler theology than the church taught. Then, between 1513
and 1518, he finally found the peace he had been looking for. Luther had a
new insight into the letter to the Romans, which he believed was in keeping
with Paul and Augustine. Instead of condemning him, Luther saw 'the just
shall live by faith' as freeing him. Faith was the means by which a person could
receive God's saving grace. Being saved was a gift, not an effort. Faith meant
that God saves people freely, not because of their good works. Good works,
therefore, are not the way to be saved, but the natural result of loving God.
Luther's understanding was transformed and his life was changed.

Luther's beliefs were not formed overnight. They did not become part of
Reformation teaching until the 1520s.

The spread of Luther's ideas

Archbishop Albert of Mainz complained to the Pope about Luther's actions,
but the Pope dismissed it as a local quarrel. Luther had questioned the
authority of the Pope, however, and the dispute grew into this wider issue.
At the same time Luther's theses, which he had fastened to the church door,
were published and circulated. His views gained public support and he
became a hero almost overnight. It became dangerous for Tetzel to walk the
streets. The local ruler, the Elector Frederick of Saxony, decided to protect
Luther. Frederick was tired of Italian popes interfering in German affairs
and enjoyed displeasing the Archbishop.

So it was that the Reformation became a powerful mixture of religion
and politics. Luther's aim was to purify the Roman Catholic Church and
preserve its truth. Very soon, however, he was overtaken by events and his

new vision became the spiritual and moral reformation of the whole of the Christian world. Even so, neither Luther nor his colleague Philip Melanchthon thought they were founding a new church. This came about gradually, until the Formula of Concord finally established Lutheran orthodoxy in 1577.

At the Diet of Augsburg in 1518, Luther refused to withdraw his views. He was presented with choosing either the Pope's authority or rebellion – and he chose rebellion. Luther's friends had to smuggle him out of Augsburg at night for fear of his safety. In 1519 he went to debate at Leipzig with a skilful man called John Eck. Eck forced Luther into a corner, to choose the Bible or Rome. Luther chose the Bible. From then on there was no turning back. By 1520 Luther was famous. His pamphlets in German and Latin were straightforward and easy to read, and many read them. Among his writings of 1520 were:

'TO THE CHRISTIAN NOBILITY OF THE GERMAN NATION': Luther considered this work as the blast of the trumpet which brought down the walls of Jericho. He called on the rulers of Germany to reform the church. He urged that reform in Germany was impossible unless the Pope's power was destroyed. Luther called the kings and princes of Germany to rise up and destroy that power. He entrusted the secular powers with a sacred task.

'THE BABYLONISH CAPTIVITY OF THE CHURCH' was an assault on the seven sacraments preached by the Roman Catholic Church. Luther reduced these to baptism and communion (the two sacraments which Christ himself had founded), and confession.

'OF THE LIBERTY OF A CHRISTIAN MAN' set out 'justification by faith'. This was Luther's belief that God saves freely through faith and not works.

For Luther the Pope became the Antichrist, like the devil himself. He wrote: 'It would not be surprising if God were to rain fire and brimstone from heaven and cast Rome into the pit, as once he cast Sodom and Gomorrah.'

On 15 June 1520 Rome issued the Bull *Exsurge Domine*, condemning Luther as a heretic. Faithful Christians were ordered to burn his books. Luther's answer was to burn the Bull, a papal document, in front of a public crowd.

Charles V, the Holy Roman Emperor, wanted peace. He knew that he could not allow a national German church to form without dividing up his own kingdom. He summoned Luther. At the Diet of Worms in 1521, Luther declared in front of the Emperor: 'Unless I am proved wrong by scriptures or by evident reason, then I am a prisoner in conscience to the Word of God. I cannot retract and I will not retract. To go against conscience is neither safe nor right. God help me. Amen.'

A month later Luther was banned and outlawed. He went into hiding at a castle called the Wartburg. There he began to translate the Bible into German. He completed this huge task in 1534, and his translation helped shape the German language as it is today. Luther's Bible and hymns became important in the Reformation. He believed that everybody ought to be able to read the Bible, from the very highest to the very lowest. Previously the Bible had been in Latin and only for priests and scholars. Translated into German and published by means of printing, now every Christian could read the Bible.

As well as reforming certain central beliefs, Luther wished to reform church practice. He did not approve of monks and nuns, nor of clerical celibacy that priests should not marry. Luther himself married an ex-nun called Katharina and they had several children.

Luther's forceful stand on the Peasants' Uprisings of 1524-25 strengthened the German princes in their power. Germany became divided. After 1524 there would have been civil war if Rome had taken any further steps to silence Luther.

At the Diet of Speyer in 1529, the princes who agreed with Luther's Reformation delivered a 'protest' against the Emperor and the Catholic princes. This was the 'protest' from which the word 'Protestant' comes. In 1531 the Protestant princes and cities formed a political body called the Schmalkaldic League. These rulers were determined to resist the Emperor and the Catholic princes. This league was a new power in Europe and was successful in its aim. Meanwhile, the Reformation spread further and further into all the countries of Europe. By the time of his death in 1546, Luther had seen the face of his continent change.

John Calvin and Geneva

The other great figure of the Reformation was John Calvin (1509-64). Born at Noyon in France, Calvin studied at Paris, Orleans and Bruges. He was converted around 1532 and devoted himself to theology. In 1533 he was associated with Protestantism and had to escape from Paris. Calvin went to

Basel in Switzerland where he wrote *The Institutes of the Christian Religion* in 1536. This book of Protestant theology went through four editions in Calvin's lifetime. The last edition of 1559 was five times as long as the first.

A severe man, ruthless in applying his principles, Calvin was a man of books, texts and authorities. He passed through Geneva by chance in 1536 and was asked to stay. A row over church government forced him into exile from 1538 to 1541. Then the magistrates of Geneva begged him to return. Calvin drew up reforms to bring order and decency to the city. Geneva was to become a city of God. In the vacuum left by the collapse of Roman Catholicism, the Protestant church had to find new ways of organizing itself. Calvin persuaded the city council to impose the 'Ecclesiastical Ordinances' on the city. These were rules even about what people could wear, and dancing was banned. Calvin tried to close the pubs. His plan was to open sober cafés where grace would be said before and after meals. Despite Calvin's strict ideals, the people of Geneva were not prepared to accept everything and the pubs had to be reopened.

Calvin was never popular; people were either followers or enemies. In 1559 he complained that 'never was a man more assailed, stung and torn by calumny' than he was. Yet his inflexibility cast a shadow across the city and he was kept in power by the tide of Protestant refugees continually sweeping into Geneva. He was a prolific writer and regular preacher. He appointed elders to oversee the morals of Geneva. These elders refused sinners holy communion and reported to the pastors in a body called 'consistory'. Consistory made rules about all aspects of life. Punishments were common and severe.

Calvin's teaching has given rise to 'Calvinism'. Calvinists were disciplined believers, determined, hardworking and devout. Modern theologians claim that it is unjust to judge Calvin by the Calvinism his theology spawned. Calvin did, however, set out the doctrine of 'limited atonement'. This doctrine states that Christ did not die on the cross for everybody, but only for the 'elect'. Protestant theology abolished purgatory, but some scholars have claimed that a grimmer doctrine was put in its place. Calvin believed that Christ died only for a limited number of chosen people and not for the whole world. This view, called 'predestination', exists in Paul and Augustine, but Calvin heightened it. He claimed that everybody deserves to be punished by God and so it is a measure of God's goodness if even only a few are saved. God's justice, Calvin stated, is beyond human understanding and should not be questioned.

Other leaders and national churches emerged from the Reformation.

Ulrich Zwingli and the church in Zurich were among the earliest. Along with them came a new stress on certain central beliefs:

* Everyone should be able to read the Bible in their own language, because the Bible is the supreme authority, not the church.

* Justification is by faith, not by works.

* Each individual needs a faith relationship with God.

In large parts of Europe the power of Rome was overturned and the political and religious map changed completely. These changes have largely stayed with us until today.

The Reformation in Britain

In England Henry VIII accomplished the Reformation at a stroke. He wished to divorce his first wife and marry his second. The Pope would not agree and in 1534 Henry VIII declared himself 'only supreme head on earth' of the church in England. The Anglican church developed slowly and retained many of the old Roman Catholic ways. Profoundly influenced by the new Protestant teaching, it became a reformed Catholic church, rather than an entirely Protestant one. In Scotland the Reformation was more severe. In 1559 John Knox preached and his preaching caused a storm throughout the country. Knox had been in Geneva with Calvin and had spent time in exile. His attacks against Mary Queen of Scots (a Roman Catholic) were fierce and uncompromising. Knox helped draw up the 'Scots Confession' which was passed by the Scottish Parliament in 1560. He led a Reformation in Scotland which sought to drive out any trace of Roman Catholicism, including bishops and liturgy which some other Reformed churches retained. The Church of Scotland still exists today as a national church, while the Church of England is a State church.

The Counter-Reformation

In 1534 Ignatius Loyola founded the Jesuits (the Society of Jesus) in Spain. Loyola had been a soldier and was determined to become a soldier of Christ.

The aim of the Jesuits was to reform the church from within (especially by education), to fight heresy and to preach the gospel. The Jesuits have been a powerful force within the Roman Catholic Church. Their zeal and determination have ensured their success in many parts of the world. They remain a powerful order. In response to the Reformation, the Council of Trent met in three stages between 1545 and 1563. Two-thirds of the bishops who attended were Italian, and the Council was not representative of the Roman Catholic Church as a whole. The purpose of the Council of Trent was to define what Roman Catholicism believed in opposition to Protestantism, and to introduce reforms within the Roman Catholic church. In 1564 Pope Pius IV confirmed all the decrees of the Council. Trent's conclusions set the standard for Roman Catholic teaching for 400 years until the Second Vatican Council in 1962-65.

Interpreting the Bible Today

Conservatives and Radicals

What kind of books do you like reading? Maybe you don't like reading books, but prefer watching films or TV or videos. But if you read a book or watch a film, what happens? If it's good, you become lost in the book or the film. You become caught up with the characters and the story. Then the book or the film affects you: it makes you excited or terrified; it makes you laugh or cry.

Many religions have a Holy Book which holds a high place in the faith of the believers. For Christians, the Holy Book is the Bible. When Christians read the Bible they, too, are caught up in the worlds of the Old Testament and the New. But there is more than that. Christians believe that the Bible shows them how to live and how to have faith in God. They believe that the gospels of Jesus show how it is possible to have a new and lasting life with God. Christians believe that, somehow, God speaks and reveals himself through the words of the Bible. For them, the Bible is more than just a book; it is a key to understanding the universe.

Reading the Bible

A question facing each new generation of theologians is: 'How do we read the Bible?'

Rationalism states that many of the miraculous Bible accounts cannot be taken at face value; they are fantastic or impossible. For the scientist, the world is governed by uniform laws. The supernatural elements in the Bible need a new interpretation as they are scientifically impossible. And historical criticism states that the Bible writers expressed their experiences in a pre-scientific understanding of the world. Episodes in the Bible, such as the miracle accounts, are only stories. They tell us something about the meaning of Jesus for the early Christians, rather than about his supernatural power.

These and other modern types of criticism have changed the way Christians have to respond to the Bible. Many modern scholars claim that because we live 2,000 years after the last of the biblical events took place, we now have a completely different understanding of the world. The Bible has to be interpreted afresh in that rational and scientific light.

But we need to ask, in what sense is the Bible revelation?

The Bible never tries to prove the existence of God. Its writers were conscious of God acting in their lives and affecting all of reality as they knew it. All sixty-six books of the Bible are written from that same, universal standpoint of faith.

Christians have taken one of two broad views of what it means for the Bible to be a Holy Book containing God's revelation.

ONE IS THAT THE BIBLE IS A DIVINE RECORD OF RELIGIOUS TRUTHS. Many Christians believe that the Bible is a record of God's words expressly as God wished them to be recorded. There were different writers involved, but these writers were inspired by God to write as they did. This view is called 'verbal inspiration', because the very words are God-inspired. Statements in the Bible have, in a way, been guaranteed by God. This propositional view dominated the medieval world. It is still the official view of the Roman Catholic Church and is also held by Protestant Conservative Evangelicals. Evangelicals often claim that the Bible is 'the word of God'.

THE OTHER IS THAT THE BIBLE IS A RECORD OF HUMAN FAITH IN GOD. Many Christians believe that it is misleading to think of God's revelation as a set of statements. These Christians would prefer to think of the Bible writers as recording how God acts in human history and human experience. The Bible, they claim, has grown out of humankind's relationship with God, it is a set of human documents. These Christians would concentrate on Jesus as the Word of God, and the Bible as a witness to that Word.

A key point in Matthew's account of Jesus comes when he questions his followers:

> 'Who do people say the Son of Man is?' They replied, 'Some say John the Baptist; others say Elijah; and still others, Jeremiah or one of the prophets.' 'But what about you?' he asked. Simon Peter answered, 'You are the Christ, the Son of the living God.'

Peter's confession is a turning-point. Jesus' disciples have spent time with him and they know that he is a great teacher and prophet. But is he something more? Peter realizes that he is; Jesus is God's own Son.

This realization came to Peter by faith. If there had been a film camera recording Jesus on his travels, the film would simply have shown a man going about his business in Galilee. To understand Jesus as God's Son, or a Messiah whose mission is to save humankind, requires religious belief which comes through faith and experience. All theologians believe that faith and experience are important. The question is whether faith and experience are responsible for the picture of Jesus in the gospels – was it altered by the early church to prove Jesus' divinity? And what about the supernatural events surrounding Jesus? Are they historically true or were they 'added' to the picture of Jesus to enable people to have more faith in him? And – are the words of Jesus' teaching his actual words? Did the early church take the 'Jesus of History' and fashion a 'Christ of Faith' to suit their religious needs? These are complicated questions which many scholars still have difficulty in answering.

Biblical criticism

Modern interpretations of the Bible began in earnest in the nineteenth century. Much of the impetus came from Germany.

Georg Hegel (1770-1831) influenced German thought to a great extent. He believed that history is a metaphysical process leading to perfection. In other words, Hegel believed there is a hidden meaning in history behind the day to day events in the world.

Germans have two words for history. Theologians came to use these two words with reference to the Bible:

> 'HISTORIE' is what happened: facts, dates and events. 'Historie' contains no interpretations.

'GESCHICHTE' is the 'meaning' of what happened. 'Geschichte' looks for the pattern in events, the story. German theologians began to write about *Heilsgeschichte* or 'Salvation-history'. They claimed that the Bible recorded God acting in human experience. How people experienced God was important, not what God did in an objective, historical sense. Miracles and supernatural events had to be understood in that light, as pointers to the hidden meaning of history. This meaning was given by God.

Another approach centred on historical criticism was a professional and rigorous approach to history. This employed new techniques of scholarship. Instead of holding the Bible up as an 'authority', historical critics treated the Bible as a 'source' to be analyzed. Historical critics wanted to peel away the 'husk' of Jewish legend and Greek philosophy which they believed surrounded Jesus. They wanted to find the real, historical Jesus. By coming close to this Jesus, these scholars believed it would be possible to come closer to his true message, the message Jesus preached before it was 'tampered with' by the early church.

Liberal theology

The founder of liberal theology, indeed the whole of modern theology, was Friedrich Schleiermacher (1768-1834). Schleiermacher separated faith from reason and experience from history. He treated the Bible as a record of human experience rather than divine revelation. For Schleiermacher religion was feeling and experience; God was not to be found objectively in the Bible or in the world.

Schleiermacher put forward the liberal view that Jesus is an example. The broad liberal understanding of Jesus is that his mission was not to save humankind by dying and rising, but to raise people's awareness of God and call them to live good, moral lives. Jesus had 'essential sinlessness and absolute perfection' and 'a real existence of God in him'. This is all that is necessary for saving humankind; the resurrection, ascension and second coming are legendary extras.

Liberal theology reached its highest expression in the work of Adolf von Harnack. Von Harnack was a professor of theology at the University of Berlin from 1888 until 1921, and the greatest expert of his generation on the Church Fathers. Von Harnack believed that the message preached by

Jesus had been corrupted by Greek philosophy. He claimed that Paul had changed the religion of Jesus into a religion *about* Jesus. This had led to the mistaken belief that Jesus was God. This belief in the 'incarnation', von Harnack claimed, was created by the early church and was not held by Jesus himself.

The nineteenth century saw a quest for the historical Jesus. In 1835 David Friedrich Strauss published the first volume of *The Life of Jesus Critically Examined* (translated into English by the novelist George Eliot, who also translated Feuerbach). Strauss had been influenced by Hegel and taught at Tübingen in South Germany. He was dismissed on the publication of the second volume.

By applying historical methods of criticism to the gospels, Strauss believed he had separated the 'Jesus of History' from the 'Christ of Faith'. He separated Jesus, the historical individual, from the being worshipped by the early church, the divine God-man. Everything supernatural about Jesus – from his conception to his ascension – was stripped away. Strauss believed that through the historical Jesus a 'universal idea' had entered into human history. (He took this idea from Hegel.) Strauss believed that Bible statements and accounts were only myths. He was accused of atheism and of attempting to destroy the Christian faith. Certainly he was replacing theology, to some extent, with anthropology.

The quest for the historical Jesus ended with Albert Schweitzer's book, *The Quest of the Historical Jesus* (1906). After decades of scholarship, it appeared that the Jesus uncovered by this method was an alien Jew from the first century who had little to say to the modern world. More usually, however, the Jesus uncovered appeared to be liberal and Protestant; curiously like the scholars themselves. A strong criticism has been that, while the quest for the historical Jesus was useful in many ways, it was often like people studying a mirror.

Barth and Bultmann

In the first half of the twentieth century, two great theologians had a strong influence:

KARL BARTH (1886-1968) reacted against liberal theology after the First World War. He introduced 'neo-orthodoxy'. Barth believed that liberal theology was only human-made religion. God was God, wholly other, sovereign over humankind. Barth's *Church Dogmatics* is the greatest systematic theological work since Thomas Aquinas' *Summa Theologiae* in the thirteenth century. Barth believed that God's word acts through Jesus and affects the whole world. The Bible is a witness to that event. The Bible is the word of God, while Jesus is the Word of God. The Old Testament points forward to Jesus, the New Testament points back to him. Their function, like that of John the Baptist in the gospels, is to say: 'Behold the Lamb of God.' Barth's view of the word of God is that it is dynamic – it does things, it is not static, like words written down in a book. Barth was one of the most influential and outstanding theologians of the twentieth century.

RUDOLF BULTMANN (1884-1976) was Professor of Theology at Marburg in German from 1921 to 1951. He believed that most of the recorded sayings of Jesus were created by the early church, and were not spoken by Jesus himself. Bultmann came to believe that it is impossible to reconstruct the historical Jesus. He rejected liberal theology, but not as extremely as Barth did.

In his view justification is by faith, not by history, and so history is unnecessary. Bultmann is best known for 'demythologizing' the New Testament. For the first-century world to speak to modern times, the 'mythical' world-view of that era has to be stripped away. These 'myths' have to be reinterpreted; they must not be cast away as the liberal theologians wished to do, for they contain valuable insights. Bultmann reinterpreted the New Testament existentially. According to him, the resurrection should not be seen as a historical event, but as a miracle of faith in the lives of the disciples. Critics of Bultmann have complained that he accepted the modern, scientific world-view at the expense of the Bible. Bultmann replied that he was merely sacrificing a pre-scientific view of the world and not the essential heart of the Christian message, that Jesus calls us to a new kind of life.

Barth and Bultmann have both influenced the course of theology in the twentieth century, but there are other outlooks which are also important. Conservative Evangelicals see themselves as defending the gospel (the word 'evangelical' comes from the Greek word meaning 'gospel' or 'good news'). Evangelicals do not think that it is very good news if Jesus did not really perform his miracles or rise bodily from the dead. They give a high place to the Bible and reject most of the modern theological ways of reading it.

Evangelicals are generally not fundamentalists. Fundamentalists believe that every word in the Bible is literally true – God did create the world in six days and there was a real Adam and a real Eve. Evangelicals believe that the Bible contains different forms of literature, and have harmonized their views with modern science. They would maintain, however, that the gospel writers are reliable and historical. Jesus' words in the gospels are what he really said, not additions by the early church, and his miracles took place as the Bible claims.

The appeal of evangelicalism is mainly emotional and spiritual. That is not to say that evangelicalism is unintelligent, only that it does not tend to speculate. Evangelicals are a vigorous group within Protestantism. They may not be well-represented at the universities in theology departments, but they are well-represented in the churches. Carl Henry, a leading evangelical scholar, wrote:

> The strength of evangelical theism lies in its offer of religious realities that human unregeneracy desperately needs and cannot otherwise provide. In a time of spiritual rootlessness Christianity proclaims God the self-revealed heavenly Redeemer. In a time of intellectual scepticism, it adduces fixed truths about God's holy purpose for man and the world. In a time of ethical permissiveness, it offers moral absolutes and specific divine imperatives. In a time of frightful fear of the future, it presents a sure and final hope. In a time when daily life has turned bitter and sour for multitudes of humans, it offers life-transforming dynamic.

Evangelicals would claim that their faith has given them a certainty and a sure way of reading the Bible which other modern theologies lack.

Theology from the grassroots

An important insight resulting from liberal theology is 'enculturation'. On this understanding the gospel was shaped by a first-century understanding of the world. Modern theology has tended to be Western, white and dominated by men. This also has led to another, different kind of cultural shaping. Now modern theologies are emerging which have challenged traditional theologies. These include:

* Latin American liberation theology.

* Black theology.

* Asian theology.

* Feminist theology.

These new theologies involve new ways of reading the Bible. Latin American liberation theology, for example, is a theology of poverty. This theology states that in the Bible God is on the side of the poor and the oppressed. Accordingly, liberation theology stresses freedom from oppression, with the goal of transformation.

While Protestant theology has concentrated mainly on the individual's relationship with God, liberation theology examines the factors which make up society as a whole. In Latin America slavery, exploitation and Christianity arrived hand in hand. Christianity arrived with the conquerors and was their religion. Liberation theology addresses not just philosophical questions to change people, but sociological questions to change society. Its theologians want to transform society as well as save souls. It is a mixture of political theology and grassroots communities, which uses some Marxist ideas.

Along with Marxism it realizes that while circumstances can form people, people can also change circumstances. Standing up for the poor, it identifies Jesus as a rebel, and an outcast. It sees him as a poor person, identified as the Suffering Servant written about in the prophecy of Isaiah.

Liberation theology is a powerful movement which has grown out of the Spanish-speaking world of Latin America. As other countries develop their own theologies, this will have an impact on how the Bible is read in the future.

Most people reading the Bible today can read it in their own language, with many translations to choose from. A reader will come with her own preconceived ideas, with many interpretations on offer and many possible approaches. Whatever the case, the Bible remains the fundamental record of Jewish and Christian experience in dealing with God. Its status as a cornerstone of Western civilization has been secured. People are freer to read the Bible today than ever before. No one view is imposed by a single, powerful church or by society. Anyone who opens and reads the Bible nowadays is entirely free to respond to what they find.

Does Science Have the Answers?

SCIENCE AND BELIEF

Creation and Evolution

Charles Darwin

'What is the question now placed before society with a glib assurance the most astounding? The question is this: Is man an ape or an angel? I, my Lord, I am on the side of the angels.' So spoke Benjamin Disraeli, a nineteenth-century British Prime Minister.

The nineteenth century was an age of extraordinary and rapid change. The Industrial Revolution altered the face of the country within a generation, and the invention of the railway enabled people to travel long distances at speed for the first time ever. The British Empire expanded confidently across the globe, while at home squalid conditions cried out for something to be done. People believed in progress and the future; yet they were pessimistic and appalled at human degradation.

It was an age of expansion, and of transition.

The Victorians were aware of this themselves. They were aware that life had changed and that, in the process, they had both gained and lost. Novelists as different as George Eliot and Thomas Hardy turned back to their rural childhood years as a kind of Garden of Eden from which they had been expelled. For the nineteenth century was also an age of religion and science, faith and doubt.

The certainties of Christianity came to appear increasingly uncertain as the century progressed and many people found themselves slipping into agnosticism and atheism. The great religious and scientific conflict of the age was symbolized in the work of one person: Charles Darwin. Darwin's theory of evolution represents a watershed in human and religious understanding.

A naturalist's voyage

Charles Robert Darwin (1809-82) was born in Shrewsbury, England. His father was a doctor and son of a more famous doctor, Erasmus Darwin. Darwin's mother was a daughter of Josiah Wedgwood, founder of the famous pottery. Darwin went to Edinburgh to study medicine, but left for theology at Cambridge and a future as an Anglican priest. While at Cambridge he became interested in science and botany.

In 1831 Darwin joined HMS Beagle as a naturalist and, for the next five years, sailed round the world studying animals and plants. He published his findings in *A Naturalist's Voyage on the Beagle* in 1839. He formed his theory of evolution from 1837 to 1839 and condensed his findings into *The Origin of Species* (1859). That and *The Descent of Man* (1871) are his two most famous books, though Darwin wrote copiously on many forms of wildlife.

Darwin married his cousin Emma Wedgwood and, shortly after, his health began to deteriorate. The family moved to Down House, Kent, where Darwin spent the rest of his life. He rarely travelled, apart from trips to visit his family, to London or for occasional health cures. He had a private income and was able to live from that and from the sales of his books. He made friends with the leading scientists of the day and his life was characterized by modesty and hard work. When he died in 1882 he was buried in Westminster Abbey.

The theory of evolution is well known, at least in outline. What is not so well known is that evolutionary ideas had existed a century before Darwin. Darwin was the first, however, to give a natural and scientific cause for evolution. Earlier, Hegel's dialectic had substituted a philosophy of progress for a static universe, and the German Romantic writers had been preoccupied with notions of change.

At the beginning of the nineteenth century, these ideas entered the realm of science. In doing so they immediately challenged a literal interpretation of the Bible and some of people's most deeply held beliefs.

The Bible faces a scientific challenge

At the beginning of the nineteenth century most people still believed that the creation account in the Book of Genesis was literally true. They believed that God made the world in six days and that he made every plant and animal separately. They accepted the timescale calculated by Archbishop Ussher that the world had begun in 4004BC. They also accepted the idea, stemming from Aristotle, of the Great Chain of Being which gave everything a place on a cosmic hierarchy. Humankind was at the midpoint between the earthly and the divine. The world, as described by William Paley in his Argument from Design, was like a watch, a carefully constructed mechanism in which each part of creation had its place.

Between the 1820s and the 1840s this understanding of the world changed completely.

The first challenge came from geology with the work of Sir Charles Lyell (1797-1875). Lyell's work described the earth in process of change rather than a result of a once and for all divine creation. Lyell also showed that geological processes such as uplift, erosion and sedimentation had taken place over millions of years to form mountains and valleys. Lyell's work was scientifically convincing and persuaded the public that a long process of change, and not the immediate miracle of creation, was responsible for the physical characteristics of the world.

Then scientists began to uncover fossils, remnants of extinct species, which had no place in the 'watchmaker' notion of the world or any part in the Great Chain of Being. These fossils were reckoned to be millions, not thousands, of years old. Bones were dug up and monstrous dinosaurs pieced together. These nightmarish creatures suddenly appeared to bring one nightmare true: the world was much older than 4004BC; animals had come and gone, and there was no Great Chain of Being. As a result, the Bible was obviously not true literally. At that point Christianity received a blow from which many would claim it has never recovered.

The theory of evolution

Lyell's second volume of *Principles of Geology* reached the young Darwin aboard the Beagle while he was in South America. The book had an enormous impact on him:

> I always feel as if my books came half out of Lyell's brain, and that I never acknowledge this sufficiently; for I have always thought that the great merit of the *Principles* was that it altered the whole tone of one's mind.

When Darwin began his study of wildlife, there were three ways of classifying species, which went back to Aristotle:

* Distinct type: a cat is a cat as opposed to a dog or a horse.

* Family type: a leopard is a member of the cat family.

* Hierarchical type: a human being is further up the scale of creation than an amoeba.

This understanding was reinforced by Platonism which viewed all cats as sharing in 'catness' and therefore as being distinct from all other animals. It was further reinforced by Genesis which claimed: 'Now the Lord God had formed out of the ground all the beasts of the field and all the birds of the air.' In other words, God had created each creature separately and spontaneously.

Even before Darwin, Swedish botanist Linnaeus, in his *Systema Natura* (1735), had begun by thinking every species distinct and separate, but had ended by being unsure.

Darwin's theory controversially claimed a common ancestor for humankind and the apes. Humankind was an animal who had evolved like all other animals. The cherished status afforded to human beings by belief in a single act of creation was suddenly swept away. Darwin's theory examined species, adaptation and evolution.

Darwin's claim was that natural selection is the mechanism of evolutionary change. He proposed that the strongest, fittest and best adapted of each generation are the ones which survive and pass on these characteristics to their offspring. This accounts for changes in animal forms over a long period of time. Animals and plants, Darwin stated, evolve to cope with and survive in their environment. Some species, such as humankind, have evolved quickly; others, such as fish, have remained relatively unchanged. It was actually Herbert Spencer who coined the well-known phrase 'survival of the fittest'.

Darwin's theory of evolution had several immediate consequences:

THE DIFFERENCES BETWEEN SPECIES DISAPPEARED. As the fossil record was uncovered and examined throughout the nineteenth century, so the differences between species began to dissolve. Darwin pictured all animal life as a kind of tree, with all animals, perhaps, having a common ancestor. He wrote that mentally 'man and the lower animals do not differ in kind, although immensely in degree. A difference in degree, however great, does not justify us in placing man in a different kingdom...' In other words, humankind has to be viewed as an animal species pure and simple.

EVOLUTION TOOK PLACE OVER A LONG PERIOD OF TIME. Instead of the six days of Genesis, it became rapidly clear that complex animals must have taken millions of years to develop. A single generation was not long enough to evolve an elephant. As a result, the Bible appeared discredited.

EVOLUTION ALTERED THE MEANING OF LIFE. People had believed that human beings were made by God, who had a purpose and plan for them. Suddenly, human beings appeared to be only the result of a blind, random, selfish, natural process. This came as the most enormous psychological shock. Instead of being children of God, people found themselves adrift in a meaningless world, and this fuelled the instinctive protest which many felt against the theory of evolution.

Darwin did not form any philosophy out of his theory, though it was taken up by his age. He did not apply it to economics or progress, as Herbert Spencer was to do. He did believe, however, that different moralities evolve with different groups and this led him to question the unique moral authority of God.

Darwin and Christian faith

Darwin's own Christian belief suffered as the years passed and he slowly became an agnostic:

> Disbelief crept over me at a very slow rate, but was at last complete. The rate was so slow that I felt no distress, and have never since doubted even for a single second that my conclusion was correct. I can indeed hardly see how anyone ought to wish Christianity to be true; for if so, the plain language of the text seems to show that the men who do not believe, and this would include my Father, my Brother and almost all my best friends, will be everlastingly punished. And this is a damnable doctrine.

The debate raged. In 1860 there was a famous confrontation between Samuel Wilberforce, the Bishop of Oxford, and T.H. Huxley, who had become a great spokesman for Darwin's ideas. After the bishop had finished speaking, mocking evolution, he asked Huxley if it was through his grandfather or grandmother that he claimed descent from an ape. One witness reported:

> On this Mr Huxley slowly and deliberately arose. A slight, tall figure, stern and pale, very quiet and very grave, he stood before us and spoke those tremendous words – words which no one seems sure of now, nor, I think, could remember just after they were spoken, for their meaning took away our breath, though it left us in no doubt as to what it was. He was not ashamed to have a monkey for his ancestor; but he would be ashamed to be connected with a man who used great gifts to obscure the truth. No one doubted his meaning, and the effect was tremendous. One lady fainted and had to be carried; I, for one, jumped out of my seat.

Evolution had carried the day. The publication of Huxley's *Evidences as to Man's Place in Nature*, published in 1863, finally settled humankind's relationship to the apes. That same year Lyell's *Antiquity of Man* showed that human origins lay millions of years back. In The *Descent of Man* (1871) Darwin summed up the argument tying humankind into an evolutionary scheme. The Bible had lost; science had won. Science was triumphant.

In the face of this Christians had three straight options:

THEY COULD REJECT DARWIN'S THEORY. Many 'creationists' still believe that Genesis is literally true. Creationists point out that Darwin's theory of evolution is only a theory and that God's word is more reliable than Darwin's.

THEY COULD REJECT CHRISTIANITY. Many people found science and religion incompatible and either lost their faith or became agnostics.

OR THEY COULD ACCOMMODATE CHRISTIANITY AND EVOLUTION. This is what the majority of Christians have done. They see no conflict between science and religion, between Darwin and Genesis. How is this possible?

Christian theology developed alongside Greek philosophy. This led Christianity to claim a static, unchanging universe. Science challenged that view, but, in doing so, did it necessarily challenge Christianity?

Science is a kind of knowledge, a method of finding out about the world. Strictly speaking, science is not a philosophy concerned with the meaning of the world.

Religious knowledge is different from scientific knowledge. If God exists, he cannot be studied as part of natural science as God does not exist 'in the world' in that way, nor does he exist as an object. As a result, talking about God scientifically involves great difficulties, as theological language has not been developed to meet with the language of science. Because a scientific view has come to predominate, many people now feel that science is founded on facts and religion on fancy, that they can put their trust in science but not in religion. Yet science and religion are distinct. They speak two different languages, have two different areas of concern.

The misunderstanding lay in treating Genesis as an account which had to be scientifically true. But equally, some scientists used evolution wrongly. They put forward a philosophy of humankind in competition with Christianity, instead of merely putting forward a scientific theory. Chance and natural selection are not necessarily in conflict with belief in God as a creator who gives meaning to human life. Biology is distinct from theology.

How then is the Genesis account of creation to be understood? While some Christians still maintain that Genesis is literally true, many do not. In Genesis there are two accounts of creation. The later account (which opens the Bible) was written while the Jews were in captivity in Babylon. The Jews had been defeated, but they still believed that their God was the true God. This creation account depicts God as God, creator of the sun and moon (which the Babylonians worshipped) and as Lord of the Universe. There are, therefore, important human experiences underlying such writing – insights into God's purpose and character. The Genesis account was not written as a scientific document, but to show God as Lord and Creator. The creation accounts, therefore, contain religious truths, not scientific truths. Distinguishing these truths and applying them to ourselves will, perhaps, give us a clearer understanding of the world.

Theologies of evolution

Christianity retreated from natural theology, that is, looking at the world to find out about God. It moved to such approaches as those of Rudolf

Bultmann (1884-1976) and others who considered the Bible accounts of the creation as 'myths' which contained important truths about human experience.

Other thinkers used Darwin's theory of evolution to form new theologies, new ways of understanding God and his action in the world.

Pierre Teilhard de Chardin (1881-1955) was a Jesuit scientist who studied extinct species. He had a lifelong interest in the origins of humankind. Teilhard de Chardin tried to relate Christianity to evolutionary thought, but his work was regarded as suspect by his superiors and only published after his death. He believed that creation is the process of evolution – sin accompanies evolution and perfection is impossible and that the 'Cosmic Christ' is at least as important as the 'Historical Jesus'. The 'total Christ', or Christ's mystical body, is evolving within evolution, therefore redemption is evolutionary and not one single act. For Teilhard, human history is evolving towards a climax which will be reached in Christ. He called this the 'Omega point'. God is not unchanging and transcendent (beyond the world), but active in the here and now. God is in the process of evolution and cannot be separated from it. Teilhard de Chardin's best known books are *The Phenomenon of Man*, *Le Milieu Divin* and *The Future of Man*, which appeared in France from 1955 to 1959. He wrote:

> I believe that the universe is an evolution;
> I believe that evolution proceeds towards spirit;
> I believe that spirit is fully realized in the form of a personality;
> I believe that the supremely personal is the universal Christ.

Process Theology emerged after the First World War in the work of A.N. Whitehead and Charles Hartshorne. Its influence has been felt mainly in the United States. Process theology declares that 'I' am not a fixed entity which passes unaffected through time. Instead 'I' am a result of all the changes and experiences I have had. 'I' (all the things that make me 'I') am, in fact, a process. The same is true of God.

Process Theology goes back to the Greek idea of the One and the Many, or permanence and change. The Christian God, based on Greek permanence, presents God as unchanging and remote (so Process Theologians complain). Process Theologians claim that God is actually part of the process of evolution and change, actively involved in the world and affected by events in the world, sometimes to the point of changing his mind.

God has an existence 'out there', but God's actions in the world reveal God's character. Process Theologians further claim that God travels with us in time. The future is the future for God, not only for us. In other words, although God has a fixed character, God is subject to change as we are subject to change.

The theory of evolution represents a turning-point in human understanding. New findings challenged old philosophies and religion was forced to rethink some aspects of its claims to 'truth'. But if science appeared to triumph over religion that was not necessarily science's gain, but humankind's loss. Understanding the questions posed by existing in the world cannot be reduced to science, though science has clarified many issues. The challenge to science surely is to fight for its truth in the face of prejudice; the challenge for religion is to present its truth afresh to each new generation.

The Meaning of Modern Science

Einstein and the New Physics

There was a young lady named Bright
Who could travel much faster than light.
She started one day,
In a relative way,
And got there the previous night.

Every age has its way of understanding the world. The world can be understood in terms of consciousness, what we believe; or of science, what we know. A total way of understanding the world is called a 'paradigm'. A paradigm is a model of reality, a complete thought-system – for understanding what is important, and for understanding how the world works.

Certain works have marked a change in such paradigms. Aristotle's *Physics* is one such, also Ptolemy's *Almagest*, Newton's works *Principia* and *Opticks*, Franklin's *Electricity*, Lavoisier's *Chemistry*, Lyell's *Geology* and Darwin's *Origin of Species*. These works have done more than change our knowledge of the world, they have changed our very understanding of existence.

In religious thought Augustine, Aquinas and Luther all set new paradigms in place. They radically altered humanity's understanding of itself and its relation to God.

In science, revolutions in thought took place when Copernicus succeeded Ptolemy (in saying that the earth went round the sun) and when

Newton succeeded Aristotle. The twentieth century began with a new, profound scientific revolution. In the work of Albert Einstein the whole course of physics changed, and with it humankind's understanding of the universe. Relativity theory and, subsequently, quantum theory are the foundations of this new physics, which has opened up a whole new approach to reality.

Albert Einstein solved several mysteries of the cosmos and rewrote the theory of gravity, finally dispensing with classical physics. His work laid down rules for governing the history and fate of the universe. His theories anticipated nuclear power, the atom bomb, space travel, radar, laser beams and atomic clocks. He revolutionized the ideas of time, space and motion. He is, without doubt, one of the greatest scientists who has ever lived.

The life of a genius

Albert Einstein (1879-1955) was born in the German city of Ulm, but grew up in Munich. He was a dreamy child who showed no real genius. He loved music and hated games. He left school, partly as a result of the failure of his father's business, and joined his parents in Milan. He gave up his German citizenship and became a Swiss citizen in 1901. Einstein failed the entrance exam to Zurich Polytechnic to study electrical engineering, but gained entrance there a year later.

After he graduated he was unable to find an academic job and worked as a clerk in a Patent Office in Berne. Between 1904 and 1917 he remade the universe in his head. The landmarks of his work are 'Special Relativity' (1905), which deals with high-speed motion, and 'General Relativity' (1915), which deals with gravity. After several years of poverty, Einstein's reputation grew. The rise of Nazism in Germany caused him to flee from there to Belgium in 1933. His summer home in Berlin was searched by the Gestapo and his property taken away on the grounds that he wished to give money towards a communist revolt. Some of his writings were burned publicly in front of the State Opera House in Berlin, because his were 'Jewish' physics. He resigned from the Prussian Academy of Science to which he had been elected in 1913. Einstein went to Princeton in the United States in 1933 and never returned to Europe. He lived in a simple house surrounded by books and records. He worked for a few hours every day.

Einstein was convinced that Hitler had to be confronted by force. This led him to write to President Roosevelt, informing him of the capacities of nuclear fission. Einstein's letter was the beginning of the nuclear age – the age in which we all live – and bore fruit in the dropping of the atomic bombs on Hiroshima and Nagasaki in August 1945. Einstein had little to do with the development of the atomic bomb. When he heard of Hiroshima he said, wearily, 'Oh, woe,' and spent the rest of his life campaigning actively against nuclear warfare. Modest, absorbed, he was an admirer of the great Indian pacifist Gandhi.

Physics before Einstein

In the nineteenth century, physicists had notions of absolute space and absolute time which went back to the Ancient Greeks. Such notions form our everyday perceptions of the world, so it is hard to conceive of reality operating in any other way. But three hundred years of scientific work were needed to lay these foundations.

* Johannes Kepler (1571-1630) showed that planets move in elliptical orbits, not in circles.

* Nicolaus Copernicus (1473-1543) proposed that the earth goes round the sun, not vice versa.

* Galileo Galilei (1564-1642) demonstrated that objects fall to earth at the same speed whatever their weight.

These men observed, but Isaac Newton (1642-1727) calculated. Newton's *Principia*, published in 1686, gave a mathematical expression for the force of gravity. At last the movements of the heavens could be calculated. Newton's theory was much more useful than any pile of observed facts, for his mechanics had a deeper significance. Once the forces and initial conditions had been worked out, it was possible to calculate into the future. The entire future of the universe could be worked out by Newton's theory, if its present state and the forces operating could be known.

Einstein's inheritance at the beginning of the twentieth century included the work of Newton on gravity, and the work of James Clerk Maxwell, whose theory in 1873 showed that light is an electromagnetic phenomenon. Maxwell's work was vital for understanding electricity and magnetism.

But there was a problem. While Newton's theory showed it was possible to travel at the speed of light, Maxwell's work showed that this was impossible. Einstein asked a simple question: What happens if you move at the speed of light? His answer revolutionized physics for ever.

The Theory of Relativity

Einstein's work showed that the observer was part of the process. He stated that theories are 'free creations of the human mind'.

* If you stand still on a beach, the waves move past you.

* If you are in a boat and move with the waves, you see no movement in the waves; just a straight line.

Both are perceptions and both are true. Einstein showed that reality is like this. We may think we are resting on a fixed point, but in fact, we are moving. (The notion that we are at rest is an illusion.) We exist on a turning globe which travels on an orbit round a sun in an ever-changing universe. The fact that we are moving not only affects our idea of reality; it affects reality itself.

'The train arrived at seven o'clock.' What does that actually mean? It means that as the train pulled into the station, the hands on my watch pointed to seven and twelve. For everyday purposes this is adequate. At a far distance, however, it takes the light some time to catch up. Light takes 2.5 seconds to reach the earth from the moon. When we look up at the sky we see the moon, not as it is now, but as it was 2.5 seconds ago. We are not looking at the present, but at the past.

Imagine putting a clock on the earth and a clock on the moon, and wanting to set them to the same time. You could do this by setting off a light signal half-way between the earth and the moon. That way it would take the light 1.25 seconds to reach the clock on the earth and the clock on the moon. The two clocks could be fixed by this method to read the same time.

Now try to imagine that you are in a train travelling at sixty miles an hour. You are on a track beside a train travelling at seventy miles an hour. The train outside the window appears to be travelling ten miles an hour faster than you.

But while this may be true of trains, it is not true of light. No matter how fast you are travelling, light always travels at 186,000 miles a second. That means, even if you were travelling at half the speed of light, the light would reach you at 186,000 miles a second, and not at 93,000 miles a second.

What is the consequence of this? Go back to the two clocks on the earth and the moon. Now imagine a third clock on a rocket moving at vast speed. The light signal goes off, but the rocket is hurtling towards the earth. The clock on the rocket will not synchronize with the clock on the moon because it is closer to the earth. In other words, the clock on the moon and the clock in the rocket have two different times. Both are right; both are different. Time, therefore, is not everywhere the same; it depends on how fast you are moving, and what you are moving in relation to. The faster you move towards the speed of light, Einstein showed, the slower times goes. Absolute space and absolute time are no longer feasible – the theory of relativity has replaced them.

> Thence we conclude that a balance clock at the equator must go more
> slowly, by a very small amount, than a precisely similar clock situated
> at the poles under otherwise identical conditions.

From this Special Theory of Relativity, Einstein went on to develop the General Theory of Relativity, which replaced Newton's theory of gravity.

Einstein showed that the universe contains a finite amount of energy. If you burn something or explode something, it does not increase the amount of energy in the universe; it just changes things from one state to another. The amount of energy in the universe always stays the same. Energy, in fact, resides in mass, in objects. Energy is matter; matter is energy. From this notion, Einstein worked out his famous equation $E=mc^2$. This theory sums up all action and creation in the universe. It accounts for how stars continue to burn, how gravity bends light, how space is curved and how the universe is expanding. Einstein wrote: 'In a certain sense, therefore, I hold it true that pure thought can grasp reality as the ancients dreamed.'

What was astonishing about Einstein's work was the beauty and spareness of his calculations. Without footnotes, ignorant of the work of other scientists, and with apparently effortless simplicity, he worked out equations which brought humankind 'closer to the secrets of the Old One', as Einstein termed God.

Quantum Theory

Einstein argued against quantum theory, although his own work prepared the way for it. He wrote to Max Born: 'Quantum mechanics is certainly imposing. But an inner voice tells me it is not yet the real thing. The theory says a lot, but does not really bring us any closer to the secret of the "Old One". I, at any rate, am convinced that he is not playing dice.'

Quantum theory was first put forward by German physicist Max Planck in 1900. It severs any connection with previous physics. If the theory of relativity deals with matters on a large scale, quantum theory does the same on a small scale. It works at levels lower than an atom. Democritus, Ancient Greek philosopher, declared that matter was made up of atoms, the smallest units in the universe. Scientists used atoms as a useful idea until they discovered particles smaller than an atom. They also discovered that these particles did not behave in any determined way, but randomly. Just as light had been discovered to be made up of both waves and particles, so matter exhibited the same uncertainty. Heisenberg's 'uncertainty principle' demonstrated this. It had been found that the behaviour of these particles is not experimentally certain. Heisenberg demonstrated that this is more than mere laboratory phenomenon; matter itself is fundamentally uncertain. Any notion of absolutes had to be abandoned.

While relativity theory and quantum theory work in their respective spheres, they do not fit together. The task still facing modern physics is to develop one unified theory which will incorporate both relativity and quantum theory.

Einstein, God and the universe

Einstein rejected the notion of a personal God at an early age. He also rejected any fundamentalist reading of the Bible. If he adhered to any philosophy, it was to the pantheism of Benedict Spinoza (1632-77). Yet Einstein did have a religious reverence in the face of the universe. He wrote:

> What is the meaning of human life, or organic life altogether? To answer the question at all implies a religion... The man who regards his own life and that of his fellow creatures as meaningless is not merely unfortunate but almost disqualified for life.

Einstein confessed that he was 'a deeply religious man'. For him religious feeling was 'a knowledge of the existence of something we cannot penetrate, of the manifestations of the profoundest reason and the most radiant beauty which are only accessible to our reason in their most elementary forms.' Einstein's 'cosmic religious feeling' caused him to pursue his research to the very heart of the universe. His sense of wonder at what he found must cause us to ask once again, why is there something and not just anything at all?

Einstein's work brings us face to face with the modern understanding of the universe. The universe is a different place from the one scientists, philosophers and theologians of previous generations had thought they knew. Einstein's physics has implications for any understanding of God. In approaching the universe we now understand that our understanding of God must be cosmic as well as personal.

Some writers, such as Fritjof Capra in *The Tao of Physics* (1976), have used Einsteinian physics as a key to open up a mystical contemplation of the universe. Capra likens the behaviour of the universe as we now understand it to aspects of Zen Buddhism or the Dance of Shiva in Hinduism.

What about the Christian understanding of God?

KARL BARTH and those following his neo-orthodoxy would state that God is known through revelation and not through science and the natural world.

THEOLOGIANS BASING THEIR WORK ON AN UNDERSTANDING OF LUDWIG WITTGENSTEIN would claim that religious and scientific language are two separate languages. To speak the language of science and reject religion (or vice versa) would be like dismissing Chinese as incomprehensible nonsense just because you happened to be an Italian speaker.

RUDOLF BULTMANN and the Christian existentialists claim that God acts in experience, not in history. In that sense, science and religion inhabit separate spheres.

CONSERVATIVE CHRISTIANS claim that God does act in the universe. They claim that science can never provide an all-embracing world picture which will encompass the whole of reality, for God is the Ultimate Reality and cannot be encompassed.

One writer with expertise in both theology and philosophy of science is Thomas F. Torrance. Torrance studied at Edinburgh and at Basel with Karl

Barth. He was professor of Christian Dogmatics at Edinburgh from 1952 until he retired in 1979.

Torrance has taken a different approach to religion and science from other theologians. He believes in religious facts, not in religious myths. Torrance asserts strongly that reality is a given thing. If science is true, religion is true. If religion is true, science is true. If religion and science both have their own areas of concern, that does not mean that they have to contradict one another. Rather, religion and science must fit together to give an overall picture of reality.

Torrance believes that in order to search for a true scientific and religious understanding, all old cultural habits and personal habits of mind must be discarded. People must approach the universe with an open mind, not with prejudice. In his view, the new physics has opened up deep cosmological questions which have created a new attitude to the universe as a whole. This new questioning attitude means:

INVESTIGATING GOD ACTUALLY HELPS US INVESTIGATE THE UNIVERSE.

SCIENCE HELPS THEOLOGY in terms of its method: scientific and theological method should be similar, even if their areas of concern are distinct.

SCIENCE GIVES US A LARGER UNDERSTANDING of the universe in which God is involved. Torrance maintains that the truth shines through 'transparencies' or 'disclosure-models': truths about the universe which both religion and science share. Reality discloses itself to both theology and science in such a way as to lead to a deeper understanding of the inner relations of the universe.

BOTH THEOLOGY AND SCIENCE are built on human experience.

BOTH THEOLOGY AND SCIENCE are motivated by belief.

Torrance believes that Einsteinian physics is an 'astonishing revelation of the rational structures that pervade and underlie all created reality'. Physics, like theology, draws people towards thinking about being, reality and, ultimately, God.

If Torrance is correct, science and religion are not rivals but twins. It may be that we are moving away from nineteenth-century attitudes of conflict between science and religion, towards the discovery that science actually enhances religion.

Miracles in a Scientific World

The Argument with Hume

The word 'miracle' is quite commonly used:

* I got up at six this morning – for a miracle.

* A baby at her age? It's a miracle.

* It's a miracle what engineering can do these days.

* The cancer just vanished; it was a miracle.

* She was dead for twenty-four hours and then she came back to life. It was a miracle.

* His dog started to recite Shakespeare on the bus. It was a miracle.

In the modern scientific world there is one great flashpoint of conflict with religious faith. That is the belief in the occurrence of miracles. The miraculous, taken for granted for so many centuries, now appears discredited in the light of increased human knowledge. Miracles, like belief that the earth is flat, or the sun goes round the earth, now seem a thing of the past to many people. But are they? And what exactly is a miracle?

The notion of 'miracle' is open to many interpretations. Many people still believe in miracles; many theologians still wrestle with trying to decide what a miracle actually is. The Roman Catholic Church, which continues to canonize saints, can only do so if two miracles are ascribed to that particular person. Belief in miracles is alive and well even if miracles themselves are not.

Whatever a miracle is, it is clearly a marvellous event which is unexpected and causes wonder. Miracles in the Bible were recorded to provoke wonder at God's power and goodness. Many people claim to find miracles in nature or science, but these are not true miracles in the traditionally understood sense.

Miracles have been understood in different ways:

AS RESULTING FROM A LACK OF SCIENTIFIC KNOWLEDGE. Miracles are put down to a 'God of the gaps'. In other words, people with deficient scientific understanding give God the credit for a miracle which can later be explained as 'natural' by science. As science advances, so God retreats. Scholars who hold this view believe there are no real miracles, just interpretations of events which can be better explained by scientific rationality.

AS COINCIDENCES. If you find you have no money at the railway station, pray, and suddenly bump into a friend who gives you what you need, that is a coincidence. Some religious people might say this was a miracle. A miracle can take place when two 'natural' events 'collide' and have some religious significance for the person who experiences them.

AS VIOLATIONS OF NATURAL LAWS. This interpretation of a miracle is closer to that traditionally understood by Christianity and other religions. A miracle is a supernatural event, an extraordinary happening which appears to defeat the normal course of nature. In the Bible, Jesus walked on water and raised the dead. Such miracles appear to contradict our modern, scientific understanding of the world.

Theologians who believe in miracles claim that there are certain things which miracles are, and certain things which they are not.

Miracles do not result from a 'God of the gaps' understanding of the world but are events which have to be understood seriously on their own terms. And miracles are not magic. Floating in the air or walking on water may appear to contravene the laws of nature in a miraculous way, but they are not necessarily miracles as understood theologically.

Rather, miracles have a double nature. They are events of power, but they must also have a religious significance. In other words, miracles exist to show something of the nature and power of God at work in the world. They are not primarily concerned with a violation of our reality, but with pointing beyond to that greater reality which is God. This is especially true in the gospel of John where the word used for miracles means 'signs'. Miracles are signs of power. They are extraordinary events caused by God, which have a religious significance. Paul Tillich (1886-1965), a famous theologian, defined a miracle in this way:

> A genuine miracle is first of all an event which is astonishing, unusual, shaking, without contradicting the rational structure of reality. In the second place it is an event which points to the mystery of being, expressing its relation to us in a definite way.

Miracles and the Bible

At the heart of the Bible's understanding of God are the supreme beliefs that he is the Creator, who made humankind, and the Redeemer, who has acted to save humankind.

The Old Testament and the New are each built on a mighty miracle. The Old Testament claims that God rescued his people from slavery and brought them out miraculously from Egypt to allow their escape. The New Testament claims that the greatest miracle is that God became human in Jesus. By dying and rising, Jesus opened up a new way to God and a new life with God. Such beliefs about the nature of God, and the acceptance of these two miracles of God, provide the theological framework in which to examine the other miracles recorded in the Bible.

But are the miracles in the Bible historically true? Or are they to be understood differently – as events which arouse wonder, but which can now be understood as natural happenings? Are the miracle stories a literary form expressing traditions which contain the experiences of a particular religious community?

The Old Testament contains many marvellous occurrences such as the ten plagues of Egypt, the burning bush, the collapse of the walls of Jericho and Elijah's fiery chariot taking him up to heaven.

Jesus' miracles in the gospels provide a scheme and a meaning for understanding the nature of miracle in the Bible. Altogether in the four gospels there are about thirty-five occasions on which Jesus performs a miracle. These miracles fall roughly into four groups:

* Jesus heals the sick.

* He raises people from the dead.

* He casts out demons.

* He shows his power over nature.

Jesus' miracles have been understood in a variety of ways. Here is one miracle, set alongside some current interpretations of it:

One day Jesus said to his disciples, 'Let's go over to the other side of the lake'. So they got into a boat and set out. As they sailed, he fell asleep. A squall came down on the lake, so that the boat was being swamped, and they were in great danger. The disciples went and woke him, saying, 'Master, Master, we're going to drown!' He got up and rebuked the wind and the raging waters; the storm subsided, and all was calm. 'Where is your faith?' he asked the disciples. In fear and amazement they asked one another, 'Who is this? He commands even the winds and the water, and they obey him.'

The gospel-writers included the miracles of Jesus for a reason. Miracles did not merely show Jesus as a marvellous person; they revealed something of his power and nature. They revealed God and they revealed what Jesus had come to preach – the kingdom of God, the rule of God in people's lives. The miracle of Jesus calming the storm shows some central truths about him:

JESUS WAS POWERFUL; the storm calmed when he ordered it to.

HE WAS MYSTERIOUS, and had unusual powers. His disciples were amazed and afraid at him. They already knew that he was a teacher and prophet, but this miracle showed that he was more than that.

HE RESPONDED TO PEOPLE'S REQUESTS; he calmed the storm because his disciples asked him to. It was not his idea.

JESUS HAD FAITH, he had no doubt that the storm would calm down when he ordered it to. And this was the same faith he wanted his disciples to have.

Some scholars believe that these are the reasons why this miracle story has been included in the gospel narrative. The miracle is a legend about Jesus, but it contains religious truth about Jesus' person and mission. In other words, the miracle is not historically true, but it contains an existential truth.

Other scholars believe that the miracle story happened as recorded in the Bible, as the gospel-writers are reliable witnesses. Others that the miracle is merely a legend which has grown up around the historical Jesus. Others still that the miracle is allegorical or figurative, a story with a deeper meaning.

On this last understanding, we draw on the fact that the gospels were written after the death and resurrection of Jesus at a time when the early church was undergoing great persecution, and interpret the miracle of Jesus calming the storm in a way that fits that situation. The stormy sea is not a real sea; it is a picture of the troubles the early church is undergoing. The boat is a symbol of the early church, and the disciples are Christians crying out for Jesus to save them. The boat is filling with water because even in times of hardship and trouble Jesus hears the cries of his followers and comes to save them.

The true miracle then is the miracle of faith, which recognizes Jesus as saviour and redeemer and calls on him for help.

Miracles and science

The 'non-miraculous' readings of the miracle stories result from Christianity coming to terms with the modern scientific understanding of the world. For many centuries the miracle accounts in the Bible were accepted unquestioningly. People believed that the world was sustained by God and that God could tamper with the natural order when he so desired.

The scientific revolution of the seventeenth century changed all that. With the work of Isaac Newton (1642-1727) dawned the understanding that the universe was governed by uniform laws which could not be challenged. Rationality dethroned credulity. In the eighteenth century (the 'Age of Reason') Deism became a popular doctrine: the belief that God had set the universe in motion as a perfectly constructed machine and then withdrawn. People still believed in God as Creator, but they found it more and more difficult to believe that he interferes in events in the world.

The most decisive rebuff to belief in miracles came from David Hume (1711-76) in his *Enquiry Concerning Human Understanding*. Hume devoted a

whole section of his work to miracles. He declared that 'a wise man...
proportions his belief to the evidence'. With his customary force and
scepticism, Hume proceeded to show that miracles were, more or less, a
logical impossibility both humanly speaking and scientifically speaking:

> A miracle is a violation of the laws of nature; and as firm and
> unalterable experience has established these laws, the proof against a
> miracle from the very nature of the fact, is as entire as any argument
> from experience can possibly be imagined.

As unalterable laws govern the world, Hume stated that miracles were
simply impossible. An event such as the sun stopping, which is recorded in
the Book of Joshua in the Old Testament must therefore be legendary and
fabulous. Hume then turned his attention to those who claim to have
experienced miracles:

> No testimony is sufficient to establish a miracle, unless the testimony
> be of such a kind, that its falsehood would be more miraculous than
> the fact which it endeavours to establish, and even in that case there is
> a mutual destruction of arguments, and the superior only gives us an
> assurance suitable to that degree of force, which remains after
> deducting the inferior.

As miracles are scientifically impossible, Hume maintains that it is therefore
impossible to believe anyone who has claimed to have witnessed a miracle.
He goes on to make four further points:

'THERE IS NOT TO BE FOUND, in all history, any miracle attested by a
sufficient number of men, of such unquestioned good sense, education
and learning, as to secure us against all delusion in themselves.' In other
words, people who believe in miracles are superstitious not scientific.

'IF THE SPIRIT OF RELIGION join itself to the lore of wonder, there is an end
of common sense; and human testimony, in these circumstances, loses all
pretensions to authority.' In other words, people believe in miracles
because they want to believe in miracles.

'IT FORMS A STRONG PRESUMPTION against all supernatural and miraculous
relations that they are observed chiefly to abound among ignorant and
barbarous nations.' In other words, belief in miracles results from
ignorance about how the world actually works.

'IT IS IMPOSSIBLE that the religions of ancient Rome, of Turkey, of Siam, and of China should, all of them, be established on any solid foundation. Every miracle, therefore, pretended to have been wrought in any of these religions... has the same force, though more indirectly, to overthrow every other system. In destroying a rival system, it likewise destroys the credit of those miracles, on which that system was established.' In other words, all gods cannot be the true God, therefore there are no miracles and they are just religious propaganda.

Hume is still quoted with force and his arguments have to be reckoned with. Just because a miracle is unlikely, however, does not make it necessarily impossible. And is well-attested testimony really to be so easily discredited? Hume's objections are strong, but they are not watertight.

The meaning of miracles

The meaning of miracles is not in doubt: they are events or marvellous occurrences which bring an awareness of God with them. And they always involve faith. There must always be room for the individual to respond, and, for that important reason, there must always be an element of doubt concerning miracles. God does not demand slavish obedience through remarkable demonstrations of power; rather he demands love and faith from those who believe in him.

In the New Testament Jesus is tempted to reveal his naked power so that people will be forced into believing in him. But he resists this option, and instead spends a great deal of time asking people to be quiet about the miraculous things he has done for them. This is because Jesus (and the gospel-writers) do not want to stress the miraculous; they want to stress faith. John Hick, in his book Philosophy of Religion, writes:

If a miracle is defined as a breach of natural law, one can declare *a priori* that there are no miracles. It does not follow, however, that there are no miracles in the religious sense of the term. For the principle that nothing happens in conflict with natural law does not entail that there are no unusual and striking events evoking and mediating a vivid awareness of God.

What about the fact of miracles? We now know that laws govern the universe, though we also know that there are aspects of reality which cannot be conclusively proved, but are only statistically probable. Bias can work both ways. Just as religious believers can be too predisposed towards believing in miracles, so scientists can be too predisposed towards disbelieving in them. If a purely superstitious understanding of the universe is inadequate, so is a purely mechanical scientific outlook. Neither is fully human. Francis Bacon (1561-1626) wrote in his *Novum Organum*:

> The human understanding is of its own nature prone to suppose the existence of more order and regularity in the world than it finds. And though there be many things which are singular and unmatched, yet it devises for them parallels and conjugates and relatives which do not exist. Hence the fiction that all celestial bodies move in perfect circles.

Bacon's words have a curiously modern ring as scientists have come to realize that, to some extent, the universe appears as it does to us because we perceive it that way. Many people still claim to have witnessed or experienced miracles. We interpret their accounts according to our previous understanding of the world. Yet it is futile to set religion against science in a tit-for-tat fashion. A miracle is, by definition, an exception, pointing beyond what we understand as reality to something greater. Maurice Wiles writes in *God's Action in the World*:

> The only way in which God can be known is in and through our experience of him; it is a way that has more in common with the acquisition of knowledge through personal love or poetic insight than with the way in which scientific knowledge of the world is established. The knowledge thus obtained cannot be extrapolated from its given relation to human experience and human existence, and then expressed in a form that would enable us to speak of God's relation to the inanimate order of creation as such.

Whatever we believe about the fact of miracles, they stand as events which challenge our day to day beliefs. Because of this, perhaps, miracles should be used to help us turn once again to the larger questions of human existence and reality.

PART

12

The Nature of
Meaning

SCEPTICISM AND PLURALISM

The Enlightenment
Immanuel Kant

What do you think makes a great teacher? Here is what one eighteenth-century pupil, Johann Herder, said of his teacher of philosophy:

> I have had the good fortune to know a philosopher... In his prime he had the happy sprightliness of a youth; he continued to have it, I believe, even as a very old man. His broad forehead, built for thinking, was the seat of an imperturbable cheerfulness and joy. Speech, the richest in thought, flowed from his lips. Playfulness, wit, and humour were at his command... he was indifferent to nothing worth knowing... He incited and gently forced others to think for themselves... This man, whom I name with the greatest gratitude and respect, was Immanuel Kant.

Immanuel Kant was a philosopher of the Enlightenment. This was an intellectual movement in the eighteenth century which generally applied the methods of the new sciences, pioneered by Newton, to other philosophical and intellectual areas of thought. Often, though not always, the Enlightenment was free-thinking and anti-religious. In some places, notably France, thinkers risked suffering and imprisonment for their ideas.

A man with greatness of mind

Kant (1724-1804) was born in Königsberg in Prussia. His father was a saddler. He received a good education and eventually went to Königsberg

University where he became an unsalaried lecturer in 1755. In 1770 he was elected Professor of Logic and Metaphysics. He remained there until three years before he died.

Without exception all commentaries on Kant's life portray his existence as extremely regular and uneventful. He was an orderly man, given to extreme punctuality so that the local people would set their time by his daily walk through the town. He travelled very little, never married but liked the company of women. He had many friends, and was admired and respected by all who knew him. Yet the overwhelming consensus is that Immanuel Kant was a rarity, a man with true greatness of mind. He was a thinker.

It was said of him by A.M. Quinton that 'he came as near as anyone ever has to combining in himself the speculative originality of Plato with the encyclopedic thoroughness of Aristotle'.

In 1784, Kant wrote an article in a magazine asking the question: What is enlightenment? His answer was that enlightenment consists of 'man's emergence from his self-incurred immaturity'. Men and women had relied childishly on external authorities, preferring them to their own understanding. The motto of the Enlightenment was therefore, 'Dare to know!' 'Dare to use your own understanding.' In context this applies especially to religion. The destiny of human nature lies in progress, not in past beliefs. The world is coming of age. Reason is coming centre-stage.

In 1781 Kant published his *Critique of Pure Reason* in which he set out an enlightened approach to human knowledge. He aimed to reappraise:

* Metaphysics: what can I know about the world?

* Religion: what may I hope?

* Ethics: what should I do?

* Anthropology: what is humankind?

Kant's major writings were:

* *Critique of Pure Reason* (1781).

* *Prolegomena to any future metaphysics that will be able to present itself as a science* (1783).

* *Groundwork of the Metaphysic of Morals* (1785).

* *Critique of Practical Reason* (1788).

* *Critique of Judgment* (1790).

It is important to grasp the intellectual climate of philosophical thinking in Kant's time if one is to understand Kant's thought. His work on the theory of knowledge was produced at a time when there was tension between the continental approach, which emphasized rational thought, and the British school, which emphasized sense experience as the foundation of knowledge.

Kant opposed the two extreme positions that all knowledge arises out of experience, and that there is knowledge which is absolutely independent of experience. In contrast he believed that all knowledge is related to experience, but that it cannot all be reduced to what we experience.

Kant steered a middle course between empiricism and rationalism. He called this 'transcendental idealism'.

Kant and Metaphysics

Kant described transcendental idealism as the belief that we have knowledge only of 'appearances' and not of 'things as they are in themselves'. Kant is not always clear on what he means by this. Sometimes he writes as though appearances are 'appearances of' some sort of reality which is hidden from us. Elsewhere he writes as though appearances were independent entities which we observe and discover.

We can assume that Kant believed that appearances are known through experience, but 'things in themselves' are not knowable at all, since nothing is knowable by thought alone without us experiencing it.

Kant's theory can be summarized:

* Empirical objects are real.

* We cannot perceive a transcendental object because it does not belong to the world of space, time and causality.

* Empirical objects are 'whatever objects are discovered or postulated through experience'.

Kant's aim is to show that we cannot know the 'world as it is', meaning the world conceived apart from the way it appears to us. Although Kant did not think the noumena was accessible to us, because of the effects of space and time through which we see everything, he did not rule out the possibility that our senses did in fact picture reality as it is in itself. The only thing he ruled out was certainty on our part that we can picture reality accurately. It is important to understand that, for Kant, *phenomena* are things as we experience them, *noumena* are things in themselves independent of the way they are experienced.

Kant and Practical Reason

Kant's famous work *Critique of Practical Reason* revives discussion of ancient ideas. In it he contrasts the distinction between theoretical and practical knowledge. According to Kant, everyone who is rational sees the distinction between knowing the truth and knowing what to do about it.

Practical reasons concern either ends or means. If I have an end in view then I think over the means to achieve it. Some philosophers argue that all reasoning involves means and that reason is 'a slave of the passions'; it is only feeling and passion that motivate us to act.

The crucial question is: Can we know what to do objectively, or do we have to rely on our subjective inclination to guide us?

This is the enormous problem that Immanuel Kant tackled in his thinking. And in answering it he produced a complex metaphysical and abstract basis for common morality. In this chapter we can scarcely begin to touch the breadth of his ideas, but we will try to give you a beginner's guide to some of the most important ones.

Kant's religious and moral ideas

Kant considered philosophy to have priority over theology. He insisted that religion must be within the limits of reason alone and that we must use human reason to interpret Christian doctrines.

Among his most important areas of thought were:

* The existence of God could be postulated based on practical reasoning.

* His insistence on immortality.

* The issue of human freedom and morality.

In his thinking on the existence of God, Kant criticized the ontological argument at length (see Chapter 7). Although he was a rationalist, he stressed the importance of a philosophy that embraced both feeling and faith. He wrote:

> It is absolutely necessary to be convinced of God's existence; it is not equally necessary to demonstrate it.
>
> It is a good thing that we do not know, but believe, that there is a God.

For Kant, rational proofs of God are not possible because they are dependent on inference. God is not in space and time, and therefore he cannot be proved from our space-time experience. He argues against 'proofs' for the existence of God on the grounds that it does not follow that to think about God implies the reality of God; that human reason is limited to the world of appearance; and that it is impossible to substantiate a belief in a universal principle of causality.

When Kant argues that the proofs of God's existence do not succeed, it does not mean he destroys the belief in God itself.

Central to Kant's thinking was that God was a wholly rational being who was not affected by anything other than reason, so we should strive to be wholly rational to be like God. Similarly, our understanding of religious faith should be dominated by reason – religion should be confined 'within the limits of reason alone'. He argued that humankind has a specific, metaphysical need, naturally rooted in human nature. Because we cannot be satisfied by our knowledge of experience, we look for a unity in that which is relative; absolute, pure concepts which Kant, like Plato, calls ideas.

Although Kant is most famous for his work in the theory of knowledge and in metaphysics, he himself believed that ethics was the most important subject in philosophy. After having shown the uselessness of trying to prove God's existence through the use of 'pure reason', he used ethical arguments to establish the existence of God. He argued that moral thinking requires that a person is rewarded according to their goodness or virtue. But in our everyday lives, 'good' or virtuous people are often not as happy or as successful as others. He therefore said that there must be another existence where those who practise virtue or vice receive their just deserts, and this led Kant to the conclusion that the existence of God and immortality are 'postulates of practical reason'. Note carefully that Kant did not think God's existence could be proved, but he did consider that God was a necessary postulate for there to be morality.

Kant's view that the world of ideas or pure reason is not accessible to rational enquiry dealt a blow to traditional theology. Theology dealt with such issues as proofs for the existence of God and examination of God's nature. Kant did not say such things are non-existent, rather he could not see how we can talk about them since they are beyond our ability to perceive. God cannot be proved by 'pure reason', but it is possible to believe in him on the basis of faith. The option for Christians was now to discover God for themselves, through their own choices and their own practical reasoning. The authority for faith is not outside the believer, in the Bible or in revelation, but inside.

We human beings are thus the final authority in judging faith. Contrast this with Martin Luther when he said: 'One does not stand over the Bible and judge it, but below the Bible, to hear and obey it.' Kant's proposal is for us to stand over the Bible and judge it ourselves. On this view it is we who decide to give the Bible its authority over us. Humanity is indeed come of age.

Human freedom and morality

The starting-point of Kant's ethics is the concept of freedom. His famous phrase 'ought implies can' means that because all human beings ought to seek the summum bonum in which virtue and happiness coincide, this must therefore be possible, and so there must be a life after death in which it can be achieved. Obviously, this can be challenged.

For Kant, freedom is the ability to be governed by reason. This ability Kant called 'the autonomy of the will'. He contrasted it with actions which spring from emotion, desire or preference.

If you were asked the question: 'What is the difference between a person who acts morally and one who does not?', what would you say?

Kant believed in the importance of this sort of question. In asking it, he referred to two types of action:

* Acts done from 'inclination'.

* Acts done from a 'sense of duty'.

If I act out of inclination, then I act out of taste or preference. I could watch TV tonight or go out to the pub. It is up to me to decide what I am inclined to do. On the other hand, if I have promised my teacher that my homework will be done by tomorrow then I ought to stay in and do the work. My inclination may be one thing, but my obligation is to do something else.

'Inclination' is to be distinguished from 'obligation'. An obligation is what I ought to do despite my inclination.

Kant strongly rejected a morality which stressed acting on inclination alone. In his view, morality is closely tied up with one's duties and obligations, and depends on being a free agent not compelled to do something.

So, for example, people who drive according to the speed limit merely because they want to, or because they are afraid of being caught, are not moral people. It is only when people recognize that they ought to keep the law because there is a moral obligation to do so that they are genuinely moral.

Kant's moral thinking opposes Utilitarianism (see Chapter 27); he stressed that morality is found in the motive of the act. If people just happen to keep their promises, or feel it is to their advantage to pay an outstanding debt through fear of reprisal, they are not moral. The acts are only moral if the person concerned understands it is his or her duty to do these things. The person of 'good will' acts from a sense of duty:

> Nothing can possibly be conceived in the world, or even out of it, which can be called good without qualification, except a good will.

Human beings ought, therefore, to strive to develop 'good wills' so that they act in accordance with the dictates of reason – if they do this they will act morally.

Kant said that we think of ourselves both as empirical beings, bound by the laws of causality, and as transcendental beings, obedient to the dictates of reason alone. Reason tells you that the world is a 'field of action' in which your will is free to choose. Only from a position of freedom can you deliberate or choose at all. From this perspective you arrive at the considerations which will govern your action.

The rational person, then, is free to choose. But for the purposes of morality the practical knowledge needed cannot be expressed in scientific terms. Rather than scientific 'causes' and 'mechanisms', morality is better described in terms of reasons, rational ends and imperatives. For Kant, morality is objectively valid – accepted in the same sort of way as the laws of science. The transcendental nature of humankind generates imperatives which bind everyone unconditionally. An evil person cannot escape the force of reason any more than the good person; it is universally demanding.

Kant has shown the difference between behaving morally and not behaving morally, and the morality is based on reason, but he still has not answered the question of how a person determines what their duty is in different situations. In answer to this sort of question Kant invented the phrase, 'the categorical imperative'. Among the several ways he has of expressing this, the following are important:

'THERE IS THEREFORE BUT ONE CATEGORICAL IMPERATIVE, namely this: act only on that maxim whereby thou canst at the same time will that it should become a universal law.' Kant means that each of your actions must be judged in the light of what would happen if everybody did what you were doing. This is the reason why lying, although it may serve a practical purpose, cannot be accepted as moral under any circumstances. For if lying were to be a universal law which everyone conformed to, living together in a human community would be impossible.

'SO ACT AS TO TREAT HUMANITY... IN EVERY CASE AS AN END WITHAL, never as a means only.' This is another way of saying 'do unto others as you would have them do to you'. We should treat other people as ends in themselves, not just as instruments of achieving what we want. Kant is not saying that each individual's interest should be accepted or given in to. He is saying that in any sort of confrontation between people, each one must be counted as being of equal value. Kant, in the categorical imperative, was trying to provide the fundamental principle of morality which would enable human beings – using reason – to settle moral disputes.

Criticisms of Kant

Some have believed that Kant's principle that 'ought implies can' may be challenged. If there is no God and no immortality, morality may just be a human construct which helps people to live together.

Others have held that Kant's ethical thinking does not help when there is a conflict of duty. For example, duty says you should pay your taxes, but if you believe that a given tax disadvantages the poor or that it offends human justice, you have a conflict of duty – one to the law and one to humanity. There may therefore be circumstances where we feel morally obliged to disobey duty.

Kant's influence on philosophy has been enormous. He has rejected any attempt to claim an absolute form of knowledge which seeks to be independent of experience, and his stress on the primacy of reason has had a great effect on Western philosophy.. He believed that, although the world that we know is not merely the product of our own individual perspective, nevertheless it cannot be known except from our own point of view. Experience limits us, and if we try to ascend to 'transcendental knowledge', we are doomed to failure, for we can never be certain that such knowledge can be ours.

Do you agree with him?

Language 25 Games
Ludwig Wittgenstein

Have you ever dreamed that you were born to rich parents or that you'd won the national lottery? The thought has probably crossed the minds of most people at some time or other along with a plethora of imaginative possibilities about how the money could be spent. But would you ever contemplate giving it *all* away? The philosopher considered in this unit, Ludwig Wittgenstein, was born in 1889 to one of the richest families in Austria. He gave his inherited millions away to live the austere life of an archetypal genius.

Not only did he live a strange life; he also produced *two* contrasting philosophies which showed him to be a thinker almost without precedent. He is a difficult writer to understand. This is partly due to the intentionally enigmatic way he presented his ideas – he often refused to 'dirty' their purity with supporting arguments. It is also due to his very particular way of discussing issues in philosophy.

His early philosophy had an intensely structured, yet minimalist, style which leaves the reader aghast at its daring and originality but with many pregnant questions unanswered. In complete contrast his later philosophy is presented in an *apparently* piecemeal, disordered fashion, which seems over-burdened with words. Yet his second philosophy is as highly structured as the first. When reading Wittgenstein's philosophies, however, one is often left with a distinct feeling of confusion over what philosophical point he is making, and why such intense intellectual effort should be spent on what may appear to be trifling issues.

Arguments over the interpretation and significance of his two philosophies still rage today as, in totally opposite ways, his writings almost dare the reader to attempt an understanding of them. Despite this his thought has had an immense impact on the way twentieth-century philosophy has developed.

The life of an archetypal genius

The Wittgenstein family were the Austrian equivalent of the Rothschilds. They wielded immense industrial power in Europe and played a leading role in Viennese cultural life. As Wittgenstein grew up the composers Brahms and Mahler were frequent visitors to the family home.

Ludwig was the youngest of eight children and was considered unacademic. After he constructed his own working model of a sewing machine when he was ten, his father decided that he was to be the useful member of the family and destined for a career in engineering. At fourteen years old Ludwig was sent to study mathematics and science at an unacademic school in Linz. It is one of the interesting footnotes of history that Wittgenstein, one of the greatest and most original minds of the twentieth century, attended the school at the same time as one of its most malevolent geniuses, Adolf Hitler.

For a time Wittgenstein studied at a technical college in Berlin because he had failed to meet the academic requirements of Vienna University. In 1908 he went to Manchester University in England to study aeronautical engineering. During research into aircraft propellers Wittgenstein became absorbed in problems involving the very foundations of mathematics. His mind, driven by an intense, passionate and domineering personality, focused in a way that it hadn't perhaps done before. As a result of his interest Wittgenstein was advised by Frege, one of the leading mathematicians and logicians of the day, to study logic with Bertrand Russell, arguably the greatest living philosopher of that time, at Cambridge University.

While studying at Cambridge he attacked Russell's own research into the theory of knowledge so severely that Russell abandoned it. Wittgenstein then left the university without finishing his degree. He went to Norway, where he had decided to live in a hut on the side of a remote fiord for two years so that he could think without distractions or having to be distracted by lesser mortals.

Because all but one of his brothers committed suicide, in 1913 Wittgenstein inherited an immense fortune which he proceeded to give away to various poets and artists, until the family solicitors managed to rescue much of it by transferring it to one of his sisters.

During the First World War he rejected a commission in the Austrian army and became a volunteer gunner. He was very fortunate to survive the misery and slaughter of the Russian front. During some of the heaviest fighting of the war he volunteered to be placed in an observation post situated between the opposing front lines, and throughout his life he was plagued by thoughts of suicide. He struggled to come to terms with his own sexuality – like most of his brothers, he was homosexual – and in order to quell these thoughts of suicide his life became ever more driven by immense intensity and narrow focus.

During the war Wittgenstein had a mystical experience as a result of reading a book by Tolstoy on Jesus. An air of mysticism which leaves open the possibility of some kind of metaphysical reality pervades his writings. It was during the war that his concern for finding the foundations for all thought drove him to write his first book, the *Tractatus Logico-Philosophicus*.

Tractatus Logico-Philosophicus

The development of Wittgenstein's first philosophy was deeply influenced by the phenomenology of Edmund Husserl (1859-1938) and the logical genius of Gottlob Frege (1848-1925). With Husserl and Frege, the focus of philosophy began to shift away from a study of epistemology and the problem of how knowledge is to be given secure foundations, to a study of the more basic problem of how knowledge is attained and given meaning in the first place.

Like the philosophy of Husserl and Frege, Wittgenstein's Tractarian philosophy has an overwhelmingly tight focus on issues of meaning. It is not an *a priori* denial of the possibility of metaphysics, the problem that epistemology had traditionally found itself unable to ignore. Rather, it represents a limitation of the possibility of our *speaking* of metaphysics and a narrowing down of what kind of ontological claims – about the nature of being – can be made, to austere levels. Wittgenstein was concerned to reveal the bankruptcy of philosophical, metaphysical and ethical discussion. Such discussion, he claimed, is fooled by the illogical, untidy and complicated nature of the very language it uses. Metaphysicians like to think that language gives them a greater grasp on reality than is in fact logically and empirically possible.

Within the *Tractatus* Wittgenstein is trying to show how simple the essential nature of the world must be for a purely logical language to be able to refer to and represent reality in a meaningful way. Wittgenstein regarded the limits of language as providing the limits of thought itself. The *Tractatus* attempts to strip language of all that is inessential or veneer in order to show that it *is* possible to represent the world in its most basic and minimalist – and therefore purest – form to ourselves, by the symbolic use of an imagined perfect language.

Wittgenstein's first statement in the *Tractatus* states his belief in a metaphysical reality through his assertion that the world consists entirely of simple facts, which are not dependent on each other, and which constitute the ultimate subject-matter of empirical science.

He argued that these 'facts' could be pictured in language by mirroring the spatial relationship of objects (as they truly are) in our minds by means of the words which are used to refer to those objects. Thus, language has a structural similarity to that which it describes in reality.

Just as a sketch of a room drawn on a piece of paper can be used to represent and mirror the layout of the furniture within it, so language acts to mirror the facts that exist in reality to our minds.

Much of the *Tractatus* is concerned to support this argument by attacking and revealing the many occasions when language with its many rules and conventions is used in idiomatic ways. In England beds do not have real feet, but everyone understands the phrase 'at the foot of the bed', and no one expects to see more than one garment when 'my new trousers' are displayed, though a plural verb is always used. Wittgenstein is intent on stripping away the often illogical rules of grammar which are not a necessity, to reveal the underlying logical form of language so that we can see reality as it really is.

At the end of the *Tractatus*, with impecable logic and consistency, and perhaps with perverse enjoyment, Wittgenstein tells the reader who has truly understood him to acknowledge that the model of language and 'facts' he has presented has little relevance to everyday living. Rather, those things which are fundamentally important – morality and the good, aesthetics and the beautiful, theology and the nature of reality – may be shown and experienced but cannot accurately be spoken of.

On his own reckoning Wittgenstein's philosophy should be understood as 'useful nonsense'. It acts as a ladder one climbs in order to see things as they really are. But in becoming aware of things as they really are, one must admit that the ladder, which occasioned that new understanding, must now itself be thrown away. The pictorial relationship of words to the simple underlying 'facts' of reality 'shows' itself, and what shows itself cannot be said. In other words, philosophy, which concerns itself with all these matters of fundamental importance, is trying to achieve the impossible by describing the indescribable in words.

Perhaps the most helpful way of grasping what Wittgenstein is trying to show in the *Tractatus* comes from a consideration of the problems caused when we try to explain how language is used to refer to colour. In teaching someone what the colour 'red' is, holding up a card with the word 'red' coloured in a shade of red and pointing at it doesn't actually make the connection between the word and the colour a necessity. The demonstration might refer to a shape, a surface or even a locality. You can never reach a point where the connection between the word and the colour is inevitable. 'Redness' cannot be explained; it can only be shown. Once the connection has been made, language has the ability to picture 'redness'. But anyone who has not experienced 'redness' cannot understand the words used, and the connection must be made afresh for each new experience of 'redness'.

Such a view of language and reality is exemplified by Barnett Newman's painting *Vir Heroicus Sublimis*. In this painting a very wide canvas is painted a brilliant red, with five vertical stripes which range in colour from cream and white to shades of pink and crimson. The painting, which is to be viewed at close range, overwhelms the viewer as the sense of 'redness' creates an hallucinatory effect which seems to engulf the viewer and his senses in the experience of 'redness' itself. Thus, the reality of 'redness' is shown in the immediacy of present experience, as reality shows itself to our consciousness.

This may sound rather far removed from our ordinary experience of life, but the consequences of Wittgenstein's thought are startlingly relevant. The realization that 'facts' can only be shown and must define their relationships to us afresh in each succeeding present moment means that there is no such thing as the human subject to think or entertain ideas. Rather as Wittgenstein states in *Tractatus* proposition 5.641:

The philosophical self is not the human being, not the human body, or the human soul, with which psychology deals, but rather the metaphysical subject, the limit of the world – not a part of it.

The very act of thinking becomes another 'fact' in existence within reality. This thinking fact carries with it the *illusion* of consciousness, as part of the characteristic of what it means to be a human being as a 'fact' within reality. The fact of 'human being' marks its own space in reality over and against the many other facts that exist in the world.

Wittgenstein's philosophy challenges and replaces the whole Cartesian way of thinking with its belief in the autonomy and sovereignty of the thinking and rational human subject which dominated philosophy at the time Wittgenstein wrote the *Tractatus*.

As a result of this, his first philosophical career, Wittgenstein was convinced that philosophizing had been reduced to a meaningless and ultimately useless activity. For this reason he retired from it and took up gardening and then teaching in rural Austria.

Logical positivism

A group of philosophers called the Vienna Circle misconstrued the whole point of the *Tractatus* and read out of it a seminal support for their own developing philosophy.

This philosophy, which became known as logical positivism, was attracted to Wittgenstein's repudiation of metaphysics and philosophy. From Wittgenstein's continued reliance on the logical concept of tautologies (statements that are self-evidently true, such as for example, 'The car is red or it is not red') and relying on empiricism in order to show what a 'fact' was, the philosophers of the Vienna Circle argued that the meaning of any proposition lay in how it could be verified or checked. In the Wittgenstein sense, tautology embraces the dictionary definition but goes beyond it – it allows you to examine reality by putting two logical opposite propositions side by side. It is therefore obvious that one is 'true'.

Logical positivism maintained that for something to be meaningful it had to be either self-evident or else verifiable by observation. As a result, talk of ethics, values and metaphysics was meaningless. However, in struggling to back up its own founding proposition of what constituted a fact it struggled with the problem of being self-referentially incoherent – logical positivism was itself a value system, which therefore must also be open to question!

Yet for Wittgenstein's *Tractatus*, in complete contrast to the positivists, that which cannot be verified, but can only be shown or experienced, is of the most fundamental value. While Wittgenstein severely limits the ability of 'God-talk', metaphysics and ethics to lay hold of reality he regards them highly. They are not domesticated as nonsense. Rather, for Wittgenstein our relation to the 'facts' of reality is a highly mystical and open-ended experience. In discussion with the Vienna Circle Wittgenstein became convinced that his first philosophy had not solved and foreclosed on philosophy the way he had hoped.

In response to this realization he decided to take up philosophy again. In 1929 he returned to Cambridge University as a fellow of Trinity College – even though he still didn't possess a degree. During the next eighteen years he developed his second philosophy which, articulated in its most complete form in the *Philosophical Investigations* (published in 1953 after his death from cancer in 1951), attempted to kill off philosophy as a going concern once and for all.

Wittgenstein's later philosophy

In his later philosophy Wittgenstein rejected the use logical positivism had made of his first philosophy. While his second philosophy was expressed in an earlier version in the *Blue and Brown Books*, its most complete statement is found in the *Philosophical Investigations*. He spends much time implicitly showing how prior philosophy, including his own *Tractatus*, is in error. Arguably the new method also destroys all the traditional ways philosophy had been done in the past.

In his new approach Wittgenstein's former ideas of a purely logical language which underlies all other languages are abandoned along with the picture theory of language. The meaning of language is not to be located solely by reference to the object it represented any more.

Instead, the meaning of a word depends on its location in a sentence and the use to which that sentence is normally put. *A priori* conceptions of how the meaning of words is to be understood are rejected. This philosophy shifts away from an emphasis on language in a static and formal relationship to reality, to one in which the different ways language is used is related to people's actions.

Wittgenstein goes on to argue that there are various types of language used by human beings which have their own systems of logic, rules and grammar. These dictate the proper, accepted use and meaning of words within the particular 'language game' they form a part of. For instance, giving orders, making requests, providing advice, measuring things, asking, thanking and counting are all examples of different language games people play. With regard to measuring, he refers to the example of the 'metre'. Whereas in the *Tractatus* he could only show what a metre was by pointing to the original metre rule kept in Paris – correspondence between the 'fact' and the word – in the *Philosophical Investigations* he can explain that it exists as part of a language game human beings play which has practical and technical uses. Even the *Tractatus*' way of looking at reality with its picture theory of language forms a particular socio-linguistic language game.

Anything that fails to obey the 'rules' of a particular language game is part of another, but different, language game. Each language game contributes to a 'form of life' which is formed by the grouping together of various language games in which a way of thinking and being in the world is constructed for the human subject. In consequence the human subject's knowledge of reality is always interpreted in terms of the form or forms of life it inhabits and which it has learnt to understand and use from childhood onwards.

Though we exist within reality, with our understanding dependent on the dynamics of socio-linguistics, Wittgenstein challenges us to stop being bewitched by language, to stop letting language 'go on holiday'. He argues that we need to be careful to remind ourselves constantly of the limitations of a socially constructed language, and as a result of what limited claims can be made by it about reality. Any critique of philosophical problems is always internal to a particular language game; it is therefore difficult to escape the relative context of that culture and its way of approaching philosophical problems.

Although we may be tempted to discern through similarities and agreements between different language games proof of a meta-language or the emerging nature of reality, Wittgenstein cautions against doing so too readily. Language *may* correspond to reality. However, due to the complex nature of reality, language is complex too. In such a situation human judgments cannot escape being provisional and open to revision. The similarities that exist between different language games and their forms of life should be understood as 'family resemblances'. If the complex relationship between language and reality is kept in focus, Wittgenstein suggests that we will be able to escape from the philosophical puzzlement that often marks the human condition. As a result we may become free to get on with more useful pursuits. Indeed, his philosophy could be seen as a form of therapy for philosophers!

Much of the *Philosophical Investigations* is dedicated to using this new way of viewing language, in order to invite us to look afresh at what we think we know in order that new perspectives may be teased out. Conventional linear arguments are not used. Instead, he conducts a veritable assault on his chosen topic by the use of analogies, aphorisms and the suggestion of other possibilities for understanding.

Wittgenstein argues that the uses to which each human subject puts language is dependent on how language has been learned from the language games and the forms of life within which the particular human subject finds itself existing. This enables Wittgenstein to argue, through his 'private language argument' – despite endlessly controversial discussion over its interpretation ever since – for the inconsistency of the Cartesian idea of the autonomous human subject. For the human subject is never in control of language and incapable of creating its own private language; rather, its very mode of thought is dependent on the agreed use of language in the realm of shared public meanings.

Wittgenstein and philosophy today

Wittgenstein, although one of the greatest thinkers of the twentieth century, was a man of his time. In different ways the conclusions, if not the method, of Wittgenstein's and Heidegger's philosophy are similar. Both affirm a scepticism about our ability to secure knowledge of reality. Both arrive at what are, in effect, post-metaphysical philosophies of meaning.

While Wittgenstein has influenced analytical philosophy he has also been used and adapted by postmodernist thinkers as a support for poststructuralist conclusions which would affirm that we are unable to escape language (see Chapter 44). We cannot discern where language corresponds to reality because language stands apart from reality. But whether Wittgenstein intended to be understood in the way some postmodern thinkers like Jacques Derrida and Richard Rorty have interpreted him is an open question. This is especially so given Wittgenstein's admission in section 583 of the *Philosophical Investigations* that 'the surroundings' of language give it at least part of its currency.

In contrast Michael Polanyi, a philosopher of science, sets out in his seminal work *Personal Knowledge* another possibility for understanding the relationships between language, reality and the human subject. Polanyi's analysis of how we relate to the external reality we are part of argues that whatever has more depth of meaning and thus more attractive power to our minds, is more real. In the words of Polanyi from his article 'The Unaccountable Element in Science':

> This is in fact my definition of external reality; reality is something that attracts our attention by clues which harass and beguile our minds into getting ever closer to it, and that, since it owes this attractive power to its independent existence, can always manifest itself in still unexpected ways... If we have grasped a true and deep-seated aspect of reality, then its future manifestations will be unexpected confirmations of our present knowledge of it.

This represents a critical realist approach to language. It recognizes that we all know what we know from our own personal perspectives, and as human beings we are limited in our knowledge to our own experiences and descriptions of the external world. This means that reality is something other than the knower (hence 'realist'). It also affirms an ongoing open critical dialectic between the knower and the thing known (hence 'critical') so that our perceptions and descriptions may move towards a closer correlation with the way reality is. Such a listening to and indwelling of reality attempts to heal the split between facts and values which has dominated philosophy ever since Kant, without reducing human thought to pure subjectivism or religion to meaningless nonsense.

However, the debates between postmodernists and critical realists will continue to rage on. It is perhaps indicative of the subtlety and brilliance of Wittgenstein's later philosophy that both postmodernist and critical realist thinkers claim Wittgenstein as a friend and support. But in what tradition is Wittgenstein's philosophy?

Philosopher R. Fogelin has suggested that Wittgenstein's philosophy, in its desire to undermine philosophy as traditionally practiced and with its goal of eliminating it as a meaningful enterprise, is closest in spirit to that of ancient Greek Pyrrhonian scepticism. The complexity of his philosophy, and its openness to the possibility of the mystical, will continue to provide a rich and controversial resource for philosophers to mine. Indeed, for a philosopher who was intent on destroying the philosophical profession, it is ironic that a biography on Wittgenstein published in 1989 listed over 5,000 books and articles focusing on various aspects of his philosophy!

Pluralism
Religion is Relative

> Life is now a smorgasbord with an endless array of options. Whether
> a hobby, holiday, lifestyle, world-view or religion, there's something
> for everybody... Putting it simply, we have reached the stage in
> pluralization where choice is not just a state of affairs, it is a state of
> mind... Change becomes the very essence of life.

So wrote Os Guinness, in *The Gravedigger File* (1983). The 'pluralization' he
describes has been defined by Peter Berger as the process by which the
number of options in the private sphere of modern society rapidly
multiplies at all levels, especially at the level of world-views, faiths and
ideologies.

In a religiously plural society, rival truth-claims of different religions exist
side by side, all claiming to be true. This presents a problem in
understanding how the word 'religion' is used and understood in such a
society. If a 'religion' is just one of many on a shelf, something you can
choose if you want and leave if you don't, then it ceases to have any ultimate
truth-claim.

The committed Muslim cannot regard Islam as one among many
choosable religions. God has sent many messengers but Muhammad is the
final Messenger and the Qu'ran is far more than one of the many religious
books available to humanity. To regard Islam as one of many equal religions
is to deny its truth. Likewise, for the committed Christian God has spoken
and come to the world in Jesus Christ; he is God incarnate, unique in the
whole history of the world.

For religious believers such as these, to talk about religion is to discuss truth and ultimate reality. But since the eighteenth-century Enlightenment, ultimate realities have been in the domain of mathematics and experimental science. It is reason, and not religion, which provides a way to explore the ultimate. How then are we to understand the word 'religion' in a religiously plural society?

There are various possibilities open to us:

WE COULD LOOK AT A RELIGION FROM THE OUTSIDE as something cultural. We could 'observe' it, looking at it various rituals, beliefs and so on. This has been called 'the phenomenological approach' to Religious Education. It enables you to look at different world faiths and classify them. It has been the characteristic approach in the study of 'comparative religions'.

ANOTHER WAY OF LOOKING AT RELIGIONS is to see the way they function in society; again this approach looks from the outside. The religious beliefs and values, for instance, of those in power, or of development agencies in the third world, are considered, as well as the religious laws on which the whole of society is based.

A THIRD POSSIBILITY is to look at religious experience. On this model, all religions may be understood as different expressions of one common experience. Religious experience has a wide definition here. It can be belief in God or a mystical experience or a human awareness of the 'other'. All varieties of 'religion' or 'spirituality' are included under the same classification, that of experience.

All these approaches are being used in schools in England at the present time. They have one thing in common. All religions represent one stance among many. They are all different perspectives. All stances are open for examination, except the stance according to which one religion is absolutely true to the exclusion of the others.

A world with no orthodoxy

Sociologist Peter Berger has said that with respect to ultimate beliefs, pluralism rules. In his book *The Heretical Imperative* (1979), he argued that in modern Western culture we are all required to be heretics when it comes to religion. Heresy means making an individual decision about matters of faith, over and against the given tradition of church or society.

Berger claimed that in modern culture there is no accepted 'plausibility structure' for religion. A plausibility structure is a situation in society where it is easy to believe something because many people believe it to be true. Now we are required to choose against religion because it is not plausible. To be respectable you have to be a heretic, to make your own decisions about what to believe. There is now no such thing as orthodoxy in the old sense of the word, meaning to hold correct or currently accepted opinions on religious doctrine.

On this view, the principle of pluralism is overwhelmingly strong. The truth-claims of different world religions are not felt to need argument or resolution. They are simply different values held by different people. Lots of different truths exist side by side. The result is that religion becomes relativized. Truth is true if it's true for you. A different truth is true if it's true for me.

On this basis some religious educators have argued that in present Western culture it is impossible to have any religious education which is at its heart religious. To study the religion of Hinduism, say, or Islam in British classrooms today you have to look at them through relativized spectacles. The student, in effect, is looking at Allah or the eternal order of the Sanatanadharma as one of the possible ways of looking at things. The charge is that this annihilates the very thing being studied. Reason, autonomy and so called 'objectivity' consume the subject matter, in this case revelation.

As long ago as 1885 Pope Leo II warned: 'The equal toleration of all religions... is the same thing as atheism.'

Os Guinness (1983) put it more commercially:

Pluralization acts on Christian faith as a sort of nonstick coating. Christians and convictions were once inseparable. Pluralization, though, acts like a spiritual Teflon, sealing Christian truth with a slippery surface to which commitment will not adhere. The result is a general increase in shallowness, transience and heresy. Picking, choosing and selectiveness are the order of the day. Asked once about her beliefs, Marilyn Monroe replied, 'I just believe in everything – a little bit.'

Where does pluralism stop?

Where are the limits to pluralism? Are there some stances that cannot be tolerated? Can intolerance be tolerated? Leslie Newbiggin drew attention to the fact that even the most secular societies acknowledge some limits to pluralism. He pointed out that neither racism nor hedonism are offered as stances for living in English schools. The National Front can poll more than the Communist party, and the appeal to ethnic identity is powerful when society is undergoing rapid change. Yet British society has made the practice of racism in public affairs a criminal offence. He argues the same for hedonism: 'The view that whatever creates erotic stimulation is good and should be available to all is widely held and propagated in accepted organs of opinion. But there are serious doubts even in our secular society about whether total free trade in pornography would not be so corrupting as to destroy society... The fact is that we do not include these in the Syllabus because we know that it would be wrong to offer these as stances for living to children.'

Asad Muhammed was born in Poland in 1900 as the son of a lawyer and the grandson of a Rabbi. His name was Leopold Weiss before he converted to Islam in 1926. He worked as a journalist with his own special interest in the Arab world. In his book *The Road to Mecca* (1974), he sensitively interpreted Islamic culture and its appeal to someone brought up in a European culture. After the First World War he warned fellow Muslims of the effects of Western culture, based on secular materialistic values which are against those held by Islam.

Asad criticized Western intellectualism for its scepticism, not only with regard to Islam but to revealed religion as a whole:

> Western education of Muslim youth is bound to undermine their will to believe in the message of the Prophet, their will to regard themselves as representatives of the peculiar theocratic civilization of Islam... The explanation of this estrangement is not that the Western science with which they have been fed has furnished any reasonable argument against the truth of our religious teachings, but that the intellectual atmosphere of modern Western civilization is so intensely anti-religious that it imposes itself as a dead weight upon the religious potentialities of the young Muslim generation.

Asad identified the problems faced by Muslims living within the Western world-view:

> The contemporary Muslim sees the basic assumptions of modern Western civilization, nearly all of which are the very antithesis of the Islamic principles he cherishes... He sees the Universe reduced to a single level of reality... and all the higher levels of reality relegated to the category of old wives' tales... He sees the power of man as ruler upon the earth emphasized at the expense of his servant-hood, so that he is considered to be not the viceregent of God but the viceregent of his own ego.

There are crucial questions to be asked here:

WHAT IS GOING ON IN WESTERN CULTURE? Is there real freedom of thought? Or are we being controlled by new insidious forces: the absolutism of choice or the imperative of tolerance?

HOW CAN WE CHOOSE BETWEEN TRUTH-CLAIMS ON RATIONAL GROUNDS? How can we know enough about all the hundreds of choices to choose well?

IF ULTIMATE TRUTH AND REALITY AND REVELATION DO EXIST, would our present educational system equip us with the necessary intellectual approach or the personal humility to encounter and respond to them? Or are certain choices ruled out by the prevailing relativized truth?

IS MODERNITY ADDICTED TO CHOICE AND CHANGE? What happens when choice becomes a state of mind? How do you make a commitment to one relationship or one faith?

What do you think about this? Are you free to discover truth if it exists? Could you, if you so desired, commit yourself to one choice which comprehends all others? How would you know you had the capacity to do this? Is an open mind so open that it can voluntarily close on one option at the expense of others? Or does an open mind draw the line at truth?

PART 13

What Are the Boundaries of Reality?

THE PARANORMAL

The Quest for the Transcendent

Christianity and the Paranormal

We live on a planet that you can see. We live in bodies that you can touch and feel. We all eat food that you can smell and taste. Our world is limited by its physical appearance. Or is it? Where are the boundaries of our reality? Is there an existence beyond the visible world?

Throughout history men and women have been in search of the 'transcendent'.

This word can have different meanings: 'excelling'; higher than other things or not included in any of Aristotle's ten categories (the Scholastic Philosophers); not realizable in experience (Kantian philosophers); existing apart from or not subject to the limitations of material existence.

How does a person become aware of the transcendent?

For some it is felt in experiences of nature: the powerful surging of a stormy sea or the solitary beauty of a mountain peak or the sheer brilliance of an amazing sunset. In all this there comes a realization that there are things beyond seeing or touching; something 'other' has been encountered. T.S. Eliot described it as 'a tremor of bliss, a wink of heaven'.

Others find transcendence through prayer or through the discipline of meditation; yet others through the use of drugs which induce 'mystical' experiences.

There are other routes. The transcendent can be encountered in times of extreme depression or failure. A person may face the traumas of life:

divorce, bereavement, unemployment, terminal illness or the feeling that their lives have been worthless. Then, at some point in the midst of all the change and impermanence, they experience the perfect, the unchanging, an ultimate sense of well-being. They realize that this exists over and apart from their own situation. Bishop Ian Ramsey has described it as 'the disclosure situation', because something is coming to the person from elsewhere.

This sort of experience is interpreted in different ways. A religious person may see it as God's initiative in giving help. If the experience comes to a secular humanist it could possibly be seen as extreme emotion or some sort of psychological response. And this presents any intelligent student with the question of whether such experiences are merely subjective interpretation or whether there is empirical, objective evidence.

The paranormal

One way to answer this is through belief in the paranormal. The world of the paranormal lies outside the range of normal scientific investigation. Those who take the paranormal seriously think that the transcendent can be seen in reality which exists outside of our normal experience of seeing, hearing, touching and so on.

The Times published in 1980 the results of a questionnaire on the paranormal. 1,314 people responded. Out of that number 83 per cent believed in ESP (extra-sensory perception including clairvoyance and telepathy); 51 per cent thought it was fact; and another 33 per cent thought it a distinct possibility. The questionnaire revealed that 38 per cent believed in contact with the dead.

There are so many questions to be asked about human capabilities:

* Can human beings know someone's thoughts or actions by non-sensory means?

* Is it possible to heal illness by the use of healing words?

* Can the future be foretold?

* Can we contact the dead, or can they contact us?

* Is it possible to bend spoons or activate clocks by concentrating our will?

Paranormal experience can be encountered either as a surprise or by being sought after deliberately.

Many people claim to have been surprised by poltergeists: mischievous ghosts who usually cause damage to the house in which they 'live'. Their activity includes the sound of footsteps, creaking floorboards or furniture, objects moved and noises made. Some reports include violent breaking and smashing.

An apparition is also a form of paranormal activity. People claim they have seen ghostly figures which suddenly appear from nowhere. Or there are more specific 'sightings' like the figure of C.S. Lewis which was seen not long after his death by the well-known Bible translator J.B. Phillips. Lewis spoke pleasant words of encouragement to him and then disappeared into thin air.

Some people actively seek to make contact with the paranormal world. Spiritualism has been described as an activity grounded in the belief that people can, by means of 'mediums', make contact with the dead and receive messages from the other world. Often a medium is used by people whose close friends or relatives have died. They try to establish contact in the 'world beyond'. For many this activity is a reality, as expressed by Jay Hudson:

> The man who denies the phenomena of spiritism today is not entitled to be called a sceptic; he is simply ignorant.

Spiritism can include glass-moving, table-lifting, speaking in trances, automatic writing and ouija boards. All involve approaching the spirit world and inviting it to manifest itself to those present.

People who have seen apparitions, encountered poltergeists or experienced spiritualism generally take these matters very seriously. For them the happenings are evidence that a materialist view of the world is not a sufficient explanation of how things really are. They believe there is a spiritual world beyond, which in some way overlaps with the world in which human beings live. In other words, their world-view includes the spirit world.

Your world-view will determine the way you understand reality. The term 'world-view' has been defined as 'a set of presuppositions (or assumptions) which we hold (consciously or subconsciously) about the basic makeup of our world'. Very few people are aware that they hold a particular world-view. They assume that the way they see life is the way everybody does. Their assumption is that what they see is reality. A sizeable number of religious thinkers argue that the Western world-view has a blind spot which keeps us from dealing with subjects related to spirits, mediums, apparitions and the like. In its classical form, the Christian world-view would be familiar with the psychic and with what is now called the paranormal or the supernatural, although Christians do not agree that phenomena of this kind are necessarily good and from God.

Christianity and the paranormal

Christians are of course familiar with things happening which are not to be explained naturally:

> IN THE MINISTRY OF JESUS there were paranormal healings, sometimes effected at a considerable distance from the sufferer.

> THE CHRISTIAN VIEW OF PRAYER includes the belief that people can talk to God and he can converse with them without the use of a medium.

> IN ROMAN CATHOLIC DEVOTION, prayer to God includes the intercession of saints. Some Catholics testify to times of extraordinary sensory perception when they can see or feel saints who have long since died.

> IN THE BIBLE there are examples of special types of 'knowing' or 'insight'. Old Testament prophets had psychic abilities to 'see' what was going on elsewhere, and have visions. Even today in some parts of the church these things are still believed and practised.

> IN THE LIVES OF THE SAINTS throughout the ages there are wonder stories. For someone to be made an authentic 'saint', miracles have to occur during and after their lifetime, and these have to be verified by church authorities. A 'devil's advocate' will be employed to do all he can to oppose the stories. If they survive the test, a sainthood is proved.

> THE RESURRECTION OF JESUS from the dead was paranormal!

Although the church from its earliest days has witnessed paranormal activity, it has also warned people about activity which enslaves people, or causes them to be obsessive. The Christian world-view has traditionally included belief in a world of spiritual realities and entities. In the cosmic drama God and the devil are in conflict, and the battle is being fought for the spiritual possession of men and women. The kingdom of God is present when a man or a woman is ruled or possessed by God's Spirit. Christian tradition warns of evil spirits, or demons which can also possess a person. The Christian view through the ages is that some paranormal activity is dangerous for the spiritual condition of the individual, and is to be avoided.

Warnings against mediums are found throughout the Old Testament:

> When you come into the land which the Lord your God gives you, you shall not learn to follow the abominable practices of those nations. There shall not be found among you any one who practises divination, a soothsayer, or a sorcerer, or a charmer, or a medium or a wizard, or a necromancer. For whoever does these things is an abomination to the Lord.

Irenaeus, second-century Bishop of Lyons in his *Against Heresies* countered the heresy of Gnosticism. Gnostics maintained that the body of Jesus was not formed from ordinary flesh but out of 'psychic' substance. When Jesus died he became the fleeting apparition of a phantom deity, who left the realm of matter before the first nail was driven into the cross. (On this view the Romans only crucified a corpse.) Irenaeus strongly contrasted the ministry of the church with other practices of the day:

> Nor does [the church] perform anything by means of angelic invocations, or by incantations, or by any other wicked curious art; but directing her prayers to the Lord who made all things, in a pure, sincere and straightforward spirit, and calling upon the name of our Lord Jesus Christ, who has been accustomed to work miracles for the advantage of mankind and not to lead them into error.

Investigating the paranormal

In recent times various initiatives have been taken by the church to investigate the paranormal and to engage in discussion about it rather than dismissing all of it as the work of the devil.

In 1937 a committee was appointed by Archbishop Lang 'to investigate the subject of communications with discarnate spirits and the claims of Spiritualism in relation to the Christian Faith'. The Christian mystic Evelyn

Underhill resigned after the first meeting. The majority view was sympathetic to spiritualism and this shocked the Archbishops. The reports of the committee were never published. But a spiritualist newspaper obtained the majority's view and it made news.

In 1953 a private venture started within the church. The Churches' Fellowship for Psychical and Spiritual Studies was formed. The aim of the Fellowship is to help Christians to integrate their psychic sensitivity with their Christian spirituality. They started publishing a quarterly magazine *The Christian Parapsychologist*.

In the United States the United Presbyterian Church received a report in 1976 on Occult and Psychic practices. This resulted in guidelines for Christians on what questions need to be asked about psychic phenomena:

> * Does the psychic event or phenomenon lead us as total persons – heart, soul and mind – to love the Lord our God, putting no other gods before him, and to love our neighbours as ourselves?

> * Does it witness to the sovereignty of God as the ultimate source of possibility, power, and resources; or is it egocentric and concerned primarily with private power?

> * Does it honour God's chosen means of self-revelation: his Son, his Word and his Spirit?

The report saw that the church is partly responsible for the increased interest in harmful forms of paranormal activity:

> Our Lord has warned us that when one devil is driven out, seven more will take his place unless the vacuum is filled with the good. It is clear that many cults and novel psychic enthusiasms are pursued because of a religious vacuum in people's lives. This is a judgement on the church.

Michael Perry wrote *Psychic Studies: a Christian View* (1984). This chapter is indebted to him for his clarity of thought. He wrote:

> There are two opposite dangers in all this. One is to make the psychic into the centre and mainstay of a person's religion. The other is to ignore it altogether. The first is the temptation of spiritualism. The second has been the temptation of the religious establishment.

The Devil and All His Works

Belief in Satan Today

The Bible speaks often of the devil, as here in 1 Peter 5:8:

> Be sober, be vigilant; because your adversary the devil, as a roaring lion, walks about, seeking whom he may devour.

So does Bengali poet Rabindranath Tagore:

> God seeks comrades and claims love, the Devil seeks slaves and claims obedience.

Mark Twain, in an article *Concerning the Jews*:

> We may not pay Satan reverence, for that would be indiscreet, but we can at least respect his talents.

Milton's Paradise Lost has a famous description:

> The serpent, subtlest beast of all the field, of huge extent sometimes, with brazen eyes and hairy mane terrific.

Mark Twain again:

> A person [Satan] who has during all time maintained the imposing position of spiritual head of four-fifths of the human race, and political head of the whole of it, must be granted the possession of executive abilities of the loftiest order.

The existence of the devil

In the present Western philosophical climate, a person who believes in the existence of the devil is intellectually suspect. It is far easier to believe in his non-existence or to see him as a mythological figure or a comic strip red devil with horns than to say that he exists as a real personality. Baudelaire wrote: 'The devil's cleverest wile is to convince us that he does not exist'. And a character in Joris-Karl Huysman's *La Bas*, a study in Satanism, remarks: 'Satan is forgotten by the great majority... the wiliest thing the devil can do is to get people to deny his existence.' André Gide wrote, 'The more we deny him the more reality we give him. The devil is affirmed in our negation'.

But how can anyone in their right mind seriously conceive of an evil, malevolent figure existing in the spirit world and working against the human race for their ultimate dehumanization and enslavement to his power? Where does this belief come from? How can it be understood? Are there still people who take this view seriously and live their lives in the light of it? On what basis do they hold these beliefs? Where are the boundaries of their reality?

Belief in the devil is one solution to the problem of explaining evil. In most monotheistic faiths evil spirits are said to exist and to be responsible for moral temptation and sometimes for physical and mental suffering and even for death.

The development of the idea of Satan in Judaism is complex. The Hebrew word for 'destroyer' or 'devil', *Abaddon*, is not used in the Hebrew Bible to describe Satan, who is seen as the 'accuser' or 'adversary'. He appears mainly in the later books as in the prologue to the book of Job. Here, Satan appears as a respectable figure in the court of God given the task of testing God's servants. He was also identified with the serpent in the Garden of Eden who tempted Eve to eat of the forbidden fruit.

The description of the devil in the New Testament is much more specific. Scholars think that the literature written between the testaments such as the Apocrypha (influenced by Persian Zoroastrianism) influenced later Jewish demonology.

In the New Testament the devil is seen in:

* The temptations of Jesus.

* The lives of the demoniacs whom Jesus cured by casting out the demons.

* The theology of John's gospel, in which there is a kingdom of darkness, ultimately overcome by Jesus but still warring against the kingdom of light.

* Paul's letters where he sees the present world being under the power of 'principalities and powers', 'thrones and dominions', in the spiritual world.

* The gospels and the Acts of the Apostles contain many stories in which demons are understood as the opposition forces to the work of God.

What emerges from the writings of the New Testament is an evil, malevolent figure who is the chief of evil spirits. The devil is the supreme Evil One, the Dark Power. He not only tempts and opposes, he is 'the god of this world', 'the prince of the power of the air'. He is the prince of darkness, the angel of the pit.

In Christian theology one dominant belief, associated with Augustine, sees God as the sole author of the created universe, but one of the angels created by God rebelling against his authority. Instead of accepting the humility of a created being he insisted on equal powers with God. There was war in heaven between the devil and his followers and God. In John Milton's great poem *Paradise Lost*, the devil claims it is 'better to reign in Hell than serve in Heaven'.

This view of the devil avoids the ancient dualism which believes that there are two separate and equal forces in the universe eternally in opposition to each other. It also involves belief in the freedom to choose God's will. Church tradition holds that the devil was created good and, like human beings, free to choose. But goodness can choose to change its nature if it has freedom of the will. The devil (called Lucifer in a passage in Isaiah) wanted to be equal with God, and he fell from his goodness to become an enemy of God and his purposes.

The early Church Fathers saw this great battle between God and the devil at the heart of the gospel story. For them Jesus' death conquered the Evil One. There have been many theories of the 'atonement', as Christians call the reconciling effects of Jesus' death. In the fifth century Augustine stressed that Jesus' death as perfect man was accepted by God as a substitute for sinful mankind. From the tenth century onwards Jesus' death was seen as a sacrifice for humanity and the merit of that death was emphasized. But theologian Gustaf Aulen argued that in 1965 the classic theory of the atonement is the idea of God's conflict with the devil and victory in Christ:

> Christ – Christus Victor – fights against and triumphs over the evil powers of the world, the 'tyrants' under which mankind is in bondage and suffering, and in him [Christ] God reconciles the world to himself.

Other writers have echoed this view, as Meyendorff in 1978:

> I submit that it is impossible to understand the meaning of the Christian faith about man and the world, that it is impossible to be faithful to the significance of the Cross of Jesus, without admitting that Evil has a personalized existence, and, therefore, a strategy, a sense of reacting and planning (or rather plotting) against God's work.

The devil today

But the church is by no means united in this view and there are many who deny the existence of the devil. Among the explanations given for the preaching about Satan in the Bible are:

HE BELONGS TO THE WORLD-VIEW OF THAT TIME. A theological perspective comes from theologian Rudolf Bultmann (1884-1976), for whom the devil and demons were part of the culture in New Testament times. Christians need to reject it in order to discover an authentic faith for today.

THE DEVIL IS IMAGINARY. A psychological perspective includes the view that the devil is a projection of human fears and insecurities. Sigmund Freud (1856-1939) said a similar thing about God the Father.

HE WAS BELIEVED IN BY PRE-SCIENTIFIC PEOPLE, and science has dispelled belief in the devil. On this view many of the phenomena once attributed to demon possession are now explainable in terms of modern medical science.

HE IS INCOMPATIBLE WITH ENLIGHTENMENT THOUGHT. Writer Walter Wink in *Naming the Powers* (1984), argues that spiritual powers are central to understanding the New Testament. He writes that modern scholars do not reject the Devil because of lack of an authentic basis in the New Testament but because as heirs of the philosophical Enlightenment (and therefore a modern scientific world-view), they are not able to accept even the possibility that evil could be personified.

A *Time* magazine article in 1972 made the following comment:

> There is danger... in taking the devil too lightly, for in doing so man might take evil too lightly as well. Recent history has shown terrifyingly enough that the demonic lies barely beneath the surface, ready to catch men unawares with new and more horrible manifestations. But the devil taken too seriously can become the ultimate scapegoat, the excuse for the world's evils and justification for men's failure to improve themselves... perhaps the ideal solution would be to give the devil his due, whether as a symbolic reminder of evil or a real force to be conquered – but to separate him, once and for all, from 'magic'.

In the modern world there are still many Christians who believe that the devil is a real force to be reckoned with, an objective reality, existing in the present world and, for some time, with demons able to work evil. This belief affects the way they live out their Christian lives.

Dr Kurt Koch was a German minister whose counselling activities brought him into contact with people who had occult and psychic experience. For thirty years he documented the harmful results of such involvement. These included uncontrollable fears, fiendish nightmares and visionary experiences, and all manner of physical and mental disorders. After painstaking enquiry he linked many of these conditions with psychic and occult activities. Koch came to the conclusion that activities such as fortune-telling, levitations, clairvoyance, palmistry, magic (black and white), automatic writing, astrology, seances, are not just harmless pastimes but often lead to serious psychic and nervous disturbances. His major work *Christian Counselling and Occultism* (1972) is valued as an authority in its field. Dr Koch lectured at European universities and discussed these issues with theologians, doctors, psychologists and scientists. His lectures often started stormy arguments. He was willing to take strong opposition and intellectual criticism from those in high academic circles, as he anticipated in the preface to his book *Between Christ and Satan* (1961), where he quotes C.S. Lewis:

There are two equal and opposite errors into which our race can fall about the devils. One is to disbelieve in their existence. The other is to believe, and to feel an excessive and unhealthy interest in them.

Koch goes on:

The ones are the rationalists of every shading, the others are the magicians. Both will get upset about this book. Do they have reason to be upset? Reason to be shocked has the Christian counsellor who in his counselling sessions sees the devastating fruit of materialism and magic. Therefore this information must be made public.

Kurt Koch is interesting for his methodology. In his writings he takes a real case study of one of his clients who had been involved in a seance where a dead person was invoked by those participating. The dead person tapped out his name. It turned out that various people had known the dead man who had hanged himself years before. The whole thing was supposed to be a party game but later that night the woman began to experience real terror as she lay in bed. She saw white forms surrounding her. Neither the woman nor her relatives had ever suffered psychological disturbances like this before. Koch takes this and many more instances and asks what various professors might make of this sort of happening. How would a doctor, a psychologist, a psycho-analyst, a psychical researcher or a Christian pastor see what had happened?

Dr Koch himself is convinced that modern medical and psychological help is of no ultimate use in ultimately helping those who have been influenced by occult spiritual forces. The Christian pastor or counsellor has a specific task:

We have to proclaim the victory of Jesus Christ over all the powers of darkness. Oppressed and occultly subjected people cannot be helped through medicine, psychology and psychiatry but only through Jesus Christ. Therefore they have to be shown the way to the Great Deliverer.

What do you think? Is the devil the work of mere imagination, or simply a video best-seller, or the product of an ancient world-view? Or is there an intelligent Evil One who intends to possess and control as and where he can?

The Problem of Evil and Suffering
An Age-old Question

The world has seen a history of human suffering: pain and sickness; incurable conditions that even now medical science cannot heal; meaningless fates and senseless wickedness; the devastation, blood and plunder of wars. The world's history is one of conflicts, inequality, and social distress. And for the individual, there is the loneliness, the inner emptiness, the non-identity, worthlessness and despair that is part of the human condition. The meaninglessness of life.

People have always questioned the meaning and reason for human existence. In all the absurdity of life, all the chaos of things as they are, the big questions are asked: 'Why is this happening to me?' 'What is the point of this suffering?' 'Who is responsible for this?'

For many people, suffering has caused them to reject a belief in a good God. God is supposed to give meaning to life, but there is so much senseless suffering, how can all this happen and people still believe? At best, even if there is a God he can't be good. The problem of suffering and evil is connected at a deep level with our attitude to God and to the question of what we believe about reality.

An all-powerful God?

The belief that the world is the creation of an all-powerful God has evolved over time. In some religions, God has been thought of as being limited in his abilities. For example, in Plato's *Timaeus* the figure of the Demiurge, the divine architect, was a limited one, limited by the eternal forms by which he designed the world and the pre-existent matter from which he shaped things.

In Christian or Augustinian thought everything was God's creation brought into being *ex nihilo* or out of nothing, solely through an act of his will. This is why evil is such a serious problem for Christian thought. If all of creation came about through an act of God's will, it presents the Christian believer with a real problem: Why did God create a natural order containing the potential for so much pain and destruction?

The sceptics' charge against God is that either he cannot prevent evil or pain, in which case he is not all powerful; or else he will not prevent evil, in which case how can he be a just, holy, good God?

Or finally, what if he can and he will: how then is there all the wickedness and suffering in the world?

The question of evil

Various attempts have been made to explain evil in theistic and particularly monotheistic religions.

Dualism sees two principles or powers behind both evil and good which are ultimately equal. On this view the good God is not the only God. The forces of evil are operating against the forces of good and there is a cosmic battle.

Another answer to the question of suffering is a belief in divine punishment. Clear examples of this view from the early part of the Hebrew Bible are given by the 'Deuteronomic historian', who is believed to have edited the stories of the kings of Israel and Judah. Here, the nation of Israel is conquered because of her disobedience to the law of God. Invasion is a punishment from God and victory is a reward for obedience. Later in the Bible, in the book of Job, the holy righteous man Job meets all sorts of evil – poverty, disease, the death of his loved ones. His friends who look at all this calamity see his suffering as being evidence of his guilt.

Another view is that a great deal of suffering and evil in the world is because of the use of human freedom. The argument stresses that one of God's purposes in creating humanity was to have free agents who could enter into personal relations with himself. They therefore had to be created free in order to be able to respond to either good or evil.

The alternative would have been to create robots who were pre-programmed to do good. In which case they would cease to be real human beings. The possibility of doing wrong had to exist because without it there is no free choice. Of course, this view finds it hard to account for natural evil such as earthquakes or floods.

Some ecologists would link humanity's exploitation of the earth with so-called 'natural disasters'. The erosion of the ozone layer or the climatic changes forecast for the next century, for example.

Another objection to this view is that given the horrific disasters of human evil such as the Gulf War or the Holocaust – was creation at such a cost really worth it?

Part of the problem of evil lies in the nature and role of the physical world itself. On this view our bodies and our brains and our mental faculties are so designed and structured that they make such pain and suffering possible.

The theologian Thomas Aquinas said that 'God permits certain defect in particular effects, that the perfect good of the universe may not be hindered'.

The idea here is that the good of the universe as a whole necessarily implies the possibility of some evil. The balance of nature requires the death of some individuals and so 'God wills that some things should follow their constitutional course and die away'. This involves other beliefs in understanding God's will. There is an important distinction to be made between what God wills directly; and what he permits; that is, he wills indirectly.

How do people cope with evil and suffering?

Throughout history there have been both religious ways and non-religious ways of coping with evil/suffering.

Non-religious ways of coping with evil can be seen in the Roman poetry of Lucretius (99-55BC). He was a contemporary of Julius Caesar and philosophically a disciple of the ancient materialist philosopher Epicurus.

Lucretius believed that religion and the fears induced by it were among the worst evils. In the last days of the Roman Republic the emphasis was on free thinking. The Emperor Augustus encouraged a revival of ancient religion which caused Lucretius' poem 'On the Nature of Things' to be unpopular. It was re-discovered during the Renaissance, although only one manuscript survived the dogmatism of the Middle Ages.

> When prostrate upon earth lay human life
> Visibly trampled down and foully crushed
> Beneath Religion's cruelty, who meanwhile
> Out of the regions of the heavens above
> Showed forth her face, lowering on mortal men
> With horrible aspect...
> Therefore now has Religion been cast down
> Beneath men's feet, and trampled on in turn:
> Ourselves heaven-high his victory exalts.
> (translation R.C. Trevelyan)

For Lucretius the rejection of religion was to reject part of the world's evil and a step towards achieving peace of mind. His view, like his master Epicurus, was to contemplate lasting pleasure. This response to evil is to cultivate those things which bring happiness in the world: friendship, knowledge, truth, peace of mind.

In the modern world another non-religious response to the problem of evil can be seen in Marxism. Marx began his critique of society by attacking religion. He saw religion as a false way of helping people come to terms with suffering. The practical answer that Marxism offers to counteract evil is to struggle to overcome the social ills – poverty, injustice, inequality, and so on, that cause such suffering. Marxism sees the goal as being a classless society for which people now struggle, but the struggle will be worth it when such evil is eliminated. Marxism does not address the problem of 'natural evil' such as death, old age, and natural disasters.

The main traditional Christian response to the problem of evil was first formulated by Augustine. According to Augustine, everything that has being is good in itself to some degree. Evil exists when something that is in itself good, malfunctions. So things that are inherently good go wrong and that is evil.

Augustine cites blindness as an example. Blindness is, in itself, not a thing. The thing involved is the eye. So the evil of Blindness is that the eye

291

goes wrong. Augustine's answer to how evil first came into the world was that God created humanity and angels with free will. Some of the angels rebelled against God and then tempted the man and the woman to rebel. This fall of angels and human beings was the origin of sin and moral evil.

Even natural disasters – earthquakes, hurricanes, and so on, are the consequences of sin because human beings were meant to rule the earth and their rebellion against God has affected the natural order itself.

There is a modern Christian approach to the problem of evil in Process Theology. Process theology holds the view that God cannot be unlimited in power but that he interacts with the process of the universe. As a result, God is not using controlling power in the universe, rather he is subject to the limitations which are imposed on the universe. The universe includes rather than excludes the deity. In this way it is impossible for God to exercise a monopoly of power, so he is necessarily limited. Evil in the world is a measure of the extent to which God's will has been opposed. God is always offering the best possibility to each situation as it happens, but the created order is free not to conform to the divine plan.

Process Theology avoids the traditional problem of how God can be good and all-powerful and allow evil to happen. The Process view is that God is not the all-powerful creator, responsible for everything. Rather, God is a part (a unique part) of the universe who can influence the structure of things or change details to present possibilities. Hence God cannot be blamed for permitting evil, since it is not within God's power to prevent it.

Throughout history and in all cultures it is possible to trace religious responses to the problem of evil. Here we look at four ways:

* the path of self-denial.

* the way of mysticism.

* the via negativa: letting pain be pain.

* the way of sacrifice.

Throughout the history of religion there have always been ascetics who have chosen the path of self-denial. Asceticism is a religious response to confronting evil in the world. The ascetic is a person who commits himself/herself to rigorous self-discipline and renounces the bodily pleasures and passions of this world. On this view, the physical world is seen in a negative light. In Judaism at the time of Jesus, the Essenes cut themselves off from mainstream Jewish life. Some of them (but by no means all) settled in the desert in Qumran near the Dead Sea and awaited the coming of the Messiah, God's chosen one, to bring history to an end and to bring in God's reign.

Even today, the idea of withdrawing from the world is still a religious response, although it can be done for different reasons. In Christian faith past and present, monastic orders have inspired many Christian men and women in their faith. But in Christianity withdrawal from the world is not associated with a negative view of creation. The words of Francis of Assisi express this:

> All praise be yours, my Lord, through Sister Moon and Stars;
> All praise be yours, my Lord, through Brothers Wind and Air;
> All praise be yours my Lord, through Sister Water.

Christian religious communities often see their role as helping their fellow human beings by being a place of refuge or a place of prayer.

Mysticism has various forms both in the East and in the West. In essence, it is belief which derives from personal experience of universal unity. Mystical experience is when the individual person is absorbed into a greater whole. Mystical experience is heightened consciousness which raises people above the level of the world's suffering and evil.

One of the world's major religious responses to the problem of evil, mysticism has various expressions:

* The identification of ourselves with the divine spirit.

* The isolation of the soul or self beyond suffering.

* The union of the soul with some transcendent power.

As a response to evil and suffering, mysticism has been criticized for its self-absorption and non-social aspects. But often religious and non-religious 'mystics' guard against any practice which forgets the love and care of others.

An increasing number of spiritual writers are criticizing society for its shallowness in seeking to avoid pain and suffering. They seek to cope with suffering by entering into it. This can be termed the via negativa: letting pain be pain. Matthew Fox (1983) comments:

> Today in America... seventy-six million Valium will be swallowed. In
> addition, some thirty million people will glue themselves to soap

operas on television. It would seem that our culture is not well adapted to deal with pain. Pain is today's unmentionable reality, much as sex was unmentionable in the Victorian period. And pain is everywhere – deep, ineffable, unfathomable, cosmic pain. And it needs to be named for what it is, so that we can pray our pain, i.e., enter into it... Facing the darkness, admitting the pain, allowing the pain to be pain, is never easy. That is why courage – big-heartedness – is the most essential virtue on the spiritual journey.

Throughout the ages, spiritual thinkers and writers have embraced pain as a way of coping with pain. For some, the experience of pain and suffering is the key to having compassion for others and in this way it makes sense of suffering; others can benefit through it.

Lastly, the way of sacrifice. This is the idea that suffering comes because it is somehow carried on someone else's behalf. The idea can be seen in the Hebrew Bible in the book of the prophet Isaiah. Chapters 40-55 are thought to have been written during a time of great suffering for the Jewish people – the sixth century BC when the nation was conquered and in exile. The prophet speaks of a person who 'has borne our griefs and carried our sorrows... he was wounded for our transgressions, he was bruised for our iniquities; upon him was the chastisement that made us whole, and with his stripes are we healed'.

The religious idea here was that an individual (perhaps symbolic of the nation of Israel), could atone for the sins of the people by bearing suffering himself. In theology this person is referred to as the Suffering Servant.

Christians identify Christ with the Suffering Servant. It is central to Christian belief that Jesus Christ was somehow God in human form (incarnate) and that in dying on the cross, he entered into human suffering and took the world's suffering upon himself. On this view God himself takes responsibility for the evil and suffering in the world.

Christianity has several ways of understanding the meaning of Christ's death and suffering, called the atonement. Perhaps one of the most powerful beliefs is his sacrifice on the Cross. That in some way, because of Christ's sacrifice, God was showing his love and reconciliation to a world which had turned away from him. John's gospel puts it like this:

For God so loved the world that he gave his only Son, that whoever believes in him should not perish but have eternal life. For God sent the Son into the world, not to condemn the world, but that the world might be saved through him.

And the New Testament letter to the Hebrews says:

For Christ... has appeared once for all at the end of the age to put away sin by the sacrifice of himself. And just as it is appointed for men to die once, and after that comes judgment, so Christ, having been offered once to bear the sins of many, will appear a second time, not to deal with sin but to save those who are eagerly waiting for him.

God the Mother?

FEMINISM

The Maleness of Reason
A Feminist Viewpoint

There is an old nursery rhyme you may have learned when you were young:

> What are little girls made of,
> what are little girls made of?
> Sugar and spice and all things nice,
> That's what little girls are made of.

> What are little boys made of,
> what are little boys made of?
> Frogs and snails and puppy dogs' tails,
> That's what little boys are made of.

As a generalization you may feel this to be true. But why? Are boys really 'naturally' naughty; are girls really 'naturally' good? Does being male or female necessarily make a difference to the qualities or character a person has? Why should boys be 'allowed' to be adventurous; why should girls be 'imprisoned' into being nice? What makes male and female that way – biology or culture?

Women and society

Feminism is a broad philosophy concerned with the place and nature of women in society. There are two important strands of feminism which have been influential in modern times:

'EQUAL RIGHTS' FEMINISM – which seeks to change the position of women in society by changing the law. 'Equal rights' feminists believe that women have been oppressed by laws made by men. By changing the law (for instance, by allowing women to vote, to keep their own property after marriage, to divorce), the place of women in society must change unalterably.

'RADICAL' FEMINISM – believes that the very understanding of being a woman has been shaped and distorted by men. Changing the law, 'radical' feminists believe, will not change the deep-seated prejudices that men have about women. 'Radical' feminists wish to find a new understanding of what it means to be a woman, and a totally new way of living for women in our world.

All feminists would claim that there is an important difference between 'sex' and 'gender'. 'Sex' is the biological fact of being a woman; 'gender' is the philosophy surrounding being a woman. Feminists state that the philosophy of being a woman has, throughout history, unfortunately been formed by men. Gender, then, is a social and cultural category. Being 'female' is to have a certain anatomy; being a 'woman' is to be subject to a set of assumptions and given a specific role. Certain ideas – that men are active and women are passive; or that men go out to work and women stay at home – have attached themselves to the roles men and women play in society. Such ideas have, through time, become associated with masculinity and femininity until they appear 'natural'. This behaviour and division of roles is what feminists are sworn to fight against.

A male-dominated world

Plato's philosophy, involved with pure, abstract ideas beyond experience and history, is one which has persisted until modern times. Yet, ideas come from people – and people are shaped by their histories, their experiences and their cultures. In the Western Christian and philosophical tradition it is true that philosophers have tended to be churchmen and university professors. Inevitably, they have been men. Women have not shaped the development of philosophy as women, but only by becoming part of an overwhelmingly male world.

Can you imagine if all the books ever written, films ever made, pictures ever painted were done so by Eskimos or Black African women? Imagine that the only point of view that existed in the world was an Eskimo one or a Black African female one. Imagine if such a point of view were accepted as 'naturally' the norm. You might well feel that your point of view was different and that you had other, equally valuable things to say about the world. But – you would start at a disadvantage, because you would be seen as abnormal. You would have to start by expressing yourself away from the perceived norm. This is the position many feminists feel they are in when trying to express their ideas in a male-dominated world. What is considered 'normal' has been fixed by men. Women find themselves at the margins and have to struggle to find any voice.

The foundations of Western thinking are found both in the Judaeo-Christian tradition and in Greek philosophy. From the outset, these have contained notions of masculinity and femininity which have shaped ideas of male and female which persist to this day.

  * In the Bible Eve is created from one of Adam's ribs – she is secondary;

  * In Greek mythology Athene, Goddess of Wisdom, grows from the head of Zeus, father of all the gods – she is secondary.

Normally a man is born from a woman. In both these important stories, the woman is created from the man. Both stories contain the myth that the woman is secondary to the man.

Yet the Creation account in the book of Genesis in the Bible declares:

> So God created man in his own image,
> in the image of God he created him;
> male and female he created them.

Here, the Bible is showing that God created both male and female. Nevertheless, feminists retort, man is still seen as primary and woman as secondary. The very word 'woman' is included in the term 'man' (which includes both male and female). Woman is held to be subordinate to man.

Women and Christian teaching

In the Genesis account, Eve is tempted by the serpent to eat the forbidden fruit. She does so and persuades Adam to do so. As a result, God expels Adam and Eve from the Garden of Eden. God says to Eve:

> I will greatly increase your pains in childbearing;
> with pains you will give birth to children.
> Your desire will be for your husband,
> and he will rule over you.

Several important (and feminists would say damaging) ideas about women are contained in this passage:

THE WOMAN IS WEAKER THAN THE MAN. Women are the weaker sex.

THE WOMAN TEMPTED THE MAN; women are dangerous for men; they appeal to the senses and not to the mind. Women, therefore, are enemies of reason.

WOMAN'S IMPORTANT ROLE IS CHILDBEARING. Through reproduction she is linked with nature. Nature, the here and now, is contrasted with philosophy where ideas are abstracted from nature and placed beyond nature.

WOMEN ARE SUBORDINATE TO MEN. Men have a 'natural' right to rule over women. The Bible has been used throughout history to 'keep women in their rightful place'. Modern Christian feminists have attempted to give a positive reading of the Bible. Their position is that it is not just the Bible, but the interpretation of the Bible which has disadvantaged women. Christian feminists would point towards Paul's letter to the Galatians as containing the true Christian vision which has to be worked out for the future:

> There is neither Jew nor Greek, slave nor free, male nor female, for you are all one in Christ Jesus.

As the Christian church developed, the early Church Fathers slowly formed the boundaries of orthodox belief. Many of these scholars lived as monks and had withdrawn from everyday society. They wished to concentrate on the spirit, not the body and this led them to express a negative attitude towards women. Clement of Alexandria, writing in the second century, said:

> Nothing for men is shameful, for man is endowed with reason; but for woman it brings shame even to reflect on what her nature is.

and

> The female sex is death's deaconess and is especially dishonoured of God.

Likewise, Jerome:

> Woman is a temple built over a sewer.

And Tertullian:

> You are the devil's gateway. How easily you destroyed man, the image of God. Because of the death which you brought upon us, even the Son of God had to die.

Here it may be useful to remember some psychology:

> 'PROJECTION' is the act of projecting fears or prejudices onto another. The Church Fathers, concerned with the spirit, projected their own fears about their bodies and sexuality onto women. In doing so, they created an identity for woman both inappropriate and oppressive.

> HEGEL (1770-1831) formulated a 'dialectic' involving thesis/antithesis/synthesis. One identity is necessarily worked out against an opposite or 'Other'. Feminists believe that male identity (including male thinking – reason, rationality, firmness, aggression) has been worked out against a female 'Other' (nature, emotion, indeterminancy) and this has resulted in an unfair imbalance between the sexes.

Women in Greek thought

Alongside the Bible, Greek philosophy also gave women a subordinate role. In his play, *The Eumenides,* Aeschylus puts the following words into the mouth of the God Apollo:

> The mother of the child that men call hers
> Is no true life-begetter, but a nurse
> Of live seed. 'Tis the sower of the seed
> Alone begetteth. Woman comes at need,
> A stranger, to hold safe in trust and love
> That bud of her life – save when God above
> Wills that it die.

The Greeks believed that the male gave the principle of life and the 'form' to the unborn child. Therefore:

* Men are active; women are passive.

* Men give; women receive.

* Men give form; women are vague and indeterminate.

In the *Timaeus*, Plato also contrasted the father's role in giving form with the mother's role in containing indefinite matter. Men, therefore, literally shape the world.

Because of childbearing, women are linked to the world and to nature. Their bodies have a significance that men's bodies do not. Plato's idea of the rational soul overcoming and ruling the body contains within it the idea of male rule over female. By transcending matter, the soul necessarily has to transcend the feminine. The feminine, by its nature, is secondary and inferior.

A bias against women

Thinkers who married Greek philosophy and the Judaeo-Christian tradition formed ideas about reason which had an inbuilt bias against women.

Philo (20BC-AD50) was an Alexandrian Jew writing in the first century AD. He used Greek philosophy to interpret Jewish scriptures. In Philo's treatment of the Genesis story about Adam and Eve, Eve becomes 'sense-perception' (the source of the Fall); and man is symbolized as 'mind'. Sense-perception is an ally or helper to mind, but the woman (sense-perception – emotion-nature-body) is the cause of the downfall of man (or mind or reason).

The Greek idea of man as active and woman as passive is also used by Philo:

> ... just as the man shows himself in activity and the woman in passivity, so the province of the mind is activity, and that of the perceptive sense passivity, as in woman.

Woman, therefore, becomes symbolic of the non-rational aspects of human behaviour.

Augustine (354-430) placed reason in the spirit or mind 'where there is no sex'. He wrote in his *Confessions*, however, that women had:

a nature equal in mental capacity of rational intelligence, but made subject, by virtue of the sex of her body, to the male sex in the same way that the appetite for action is made subject, in order to conceive by the rational mind the skill of acting rightly.

In other words, while a woman's soul was as worthy as a man's, in Augustine's view her body still posed a problem and made her subordinate. Women had a symbolically biological burden to bear which men did not. In order to pursue reason, they had to overcome the fact that they were women. The soul's achievement, then, is to be male.

Aquinas (1225-74) insisted that the image of God is found equally in male and female. In the mind 'there is no sexual distinction'. However, turning to the Genesis account, Aquinas saw Adam as symbolizing the primary human functions, including reason. Eve, separately created, symbolizes generation, children (nature again). Her role, therefore, is as man's helpmate. Aquinas wrote:

> It was necessary for woman to be made, as the scripture says, as a helper to man; not indeed, as a helpmate in other works, as some say, since man can be more efficiently helped by another man in other works; but as a helper in the work of generation... As regards the individual nature, woman is defective and misbegotten.

Many feminists would state that the history of Western philosophy contains an in-built bias against women. Because of this, the very ways in which we are taught to think are inherently 'masculine' and women have been expelled from the province of reason. Women have been treated largely as secondary and subordinate, associated with emotion, physicality and nature. Quite simply, feminists claim, history has placed women in a 'lower' existence than men.

 * It may be that a feminist-influenced philosophy would radically change the way we think about the world;

 * It may be that a feminist-influenced theology would radically change the way we think about ourselves, God, society and the church.

Whatever the case, many feminists are urging a return to the very foundation-stones of Western thinking – and a start to making fundamental changes.

Patriarchy and Women
Mary Wollstonecraft and Others

Tennyson expressed a classic view in his poem 'The Princess':

> Man for the field and woman for the hearth;
> Man for the sword, and for the needle she;
> Man with the head, and woman with the heart;
> Man to command, and woman to obey;
> All else confusion.

What is it that makes a male child a boy? What makes a female child a girl?

Being male or female is a result of biology, but being a boy or girl is a result of culture. These roles are socially constructed. In other words, we are born male or female, but we learn to be men and women. How does this happen, and does it make any difference?

The *Equal Opportunities Commission Seventh Annual Report* of 1982 commented:

> Phrases such as 'two strong boys to carry the desk', 'a responsible girl to sit with the infants', 'sit quietly with the girls', 'he's a cissy', 'she's a tomboy' are common. It has been estimated that at school pupils are classified by sex approximately forty times a day. Thus children learn the stereotypes of girl and boy and how they are supposed to behave.

From this we can observe that expectations are piled on us and roles are allotted to us from the moment we are born.

Patriarchal oppression

Feminists point out that our society is 'patriarchal'. Our society is dominated by and shaped by men. As a result, women are relegated to a 'lesser' sphere (usually the home – or work inferior to men). Women are contained by male structures and male expectations. To take two everyday examples: When a woman marries she is often expected to take her husband's surname and wear a ring to show that she 'belongs' to him, and a woman is usually expected to do the housework and raise the children, even if she has a paid job. Her work at home is 'invisible' and financially unrewarded, yet it is invaluable. A woman's work allows her husband to go out and earn – but he is paid and has greater status because he has a 'real' job.

Throughout the ages, feminists observe, women have been the victims of practices which have 'contained' them and rendered them subordinate to men:

* Indian Suttee: the practice whereby a wife is burned with her dead husband.

* Chinese footbinding: the practice whereby young girls' feet were bound and deformed till they could hardly walk.

* African genital mutilation of young girls.

* European Witch burnings: in the seventeenth century many innocent women were accused of being 'witches' and put to death. Their accusers were mainly churchmen.

Although the law has been reformed to a great extent in Britain, even in the nineteenth century a wife was little more than her husband's property.

Today there remains an uneasy division in society. Women are generally nurses; men are generally doctors. Women are generally teachers; men are generally headteachers. Women work, but often their status is lower and they receive lower pay. In 1982 the average pay of a woman was two-thirds that of a man. This state of affairs, feminists claim, is a result of patriarchal oppression.

The rights of women

The campaign for women's rights began in the eighteenth century during the Enlightenment. The Enlightenment, or the Age of Reason, was a period when thinkers believed that 'Man is the measure of all things'. During this period, two great revolutions took place: the American Revolution of 1776 and the French Revolution of 1789. The American Bill of Rights, which gave 'rights' to the individual, along with the French cry of Liberté, Fraternité, Egalité (Freedom, Brotherhood, Equality), had a profound influence on the individual. Individuals now acquired rights and independence – they played a part in government through participating in democracy. A new age had dawned. Thomas Paine (1737-1809) published his famous *The Rights of Man* in 1791-92.

After the Declaration of the Rights of Man in France, Olympe de Gouge published the 'Declaration of the Rights of Women' in 1789. The French school of rationalism had a strong influence on the question of women's rights. The Enlightenment philosophy stressed environment and education over and above any perceived differences between the sexes. Innate qualities in human beings were denied. Olympe de Gouge went to the guillotine as a rebel. However, the Enlightenment philosophy of reason, natural law and equality of rights was expressed clearly by Mary Wollstonecraft's *A Vindication of the Rights of Women* published in 1792. Wollstonecraft's book was one of the earliest feminist statements in Britain.

Mary Wollstonecraft claimed that if women were granted the rights and opportunities of men, and freed from economic dependence – then half the world's human resources would be released and the perfectability of humankind (a doctrine she believed in) would draw nearer.

> For my arguments, Sir, are debated by a disinterested spirit. I plead for my sex, not for myself. Independence I have long considered the grand blessing of my life, the basis of every virtue – and independence I will ever secure, though I were to live on a barren heath.

Mary Wollstonecraft's writing remained influential and the Enlightenment ideal of 'equal rights' has remained a strong current in feminism.

The next strong statement on feminism came from John Stuart Mill in his essay *The Subjection of Women* published in 1869.

In the nineteenth century, the Unitarians continued the Enlightenment tradition of reason and equal rights. The Quakers, who allowed women to speak at their meetings and to become ministers, were also influential in the growing feminist movement. By and large, however, feminism advanced farther and faster in the United States of America than in Britain.

During the nineteenth century there was a clash between two differing ideals:

LIBERAL PROTESTANTISM EMPHASIZED DOMESTIC VIRTUES. The home became a sanctuary from the outside world, tended by a doting and dutiful wife and mother. Men and women moved in exclusive spheres.

PRESSURE GREW TO OPEN HIGHER EDUCATION TO WOMEN, to extend their employment opportunities and to reform the law. There was much agitation against the 'double standard' which allowed sexual licence to men, but condemned women. In 1913, a popular slogan was: 'Votes for women, purity for men.'

Olive Banks illustrated patriarchal oppression in *Faces of Feminism* (1981):

> Alongside the doctrine of separate spheres was the development of the cult of womanhood. This was based in part on the notion of man as the stronger and harder sex. Men were less emotional, more rational, as well as physically better able to stand the stern and ruthless world of the market-place. If, however, women needed the protecting walls of home because they were weak, they also had other qualities, derived in large part from their maternal nature that made them specially fitted to be both protectors as well as protected. These were the softer virtues of patience, gentleness and loving kindness, which they could use to succour and comfort their husbands as well as their children. Above all, perhaps, their greater moral purity fitted them to be the moral inspiration of their husbands as well as the moral guardians of their children.

The title of Coventry Patmore's famous poem *The Angel in the House* summed up all the qualities a good Victorian woman was supposed to possess – and everything that imprisoned her.

Some women, however, believed that a woman's place was not in the home, but elsewhere:

* Emily Davies championed a woman's right to higher education and founded Girton College, Cambridge, in 1869.

* Elizabeth Garrett Anderson became the first woman doctor in 1869.

* Millicent Fawcett became the first campaigner for Votes for Women and handed in the first petition to Parliament in 1867.

* Florence Nightingale became renowned for her nursing work in the Crimean War of the 1850s.

* Josephine Butler fought a long, hard campaign against the Contagious Diseases Acts. These Acts discriminated brutally against women and Butler succeeded in having them repealed in 1886.

Queen's College, London, the first higher education college for women in London, was opened in 1847 and Bedford College followed in 1849. Though universities could confer degrees on women from 1875, Oxford waited until 1920 to do so and Cambridge until 1947.

Women were admitted to the British Dental Schools in 1887, and the British Medical Association in 1892.

The nineteenth century witnessed a long struggle by many dedicated women to opening up new opportunities which had formerly been reserved exclusively for men. It was not until 1918 that women were given the vote in Britain. Between 1918 and 1920, women were given the vote in Britain, Germany, Austria, the Netherlands, Poland, the United States and the USSR.

Two ideologies fed nineteenth-century feminism apart from the Enlightenment philosophy of Mary Wollstonecraft:

EVANGELICAL CHRISTIANITY, with its emphasis on individual conversion, was an important influence. Evangelical women became involved in social issues, working to eradicate oppressions such as vice, drunkenness and slavery. Their outlook, which led them to place a great importance on reclaiming the individual, led them towards reclaiming women from dependence and hardship.

SOCIALISM. Robert Owen (1771-1858) was a Utopian socialist. He founded a community called New Harmony which held everything in common ownership. His socialism influenced feminism. Because of his communitarian principles, a woman was no longer bound to a family unit. Other ideas followed suit, to grant women greater independence – relations outside of marriage, divorce and birth control. Women came to believe that by asserting rights over themselves and their bodies they could break free from dependence on men.

The vote – and after

After women gained the vote in 1918, the twenties saw women attaining new positions of power and authority. The 1930s and the Great Depression, followed by the Second World War (1939-45) and the period of reconstruction and affluence of the 1950s, however, pushed feminism into abeyance.

With the advent of the 1960s and the Civil Rights Movement in the United States, led by Martin Luther King, feminism was back on the agenda.

Now feminism was concerned with the nature of the feminine, and not just women's rights. Feminism focused on birth control, abortion, separatism, male violence and stereotyped images of women. These new, radical feminists saw man as exploiter and women as exploited. Unlike Marxists, who believed that women were oppressed by economic factors, these feminists believed that women were oppressed by sexism – by men. Several important books were published:

* *The Second Sex* by Simone de Beauvoir (1949), put forward the argument that men saw women as 'Other'. Women had to transcend this identity through their own projects and exploits. They had to become 'subject' instead of 'object'.

* *The Feminine Mystique* by Betty Friedan (1963) ripped the mask off the housewife in America. Her book and the subsequent National Organisation for Women (NOW) in 1966 spoke to a mass audience. Friedan wanted to free women from their destructive dependence on patriarchal culture.

* *The Female Eunuch* by Germaine Greer (1971) influenced a whole generation of women. 'Women have very little idea of how much men hate them,' Greer wrote.

The church remained at the edges of feminism. While several denominations admitted women as ministers, the Anglican Church and the Roman Catholic Church resolutely refused to ordain women to the priesthood. One denomination, the Brethren, excluded women even from their name – and still do not allow women to speak or take part in their services. Christian theology appeared hopelessly patriarchal, and one theologian, Mary Daly, wrote in *Beyond God the Father* (1973):

A patriarchal divinity and His son are exactly not able to save us from the horrors of a patriarchal world. Rather, only radical feminism can open up human consciousness adequately to the desire for non-hierarchical, non-oppressive society and reveal sexism as the basic model and source of oppression.

Christian feminists began to see the need to address themselves urgently to these issues. The Anglican Church has subsequently allowed the ordination of women to the priesthood.

Despite the passing of laws such as the Sex Disqualification Act of 1919, the Divorce Act of 1971, the Equal Pay Act of 1970 and the Sex Discrimination Act of 1975, feminists assert that women still do not have an equal place in society to men.

Though women's position and status have undoubtedly advanced since the middle of the nineteenth century, feminists urge that there is still a long way to go.

Male and Female in the Bible

Feminist Theology

The prophet Isaiah declared, speaking for God:

> For a long time I have kept silent.
> I have been quiet and held myself back.
> But now, like a woman in childbirth,
> I cry out, I gasp and pant.

We are accustomed to images which portray God as a strong man – God as King, God as Conqueror, God as Almighty Father. But, are these images any more than that – just images? Are they actually part of the nature of God? What does it mean to say that God is masculine, rather than feminine? Are there 'feminine' aspects of God which have been buried in our religious tradition and which would enrich our understanding of God – and of each other?

The Christian gospel claims that it is 'Good News'. But is it 'Good News' only for men, or for women too?

Women and the church

Throughout the history of the Christian church women have been reduced to silence and submission. As one writer wryly put it: 'Men make the decisions; women make the tea'. A male priesthood and male ministers have dominated. The very structure of the church has been 'masculine' and hierarchical, excluding women from study, from power, and from authority. The only spheres where women have been allotted power in the church are in the convent and on the missionary field: two areas where they are conveniently removed from the mainstream. Even today, to be a successful Christian woman is to be a good wife and mother. Liturgy and hymns have overlaid women with male language and imagery, reducing them to invisibility, so feminists would claim:

* Rise up, O men of God.

* Good Christian men rejoice.

* Onward Christian soldiers.

As a result, many radical feminists have written off the church as hopelessly patriarchal. They say the church gives little help or hope to women who wish to transform their lives with a new feminist understanding. Many Christian feminists still want to remain within the orthodox boundaries of the church, however, and have taken a fresh approach to the Bible and the Christian tradition. These feminists believe that the Bible and Christianity do have something positive to offer women, and even that the death of patriarchy is contained within the Christian message itself.

The Bible's message

In the Bible, Yahweh, as God is called in the Old Testament, is seen as a liberator from bondage. God as liberator is a positive image for women. Also, prophets such as Amos and Hosea spoke a message which overturned the existing social order. They attacked hierarchy and, in so doing, attacked patriarchy. These prophets pointed towards an apocalyptic 'Day of the Lord' when all existing divisions would vanish.

Mary's song, at the beginning of Luke's gospel, heralded a new social order: 'He has brought down rulers from their thrones but has lifted up the humble...' Here God is not acting according to a strong masculine principle, but appears as a 'maternal' God who cares for the weak and oppressed.

Jesus proclaimed his mission at the Nazareth synagogue by quoting from Isaiah: 'He has sent me to proclaim freedom for the prisoners and recovery of sight for the blind, to release the oppressed...' He rejected any kingly interpretation of the Messiah's role. Instead he identified the Messiah with the 'Suffering Servant', an altogether different figure. A recurring phrase in the gospels is that 'the first will be last and the last first', a phrase which strikes at the very heart of patriarchy.

A great deal of hostility has been aroused when feminists have attempted to picture God as 'mother' as well as 'father'. Many people are uncomfortable with a picture of God which goes against the mainstream of their religious tradition. More than that, the idea of God as a God/ess has aroused barely buried fears of old cults and heresies. Female imagery has been so successfully excluded from our understanding of the cosmos that it is now hard to integrate it. Our understanding of Yahweh is inherently masculine. The three Persons of the Trinity in the New Testament are decidedly male. Mary, the mother of Jesus, although given a high place in the Roman Catholic tradition, as a bride, a queen and a mother, is still secondary. Psychologically, she is the kind of woman who functions as a male projection. This is what many feminists have observed.

But if God created male and female, how can God be said to be more 'male' than 'female'? Are sexual labels really appropriate for God, or is s/he beyond them? Are they only 'pictures' which have become attached to God? Paul Moore, an American bishop, wrote:

> If God is male, not female, then men are intrinsically better than women. It follows then, that until the emphasis on maleness in the image of God is redressed the women of the world cannot be entirely liberated. For if God is thought of as simply and exclusively male, then the very cosmos seems sexist.

If God is understood as primarily male, then patriarchy is guaranteed by the divine order. The male ruling class are looked up to as God's 'sons', responsible for implementing his rule on earth.

Many feminists would argue that picturing God as male breaks the second commandment, that no idols or images of God were to be made. To idolize God as male in this way blots out other ways of understanding God which may be rich and valuable.

In fact, purely male images of God prove too limited even in the Old Testament. There are passages where God is pictured as a mother or in childbirth, usually when the writer wishes to stress God's unconditional love towards his people. Modern feminists would hold that a 'female' understanding of God, linked to ecology, maternal care, and compassion for the oppressed, point up valuable aspects of God's nature which should be brought into modern theology.

Elsewhere in the scriptural tradition, some of the Wisdom books, written in the period between the Old and New Testaments, describe Wisdom as feminine and as emanating from God. In the Wisdom of Solomon, Wisdom is a manifestation of God through whom God mediates creation. She is the power of the presence of God in all things:

> For she is the breath of the power of God
> and pure emanation of his almighty glory;
> Therefore nothing defiled can enter into her,
> For she is the reflection of the everlasting light,
> and a spotless mirror of the activity of God
> and a likeness of his goodness.

In the New Testament, the writers preferred the word 'Logos' to Wisdom. 'Logos' is a masculine word and identified with Jesus who was, of course, male. Unfortunately, this obscured the feminine Wisdom tradition and the female aspect of the Godhead was lost.

Jesus and women

Women had a low status in Jewish society. Legally they were minors, on a par with children, and could be divorced easily by their husbands. Widows were outcast and single women were invisible or non-existent. A girl was not taught the Torah (the Jewish law) along with her brothers and could not pass through the gentile porch of Herod's temple. Because Eve had tempted Adam, a man was not allowed to be alone with a woman unless married to her. A man was forbidden to look at a married woman, and Jewish religious leaders believed they would be made unclean by even looking at a woman.

Against this background, Jesus' treatment of women is radical and extraordinary. The story of the woman caught in adultery and Jesus' anointing by a 'sinful' woman are only two accounts which show his compassion and respect towards women. Jesus' dealings with women are found mainly in the gospel of Luke (which lays a special emphasis on women) and in the gospel of John. It is worth noting:

Although Jesus had twelve male disciples, women travelled with him and were among his closest associates.

At his resurrection, Jesus appeared first to the women, even though legally their word counted for nothing in Jewish society.

Conversation with a Samaritan woman at a well broke down very rigid social barriers.

The story of Martha and Mary describes Mary sitting at Jesus' feet in the position of a disciple. Jesus commends her – 'Mary has chosen what is better' – in contrast with her sister's domestic and traditional role.

The story of the woman with the long-term haemorrhage is remarkable. This woman's medical problem would have excluded her from all religious ceremonies. Anyone who touched her would have become 'unclean' which is probably why she touched Jesus secretly. Jesus blessed her and healed her. In so doing, he affirmed women and their bodies.

Elsewhere in the gospels, the parable of the lost coin shows God as a woman searching out the lost and stray. Another parable pictures God as a woman mixing yeast into dough, showing how the rule of the kingdom of God will permeate the whole earth.

Traditionally, Peter's declaration that Jesus is the Messiah is regarded as a turning point in the gospels. Up to that point, Jesus' disciples have formed a variety of opinions about him, but Peter's revelation set Jesus on the course towards Jerusalem, death and resurrection.

Remarkably, there is another declaration of Jesus' Messiahship in the gospels – and by a woman. When Martha came to meet Jesus after her brother Lazarus had died, she said:

> Yes, Lord, I believe that you are the Christ, the Son of God who has come into the world.

Yet history has given Martha little status compared with that of Peter.

Despite Jesus' positive attitude to women, Christianity has developed along patriarchal lines. Justification for this has been found in the Genesis account of Adam and Eve. Also, Paul's letters in the New Testament sometimes speak of wives submitting, husbands having 'headship', women being silent in church...

This has led many Christians to believe that the Bible teaches that women are secondary to men. Many Christians would still argue this in the church today.

But many other Christians believe that Paul was writing into a specific situation, giving advice relevant to his culture which is not relevant to ours. Some modern scholars claim that the greater biblical and Christian principles of transformation and liberation call for an equality between men and women and an end to old divisions. Paul himself wrote to the Galatians:

> There is neither Jew nor Greek, slave nor free, male nor female, for you are all one in Christ Jesus.

Many Christian feminists embrace this vision of overcoming ethnicity, hierarchy and gender. They see it as the true Christian vision – one that gives hope to women and men and will help build a better world.

Anything Goes?

RELATIVISM VERSUS CERTAINTY

Moral Relativism

William James and the

American Pragmatists

Think of all your personal belongings. Your bike, your Walkman, the new computer. Or maybe your mind turns to your pets or even your clothes. Some of these might be worth a lot of money. Their cash-value is high. And you are more wealthy because you have them; they make a difference to how you live your life. Now turn to your personal ideas – the concepts you hold. Your view of what is real in this world and what can be known. Your beliefs about yourself or God. The values and morals that you live by. What is their cash value? Is there a way of assessing their value? Does having them make any difference to your life?

In the late nineteenth century a method of philosophizing called 'pragmatism' developed in America. The pragmatist criticism of classical philosophy was that it had little or no cash-value. What difference does it make whether or not you believe that there is a Universal Mind at work behind all reality? The everyday problems you face will remain just the same, and you will get no help from this theory as to how to face them. The metaphysical belief about the Universal Mind may make you a little happier or sadder, but apart from that there will be very little cash-value.

Charles Sanders Peirce was the founder of pragmatism, but it was William James (1842-1910) and John Dewey (1859-1952) who made it known to the educated community at large. They developed a method for solving or evaluating intellectual problems. They shared in a basic mistrust of the sort of intellectualism that is purely theoretical. Hence the term 'pragmatism', which derives from the Greek word for 'action', 'deeds', 'business'.

John Dewey was a philosopher, psychologist and educationalist. He became Professor of Philosophy at Columbia University, and was one of the leading thinkers in pragmatism. Dewey saw pragmatism as a theory involving both logical and ethical analysis. It was science that inspired his thinking. He saw science and technology as the most successful fields in the last three hundred years. Through them humanity had acquired the best and most reliable knowledge and had mastered nature. Dewey asked himself why scientific progress had meant so much and been so successful. Part of his answer was that it has helped men and women to feel at home in their environment and in the world... Like all pragmatists, he saw science as being dynamic. Science is not made up of a mounting pile of facts which are certain, but rather a method of finding things out. In *Experience and Nature* (1925) and *The Quest for Certainty* (1929), he rejected the 'spectator' theory of knowledge. The person who wants to know is a biological organism struggling for survival. Dewey's view is sometimes called 'Instrumentalism'. He developed a theory of knowledge which included the biological and psychological role that knowledge plays in human activity.

Does pragmatism work?

William James was the major American philosopher of his time. He was born in New York City, and his father, Henry James Senior, was a theologian. His brother, Henry James Junior became a gifted and famous novelist.

James' education was unconventional. He studied at schools in Switzerland, Germany, France and England, but his real education took place in the home where his family had frequent visits from learned friends who discussed all the lively issues of the day. In 1860 he started studying to become a painter but a year later he went to Scientific School at Harvard and in 1864 enrolled for the medical school. He fell ill with smallpox on a trip to Brazil in 1865 and had bouts of illness throughout the rest of his life. He lectured at Harvard first in anatomy and physiology, then in psychology and eventually in philosophy. James was known as a lively and stimulating speaker which made him very popular. He retired from the university in 1907 and in 1909 he published *A Pluralistic Universe*, which is a brilliant discussion of the ideas of Hegel and other philosophers. He died from heart trouble on 26 August 1910.

James was convinced that experience rather than theory is the key to our understanding of the world and reality. His famous work *Principles of Psychology* (1890) sets out this conviction. For him, a person's viewpoint is of crucial importance in philosophy. We think only in order to solve our own problems, so that our theories are actually instruments employed to solve problems in our experience. Therefore theories should be assessed on their ability to succeed in dealing with particular problems. If the function of a theory is to deal with an experience, the pragmatists' test of a theory is that it is true if it works. If we apply this to classical philosophy, the only way of assessing the so-called absolute truths of Plato or Descartes is by judging them in relation to their effect on the concrete aspects of life, our experience. If they have no effect then they are meaningless. He writes in one of his philosophical essays, *The Will to Believe*:

> Let us give the name 'hypothesis' to anything that may be proposed to our belief; and just as the electricians speak of live or dead wires, let us speak of any hypothesis as either live or dead. A live hypothesis is one which appeals as a real possibility to him to whom it is proposed. If I ask you to believe in the Mahdi, the notion makes no electric connection with your nature – it refuses to scintillate with any credibility at all. As an hypothesis it is completely dead. To an Arab, however (even if he is not one of the Mahdi's followers), the hypothesis is among the mind's possibilities: it is alive. This shows that deadness and liveness in an hypothesis are not intrinsic properties but relations to the individual thinker. They are measured by his willingness to act.

In his book *Pragmatism* (1907) the opening essay contrasts philosophers as being 'tough-minded' and 'tender-minded'. The empiricists are 'pessimistic', 'irreligious' and 'sceptical' and the rationalists are 'idealistic', 'optimistic', 'monistic' and 'dogmatical'. James then comments on the inability of traditional philosophy to help the modern person deal with the problems of their generation. He pays special attention to the issue of reconciling science and religion. All of us have to face choosing between different theories and throughout the book he considers these problems from the standpoint of the person, the learner.

James' approach contains certain recognizable features. Firstly, there is no static, ready-made world. The way we talk about the world is shaped by the way we learn and our theoretical activities. This means that the learner or the philosopher is not a spectator watching out for realities that exist, but is in the world just like a player is in a play. No one can be truly objective; our thinking is shaped by living in the world.

Secondly, James thinks that our beliefs must accord with the best evidence. Where the evidence for one theory is stronger than for its challengers, we have no rational choice but to choose that theory which is better supported. Where there is a balance of choice – the evidence is the same on both sides – then our decision should be made for the theory with the better and richer consequences.

For a pragmatist, truth is not a fixed idea which we are all trying to find, but truth is something that happens to an idea. Truth develops and grows in time. So for instance, you might have a view that life exists on other planets. The idea is neither true nor false. However, when finally a space expedition discovers that life exists on Mars then the theory will become true. Some ideas yield to development. They are true in that they work, and false in that they do not work. Ideas may work for a while and are true while they work. When an idea ceases to be satisfactory, it is no longer true. James based his illustrations of truth on examples of various scientific theories that have now been discarded and replaced with better truths. Truth is that which enables us to deal successfully with the life-problems that we encounter.

William James was a prolific writer. His writings were not dry, abstract and intellectual; they were works of literary art. He wrote as a creative writer with strength and force and excitement.

Experience meant experience of any sort and of everything. It was the basic stuff of human existence. In putting forward a pragmatic methodology, he believed he was simply reflecting the ways in which all of us attempt to live in the world. He thought of the universe as a massive natural system in which many pluralities exist together. We all have to change continually so as to meet with the new situations we all encounter in our experience. James' model is an evolutionary one. Development never ceases because, like Heraclitus centuries before him, he believed everything was in flux and change – including truth. Truth is therefore relative.

In modern times the big philosophical debate has been between reason and experience. The rationalists argue that reason is the only source of all knowledge, while the empiricists and pragmatists argue that useful knowledge comes from sense experience. In their view, reason only gives definition and expresses what is known already, whereas empirical knowledge shows things that are new and useful. What is the implication of this for moral behaviour? If morality is not based on objective reason, then it has to be based on subjective or personal judgments. Morality of this sort has sometimes been called 'subjectivism', based on personal taste and preference. Or sometimes 'emotivism', based on feelings which lead to actions. For the emotivist, morality is the expression of feeling and the action that follows. Both subjectivism and emotivism can develop into 'relativism'. If morality is a matter of personal feeling and expression, then it is relative to an individual or a group of people at a specific time and place and setting. For the relativist there are no absolutes, no ultimate right or wrong. All morality depends on the particular culture or situation you happen to be in at the time. In ancient Israel it was moral to have many wives; it is different in many cultures in the twentieth century. The moral practice in a hippy commune is different from that of the local Catholic convent. But what does this matter? Morals are relative. The relativist recommendation is therefore that we should all be tolerant. Because morality is purely subjective, we should be less critical of others. On this basis it is easy for 'right', 'wrong', 'good' or 'evil' to be seen as feelings. Your perception is as good as mine, and moral integrity is about being true to one's own feelings.

James and religion

If truth is relative, then when this is applied to religion it means that a religion is not to be valued for its own sake but for its psychological and moral effects. James wrote in *Pragmatism* (1907): 'If the hypothesis of God works satisfactorily in the widest sense of the word, it is true.' James defended the idea that people are not at root concerned with an exact definition of the nature of God or about proofs of his existence; they believe in God because they need God. In his famous *The Varieties of Religious Experience*, he explained:

> God is not known, he is not understood, he is used — sometimes as meat-purveyor, sometimes as moral support, sometimes as friend, sometimes as an object of love. If he proves himself useful, the religious consciousness asks for no more than that. Does God really

exist? How does he exist? What is he? are so many irrelevant questions. Not God, but life, more life, a larger, richer, more satisfying life, is in the last analysis the end of religion. The love of life, at any and every level of development, is the religious impulse.

James did not mean to be sceptical or cynical, he energetically defended the rights of religious faith. But he has been criticized, by Bertrand Russell especially, in that the pragmatic principle is too ambiguous. What is the meaning of 'true' in James' thinking? What does it mean to say something 'works' morally or religiously? Is it not a form of commercialism to make success the test of truth? A kind of religious consumerism?

Russell asked: 'How are we to determine whether the effects of believing in Roman Catholicism are on the whole good or bad? It is far easier, it seems to me, to settle the question whether the effects of thinking them infallible are on the whole good.'

Religious objections to pragmatism include the following:

* Religious belief in God has to be proved in experience and practice, but the reasons for belief in God are more than simply practical.

* Truth cannot be equated with practical outcomes or sacrificed to the effect it has.

* Even a theory that is not followed up can still be true, and even a message that gets little response can still be right.

* The notion of God is not a mere hypothesis (like Santa Claus) which bears no relation to facts. Christian faith rests on an inner awareness and experience of God which is there before any decision is made.

James felt that his pragmatism could remove religious and moral questions from the arena of theological argument and scientific controversy. If you can view the problem of belief without worrying about whether it is true or not then you have a more satisfactory solution to the problem. Truth is what gives a better life for each individual.

Do you agree with him?

Postmodernity
Culture in Change

'What does it mean to know?'

Most of the time most of us make assumptions about what is real and consequently what is true. Think for a moment about all those things you hold to be true. If you were to make a list of what you know in the order of your ability to prove them, you would probably find that you would have effectively divided your list into two categories. Towards the top of the list would be all those things that you would hope to prove through the use of science while at the bottom would be less tangible concepts, ideas and beliefs.

If you think like this you are following the philosopher Kant. He divides up reality into two realms.

* On the one hand is the objective world of phenomena which can be tested through experience by the rational mind.

* On the other there is the more subjective realm of noumena, of things as they are in themselves independent of how we relate to them.

The problem is though, how do we know that our ideas about how things are describe truly and accurately the way reality really is? For we arrive at such conceptions through our own minds and senses.

An age-old problem

Postmodern thought has its theoretical roots in the past. Plato divided the world into underlying reality and the way it appeared to human beings.

Within Greek philosophy this threatened to reduce human knowledge to mere opinion. Philosophers have struggled with this problem ever since. In understanding how postmodern thought has developed three philosophers are especially important. They are David Hume, Immanuel Kant and Friedrich Nietzsche.

Kant's rational philosophy was a response to the empirical scepticism contained in David Hume's writings. Hume had argued that there was no basis upon which we could move from our continuous perceptions and experience of the world to say anything about reality that could escape the charge of being mere opinion. Hume stated in his *Treatise of Human Nature* that:

> For my part, when I enter most intimately what I call *myself*, I always stumble on some particular perception or other, of heat or cold, light or shade, love or hatred, pain or pleasure. I never can catch *myself* at any time without a perception, and never can observe anything but the perception.

Postmodern thought, as we will discover later in this unit, represents the empirical scepticism of Hume driven to its absolute limits. The motivation to do this comes from the hermeneutic of suspicion which is rooted in the philosophy of Nietzsche. Postmodernism marks an intense period of questioning in which the very foundations of the philosophical enterprise inherited from the ancient Greek thought of Socrates, Plato and Aristotle has come under sustained criticism. It challenges the coherence of language itself. As such it is an epistemological problem – a problem of knowing – which has important implications for ontology, the branch of philosophy traditionally concerned with the study of being, of reality in its most fundamental and comprehensive forms.

Perhaps before going on to try and unravel some of the most salient features of postmodernity it should be noted that the literature on postmodernity is vast, often complex and shows much disagreement over what being postmodern actually involves. It is a multi-layered concept which is used to cover a wide range of developments in thought, art and society with both philosophical and sociological implications.

Some philosophers argue that talk of the *post*-modern is really to talk about the heightening of factors already present in the Enlightenment, 'modern' period, rather than the dawn of a new age. However, it is hard to argue against the idea that a cultural shift of some kind is taking place within late-modern Western culture. This shift, whether given the label postmodern or not, holds continuities with the past whilst also heralding important changes in the way people think and live. Indeed, it could be said that within late-modernity we are in the middle of moving from one cultural epoch to another, from modernity to postmodernity. Three philosophers who have contributed much to this cultural shift are Jacques Lacan, Michel Foucault and Jacques Derrida.

Autonomy and reason in the light of structuralism and Jacques Lacan

How such a questioning of the very foundations of thought arose within our own time is heavily linked to problems with regard to the problems of how human beings can relate to and be shaped by the world they live in.

The concept of human beings as autonomous individuals, as it developed from the thought of Descartes, has played a key part in shaping modern Western culture. Think of the judicial system and the whole framework of laws within Britain; they assume that ordinarily we have freedom to choose how to act. As a result we are responsible to others and society for our actions. What would happen to society and the very idea of individual responsibility upon which schools, businesses and other institutions are run if that autonomy was not so certain?

The thought of Jacques Lacan is often obscure and difficult to understand but represents a complete challenge to the way of thinking Descartes had developed about the human subject and its supposed autonomy.

Lacan was born in 1901 at Paris and died in 1981. While he played a key role in developments within Freudianism and psychoanalytical theory he was deeply influenced as a thinker by structuralism.

Structuralism, while it has various applications is fundamentally a doctrine about how language works which has revolutionized the basis and form upon which theorizing over social and cultural life takes place. Ferdinand de Saussure (1857-1913), the father of structuralist thought, argued that the words (signifiers) which we use to refer to and talk about reality (the signified) are to be regarded as sets of sounds which have a meaning. However, because signifiers themselves represent particular ways of interpreting the thing in reality which they are referring to, they are not to be understood as definitively describing that which is signified.

An example which Saussure himself offers is the difference between the English word for sheep, which points to the living animal, and the word mutton, which refers to its meat.[1] The French word for sheep, *mouton*, makes no such distinction between the animal and its meat. This conceptual difference between the two languages serves to illustrate not only that language is a social construct upon which each community places an agreed network of given assumptions and meanings but also that each individual term can be understood only by considering how it *differs* from other terms. The importance of the idea of difference conferring on language its meanings, which begins to emerge in his thought, is key to much postmodern writing.

Scientific and human psychology both, in their different ways, assume that the human subject and the human ego are the same thing. Lacan opposed this view. Instead he argued that the human subject both knows and does not know itself, through the dynamic interplay of two factors upon each other.

* The first is concerned with the way language provides content for the construction and evolution of the human self. Various human qualities or positions of social status and significance are directed towards each human subject. The meaning of the word 'I' is made up of a multiplicity of messages derived from how the language of other people relates to the individual human subject. This provides the material upon which the second factor operates.

* The second factor involves the way the ego (conscious self) judges and connects all this content, and thus comes to conceive of itself as being a certain kind of person in relation to the world. While this process of personal formation never stops, it is centrally important in the early years when the parameters and nature of one's own conscious and sub-conscious self are being laid.

Lacan's way of thinking about the human subject, when linked to a structuralist view of language, threatens immense consequences for all areas of thought. As the signifier is always separated from the thing signified, and has an existence in language apart from it, no signifier is ever able to come to rest on any signified: words are never able to connect or correspond absolutely with the world we live in. Signs, symbols, significations, representations and images of every type become understood in a fundamentally symbolic and metaphorical way.

What Lacan has challenged is Descartes' idea of autonomy. The human subject is now seen as a sea of subjectivity; self-identity becomes forever unstable and never fully known. As a result, being always precedes consciousness. Prejudice – arising from subjectivity – becomes part of the condition of being conscious. Consciousness, like meaning itself, forever finds itself in process. It always contains potential but is never capable of being fully objective or neutral.

The whole basis of the scientific enterprise, as commonly perceived, is threatened. Science is a situation where the meaning of language is always to be found in its present use and immediate context. Any view of language – and consequently thought – which supposes the ability of words to provide a transparent representation of an objective reality, is radically undermined by Lacan's theory. People become detached from the real, objective world, since their relationship with the concepts of the linguistic community they belong to determines how they understand reality.

In such a situation how free are we left to be? And what does 'to be free' mean anyway? What happens to the very idea of knowledge?

The unraveling of the modern in the thought of Michel Foucault

Foucault was a French historian and philosopher, who like Lacan, was heavily influenced by structuralist thought while also being critical of some aspects of it; thus Foucault is better described as a poststructuralist. In 1926 he was born in Poitiers and died in 1984 as a result of an AIDS-related illness.

In his major thesis, later published in an abridged version in English under the title *Madness and Civilisation*, Foucault was concerned with madness and reason as they related to the institutions of psychiatry.

While considering Descartes' 'I think, therefore I am' as a rationalist foundation for knowledge, Foucault doubted everything except his own sanity, the possibility of which he had already rejected in his 'First Meditation'. Foucault focuses on what madness meant in contrast to reason and concludes that Descartes' understandings of madness and reason, far from being universally objective categories, were dependent on particular understandings of them derived from Descartes' own historical situation in place and time.

Foucault uses the term 'discursive practice' to refer to the rule-governed set of statements which provide the basis by which each human community, at any given point in time, embodies what it believes to be 'knowledge'. The study of how ideas change in relation to the culture within which they exist led him to a growing suspicion of the possibility of any conception being truer than any other, outside a particular 'discursive practice'.

The effects of historical and cultural relativism threatened to reduce all discourses about reality to relative status. As a result the critical consequences of Lacan's focus on the present use of language, its basis in the human unconscious and its subjectivity was furthered by Foucault, in his later writings. He concentrates on how particular organizations or bodies of knowledge – such as that of the scientific community – hold authority and power over people and argues that they still fail to escape the problems of subjectivism and relativism.

In such a situation no criteria to discern truth from falsehood exist outside a particular community with its 'discursive practices'. Any hope of maintaining universal standards of logic and rationality evaporate into thin air and, with them, the possibility of comparing the truth claims of different communities.

In *The Order of Things* Foucault makes the statement that

As the archaeology of our thought easily shows, man is an invention of recent date. And one perhaps nearing its end... like a face drawn in the sand.

For the Enlightenment represents

a momentary fold in the fabric of knowledge.

Foucault says this because he prioritizes Kant's statement about the Enlightenment being concerned with human coming of age, in which Kant tells us to 'dare to use your own understanding', over and against the humanistic ideal of progress.

However, Kant's division of reality into the noumenal and the phenomenal and his confidence in the scientific method becomes suspect, as the objective threatens to be always subjectivized by our methods of knowing. Therefore Foucault takes a very Nietzschean turn in advocating the throwing off of humanism and all other discourses. He rejects the power these discourses and world-views have over us, as they put a limit on the possibilities of what we can be as human beings, in favour of a liberation to new possibilities.

If everyone took such an approach, would there be anything left to guide our lives with their new possibilities, apart from living in conformity to the desires that already exist within us?

Derrida, deconstruction and the 'death' of philosophy

Jacques Derrida has been described as a charlatan by members of the philosophical community within the University of Cambridge. This comment was sparked by a proposal within the college to offer Derrida an honorary degree. But why should someone of such evident intellect who counts himself as a philosopher, be so spurned by much of the traditional philosophical community?

Derrida was born to a Jewish family living in Algeria in 1930 and is a member of the French philosophical community. His writings are notoriously difficult to understand, as he adopts an opaque style to back up his ideas. His thought challenges the entire foundations and possibility of philosophy, while offering a new definition of what to do philosophy actually means.

Derrida deconstructs or takes to pieces human understandings of reality through the use of his term 'différance' (see glossary). 'Différance' does not point to a positive identity for the thing described, or describe how two identities differ from each other. Rather, as the French verb *différer* means both 'to differ' and 'to defer', in the sense of putting off, for Derrida 'différance' is difference deferred. The way he uses the word 'différance' itself, retaining its ambiguity of meaning between two possibilities rather than giving it one positive meaning, is an example of this. All claims to unambiguous truth are placed 'under erasure' by comparing and replacing them with other possibilities of interpretation, so that the contingent and relative nature of all truth-claims can be shown.

In consequence we become lost in a sea of images and signs which we can never be certain of anchoring to the true nature of reality. You can get an idea of this by opening a dictionary at any word and trying to find the place where words end and reality appears. The distinction between representation and reality, between signs and what they refer to in the real world breaks down, or rather becomes unsolvable and unimportant. Each text which purports to describe reality is regarded with a 'hermeneutic of suspicion' – everything has its meaning called into question by deconstruction.

The whole Socratic method of questioning reality so that we may come to a clearer understanding of it is therefore rejected. Plato's prioritization of speech over writing, which has been a marked feature of philosophy ever since, is also rejected, due to the ambiguities inherent in any word spoken and listened to by human subjectivities, in the light of both structuralist and post-structuralist thought. Aristotle's logic of identity which depends on asserting:

THE LAW OF IDENTITY: whatever is, is

THE LAW OF CONTRADICTION: nothing can both be and not be, and

THE LAW OF THE EXCLUDED MIDDLE: everything must either be or not be

is reduced to ultimate incoherence. This is because any grounds on which judgments might be made to support and apply the logic of identity systematically come under deconstruction themselves.

Because of this an avowedly postmodern thinker called Jean-Francois Lyotard (born 1925) – who probably introduced the term 'post-modern' into philosophy in the first place – points to the impossibility of any narrative which claims to be able to provide us with the truth about reality being able to claim a metanarrative and overarching status over all other stories. There can be no such thing as an accurate description of the way the world is.

In essence, all philosophical and religious claims about the nature of reality and the human condition are deconstructed. Religion is being reduced to a 'language game' (*see* Chapter 35). So, does philosophy become impossible?

Derrida doesn't think so, as long as it is redefined. Philosophy must let go of its desire to find the truth about things, and think of itself as a literary genre which is attempting to examine the practise of how different genres think of themselves and interrelate with others. For Derrida this doesn't lead only to negative conclusions, because the deconstruction of any text in order to bring out its hidden content also allows for new and creative ways of reading the text to be discovered. Rather than forming the foundation upon which other areas of human thought are built, philosophy should be understood, Derrida argues, to be immanent, immediately present in all intellectual activity. Not surprisingly, many more traditionally-minded philosophers don't take kindly to Derrida's suggestion, while at the same time not being quite sure how to rebut his thesis. Hence the hostility: he doesn't play the philosophy game by the accepted rules.

Cultural transition and the rise of mass culture

Within an examination of postmodern thought, we have seen that the founding presuppositions of the Enlightenment world-view have come under the most intense pressure with regard to their validity and coherence. The ideas which used to be associated with the terms autonomy, truth and progress can no longer be taken for granted. Humanism with its ideals of 'tolerance' and 'equal rights' cannot warrant a commitment, as morality in a postmodern era is subjective and changing all the time.

The very idea of progress has been undermined by the increasing realization of the ambiguity and limits of science upon which the hopes of that ideal are largely focused.

There is uncertainty today about science and whether it can provide any real answers to planetary problems, such as environmental degradation and population levels. This only serves to exacerbate the feeling of uncertainty pervading much of contemporary Western culture. The speed of modern travel and the immediacy of communication methods through the telephone, fax and internet, add to this uncertainty the feeling of a shrinking globe, just as many societies are beginning to feel the impact of the plurality of cultures now represented within them. Within pluralistic societies, in which many diverse claims are made about the world, in which direction does progress lie?

In such a situation of cultural and religious plurality, the modern project born of the Enlightenment has begun to be challenged by a new dynamism within society itself. The barrage of cultural images, symbols, texts and narratives on the one hand and the products, entertainment choices, and communications media through which lifestyle choices are conveyed on the other have created a living symbiosis between industry, consumer and culture. This is nowhere better illustrated than by the Internet with its almost infinite possibilities and modern technology's creation of virtual worlds for us to indwell. The very form of cultural transmission today is of a fundamentally different than in the past.

In the past, cultural transmission has been characterized by Dr Andrew Wacker as a trickle-down effect from the cultural élite to everyone else. But society in late modernity could be likened to a jacuzzi rather than a shower, with culture emerging from all directions! Almost of necessity, in such a situation, meaning is discerned in local contexts alone, as claims to universal truth are almost habitually treated as suspect. Meaning becomes marked by enormous diversity and contingency.

Such mass cultural transmission may look to be offering a plurality, a heterogenity of ideas, choices and activities for the contemporary person. Yet in reality there is a danger that the market itself becomes the greatest reality for the growing number in our society, especially in the middle classes, who no longer have a rootedness in tradition or an old-style metanarrative to make sense of their lives. Consumer choice is often whimsical, unstructured and unplanned. In the religious sphere – for those who do not retreat from the challenges of contemporary culture into some form of fundamentalism (a tendency which is on the increase) – a tolerance and openness is given to the many diverse forms of the sacred found in late-modern society. This diversity reveals an underlying desire – a *need* – to believe in something. It could be argued that the diversity and growth in New Age religion reflects both this need and consumer culture itself, with its emphasis on self-selection, self-fulfilment and fragmentation of traditional faiths.

In the spirit of consumerism all is reduced to play, fad, style, convenience and ever more consumption. Pragmatism and 'I feel, therefore I am' replaces Descartes' rational 'I think, therefore I am.' No rational basis for cultural and moral choices is left. Instead, an ethic of desire is stimulated with a diet of unconstrained consumerism, leaving people open to manipulation by the media and advertisers. Late-modern culture, in some of the ways it is experienced and interpreted by a growing number of people within it, has started to undermine the very idea of 'meaning' as traditions threaten to become just another consumer choice and the private realm is extended over ever more areas of society's life.

Despite all that has been said about postmodern philosophy and the tendency of consumerist culture to accentuate the challenges posed by the thought of Lacan, Foucault, Derrida and Lyotard, amongst others, the question remains whether postmodern thought will necessarily determine the form culture takes as it develops in the future. Rather, the reductionist tendencies of consumerist culture may remain as one way of thinking and being within an increasingly fragmented and pluralistic society. On the positive side, Postmodernity allows the telling and living of stories and gives those who want to follow different religious stories and meanings to their lives the space to be. This is unlike the earlier secularism of the 1960s which was anti-religious.

Within such a context questions abound. How will developments in communication continue to impact on the way our lives are organized? What may become of national allegiances? What form will the politics of the future take? Will the mainline religious traditions with their metanarratives about reality avoid, or survive, reduction to the status of cults? Is the religion of the future to be equated with today's New Age religiosity?

Notes

1. Eric Matthews, *Twentieth-century French Philosophy*, Oxford University Press, 1996.

Fundamentalism
Reality is Certain

On 14 February 1989, Ayatollah Khomeini, the Islamic cleric and former ruler of Iran, pronounced a death sentence on the British writer Salman Rushdie. Rushdie had written a novel called *The Satanic Verses*. The book caused much controversy because of the way it was perceived by many Muslims to undermine the revealed word of God given in the Qur'an. For Muslims the revelations that were given to Muhammad and later written down in the Qur'an are sacred and believed to be part of real historical events, which must not be mixed up with, or abused by, works of fiction like that of Rushdie's.

Islam, being a religion of the Book, has its basis in an unshakeable faith in a literary miracle. For Islam, the whole Qur'an is literally the revealed word of God. Its truthfulness is beyond question. Islam is at its orthodox heart both a fundamentalist and a fideistic religion. Muslims, who see the world through the teachings of the Qur'an, are given an all-embracing way of living and being in the world, which both provides their identity and confers certainty. Although some Muslims do not agree with the *fatwa* against Salman Rushdie, the ultra fundamentalists saw it as a black and white issue.

Yet in the Western world the death threat against Rushdie was greeted with a mixture of incredulity and anger that sections of the Muslim community couldn't allow the sacred to be trivialized for the sake of art and freedom of speech. As such the whole debate over the *Satanic Verses* represents a clash between the certainty contained in a fundamentalist world-view and that of a Western liberalism which, influenced by postmodern thought and consumer culture, regards Islam as just another source of narrative to be used.

On the very day the death sentence was announced, Rushdie stated that doubt, it seems to me, is the central condition of a human being in the twentieth century. One of the things that has happened to us... is to learn how certainty crumbles in your hand.

As we have seen in the previous unit, one of the major creeds of postmodernism is a hermeneutic of suspicion which is unable to stop deconstructing our very thoughts and experiences of reality. In reacting against Rushdie's book, Muslims have challenged the world of postmodern deconstructionism and refused to accept the promulgation of doubt. They have retaliated with a forceful and violent assertion of certainty in the truthfulness of their own creed.

Those who criticize Western culture increasingly say that it rails against the very idea of absolutes, and is driven by a consumerist ideology which seeks immediate self-fulfilment. An increasing number of people lost in the sea of signs, brand names, and trivia of postmodernity find themselves burdened with mind-boggling uncertainty over how to decide what is worth pursuing and why it should be pursued in life. Within such a context, many are turning to fundamentalism. Although it precedes postmodernism, fundamentalism marks a powerful response to postmodern culture.

But how did the term 'fundamentalism' come about?

The development of the term within Protestant Christianity

The dispensationalist movement was founded by J.N. Darby, amongst others, in the nineteenth century. While within England it caused the formation of a new denomination, the Plymouth Brethren; in the United States it was a force within such mainstream Christian denominations as the Presbyterian and Baptist Churches. Theologies and beliefs concerning the end of the world were given prominence. Dispensationalism divided history into several epochs before and after the coming of Christ, and emphasized premillennial prophecy. The teachings of the movement almost reached canonical status when the Bible notes of C.I. Scofield were published, in his famous Reference Bible, as the definitive way of interpreting the Biblical text.

During the period 1909 to 1915 a series of booklets were published in the United States by a group of dispensationalists. They were given the name *The Fundamentals*. Each of the booklets referred to a key element of traditional Christian teaching. They covered such topics as the divinity of Christ, his second coming at the end of the world, the belief in heaven and hell, and the authority of the Bible. Subsequently the term fundamentalism was used by Curtis Lee Laws (1868-1946) at a Northern Baptist Convention in 1920 to describe the anti-modernist party he belonged to. The term became increasingly applied to a broad coalition of Protestant, evangelical Christians. They were typified by a belief in supernaturalist biblical Christianity and they rejected and challenged the impact of secularism and liberal theology at the time.

Towards the end of the nineteenth century a group of fundamentalist scholars connected with Princeton University, New Jersey developed a doctrine called the inerrancy of scripture. Through this theological device such theologians as James Orr, Charles and Archibald Hodge and B.B. Warfield attempted to provide an incontestable philosophical foundation for the truth of scripture. However, though they wished, through the assertion of the doctrine of inerrancy, to protect the infallibility of scripture, they were in danger of making faith in a particular theological dogma more important than the revelation of Christ. Some theologians have suggested that to make scripture, instead of God, the locus of truth may be a form of religious positivism which borders on idolatry. However, the doctrine of inerrancy still exercises a powerful hold on much of the evangelical church today.

The Vineyard Church of John Wimber, the 'New Frontiers' movement of Terry Virgo, the writings of Colin Urquhart, the ministry of Reinhard Bonnke, and tele-evangelists such as Morris Cerullo and Benny Hinn, all form varying examples of contemporary fundamentalist and revivalist movements within Christianity.

Christian fundamentalism tries to uphold the truthfulness of the Christian tradition by a call to personal holiness. This can be seen as a development of nineteenth-century American revivalism. In its turn, Revivalism shares common roots with the 'Holiness Movement' and Pentecostalism back to the ministry of John Wesley and early Methodism in the eighteenth century.

A worldwide phenomenon

Fundamentalism is a term which the media in the Western world have come to use more and more. Not only has it entered common parlance but its very meaning has become difficult to pin down. It can no longer be limited in its use to a particular form of evangelical Christianity as a seminal study on fundamentalism by James Barr did in 1977.

While the terms liberal and fundamentalist may be used to identify one's own position they are often used to label an enemy. Both terms have taken on abusive overtones. The fundamentalist is often thought of as arrogant, blinkered and culturally uneducated. The liberal is in turn perceived as timid, fickle and continually mesmerized by new fashions in thought and culture. Christian thinker, Leslie Newbiggin says that, for the liberal, the ability to doubt is a measure of intellectual maturity and honesty. For the fundamentalist, however, doubt is equated with sin.

Although the term has, as a result of its wider use within society been most often associated with religious groups, it has also been identified by sociologists in the secular realm. Some uncompromising assertions made by feminists have been labelled 'fundamentalist'.

But what characteristics can be discerned in this wider use of the term which has come about today?

Fundamentalism may be viewed as a tendency or habit of mind. It transcends specific religious and secular groups and, as such, it has a distinctive world-view. Fundamentalists tell themselves a story designed to encompass the truth about the whole of reality. They are provided with a social structure around which life is organized. In participating, its members find both personal value and corporate identity.

It has been suggested by Christian historian Martin Marty that the fundamentalist lifestyle appeals to a particular kind of personality type. They have, he argues, a psychological profile which finds that authoritarian structures provide security for living – for example, in many fundamentalist sects even personal relationships are controlled so that men and women cannot associate freely.

As a socio-linguistic phenomenon fundamentalism has several identifiable characteristics. These have been well summed up and identified by an Anglican theologian called Martyn Percy.

FUNDAMENTALISM TRIES TO CONVINCE PEOPLE OF ITS OWN AUTHENTICITY in both practice and belief. The establishment of an absolute authority which is beyond critical question becomes an essential pre-requisite for such a world-view. This is often achieved by looking back into the past in order to identify a core set of fundamental beliefs and events. So, for example, it will identify particular interpretations of a historic tradition as the basis of truth. The chosen set of fundamental beliefs, with the story used to explain and legitimate it, forms the glasses through which the member of the community looks out on, understands and experiences the world.

FUNDAMENTALISM FINDS ITS OWN IDENTITY THROUGH ITS OPPOSITION TO ANY TRADITION WHICH THREATENS ITS OWN AUTHORITY and accompanying world-view. Other approaches outside its own, even those of other fundamentalist groups, are often deemed to be in error. It forsakes a full-fledged sectarianism which would involve a retreat from the world. Instead it seeks to change the world through the imposition of its own truths. The world must receive the particular fundamentalist group on terms of their choosing. Opportunities for true dialogue and mutual learning become very limited if not impossible. The need to champion and protect its own authority is too strong.

FUNDAMENTALISM IS MOST CLEARLY IDENTIFIED THROUGH ITS ATTACK UPON LIBERALISM and any theological and ethical positions which are seen as syncretistic or promoting the cause of pluralism and relativism. Because it commonly conceives of itself as being in a battle for the truth, the metaphor of 'Holy War' is used in various ways.

While much of what has been said above may find resonances within many of the mainline traditions within Christianity, Islam, Judaism and other world-views, not all Christians, Muslims Jews or other believers are fundamentalists. The fundamentalist spirit is marked off as different by two key features.

* Firstly it needs to be remembered that it operates as a totally closed world-view which is not open to any substantive dialogue. Doctrines are held to be true in a rigidly defined way which confers power to its own hierarchical and organizational structure.

* Secondly, truth is seen as being certain and uniformly identifiable with their own interpretation. Any possibility of ambiguity is out.

It could be argued as a result of these observations that the controlling paradigm of fundamentalism is one of power. Although each fundamentalist group will have its own unique narrative to explain what it is about, each commonly seeks an organizing principle for life through the power provided by an unquestionable authority over one's own life, over the lives of others, and also over reality itself. Power is able to vanquish the fear of the unknown which is often at the heart of the need to adopt such views.

The fundamentalist orientation of 'Christian' sects

As a socio-linguistic phenomenon, fundamentalism is often parasitic upon other more established religious or secular traditions, but the fundamentalist spirit can manifest itself in very prominent and sensationalist ways in sects and cults. Two such examples are those organizations led by David Koresh and Sun Myung Moon.

The Waco, Texas sect of David Koresh was called the Branch Davidians. The sect was itself an outgrowth from a more mainstream group within Christianity called the Seventh Day Adventists. Koresh took the narrow focus on matters concerning the end-times within Adventism and pushed it to its ultimate limits. In claiming to be *the* 'Lamb of God' he took final authority over the members of his sect in all matters, including sexual activity; he took his married female disciples as sexual partners and had many children by them. As the Messiah he proclaimed that the second coming of Jesus had been fulfilled in him, and that he would bring in the final judgment of the world. In a horrific apocalyptic end, he and his followers were burnt to death through a fire which they themselves had started in order to experience the ultimate test of commitment 'through the fire of the furnace'. Within the sect one individual had became obsessed with the power and authority the particular mythic story he told gave him over his followers – with disastrous consequences.

Sun Myung Moon, as the leader of a sect nicknamed the Moonies, represents yet another manifestation of the fundamentalist phenomenon. The sect, which calls itself the Unification Church, was founded in Korea in 1954 and is a considerable aberration from Christianity. Its disciples are urged to give all their worldly possessions to the organization. As a result they become dependent on the sect, which then provides for their needs. In return members are sent on relentless fund-raising and recruitment missions. Not only has the sect been known to cause the break-up of families; it has often been charged with 'brainwashing' its members into devoted service to Sun Myung Moon, whom they believe to be the Messiah. In Britain it lost a libel suit against the *Daily Mail* newspaper, which had published an article accusing it of 'brainwashing'. Within the United States Moon has been imprisoned for tax evasion. Despite this he has owned the New Yorker Hotel in Manhatten, the *Washington Times* newspaper and considerable real estate; he even has a theological seminary in New York State.

Fundamentalism versus liberalism within Islam and Judaism

Two other religions which are struggling to come to terms with strengthening fundamentalist groups within them are Islam and Judaism.

The Salman Rushdie affair only served to highlight the tensions that exist within Islam today. At a sixth-form college in London young Muslim boys who are members of the Muslim Youth Organization, which is dedicated to the introduction of Islamic government to Britain, threatened Muslim girls for their 'immodest' dress and for daring to study modern art, which exposed them to representations of nudity. Saudi Arabia punishes women who drive cars. Kuwait has refused to give women equal rights despite its promise to do so during the Iraqi occupation in 1990.

Many countries in the Islamic world are experiencing much turmoil as hard-line fundamentalist and more liberally inclined factions fight one another for the hearts and minds of their fellow citizens. The tensions caused by those who would seek to impose Qur'anic values upon society through Shari'a law, to counteract the seductive pull of Western materialism, leads to an explosive mixture which is nothing less than a battle over the shape Islam will take in the twenty-first century. Is Islam to completely oppose and reject Western liberalism, or will it be able to find some kind of accommodation with it which will not undermine its essentially fundamentalist origins?

A particularly harsh form of Islamic fundamentalism is being imposed on much of the population of Afghanistan by a Muslim movement called the Taliban. Their interpretation of the Qur'an and Islamic law is very strict. Many Muslims reject this. The result is a fierce civil war fought between Muslims over how Islam should be lived and applied to the population. Similar tensions have surfaced in Iran, Sudan and Algeria.

Fundamentalist religious groups, perhaps because they look back to past events and cultural norms in order to find their legitimation and driving force, have a tendency to limit the role of women within society. While the Qur'an gave more rights to women in the seventh century than they have attained in the Western world until the twentieth century, the Taliban have enforced such strictures on women that many say it has reached the level of misogyny.

They have pronounced many edicts in order to enforce their particular brand of Islam on the population. One such edict stated that women are not allowed to be employed, while another imposed the wearing of a full-length covering called a *burqa* upon all women. Women found still working as nurses and women whose ankles are showing, have been beaten up by the Taliban militia.

The fundamentalist-liberal divide within Judaism

Within Judaism Hasidic Jews form a particularly powerful fundamentalist movement which has splintered into dozens of different dynasties. Again, many strictures and limitations are placed on the role and life of women.

Hasidic Judaism developed out of a Jewish revivalist movement led by Israel Baal Shem in eighteenth-century Poland. It is a strongly anti-intellectualist movement, with such a strong emphasis on the Jewish mystical tradition called Kabbalism that it has taken on some of the hallmarks of a Gnostic sect. A secret spiritual knowledge within Hasidism is open only to a few very pious and wise individuals. Each group is led by a Rebbe, who is considered to possess immense spiritual insight and powers which confound the understanding of ordinary people. To follow his example and to submit to his authority is to move closer to God in one's own life.

Hasidic groups are almost totally impenetrable to anyone who does not already belong to the sect. Only a minor group called the Lubavitch Habad actively recruit converts from non-Hasidic Jews. Yet Hasidic Judaism has shown a willingness in both the USA and Israel to use the media, its financial power, and the political system to further its own ends as a highly anti-modernist movement which is willing to challenge liberalism head-on.

Indeed, tensions within Israel between secular Jews and the Ultra-Orthodox Hasidim are a growing cause for concern for the survival of that country.

Fundamentalism as the flip side of postmodernity

Because fundamentalism as a social phenomenon is on the increase today, society finds itself with a growing set of tensions and conflicts which threaten to tear apart the humanistic commitments to tolerance and equal rights which have formed part of the fabric of Western democratic culture. Believers in an old-style world-view with its absolutes of right and wrong, God and the created order, find themselves in danger of being overwhelmed by uncertainty in the postmodern world.

In the hurry to re-establish order out of the postmodern chaos, new converts to the fundamentalist way of being are inadvertently encouraging the further fragmentation of society by their very defiance of it. For the embracing of the fundamentalist spirit entails the taking of fragmentation to its logical conclusion. One particular and specific fragment within a tradition is made the primary focus. It is then expanded into an all-encompassing ideology and world-view through which life may be ordered afresh.

With certainty given a new and unshakeable foundation, the need to listen to and be in dialogue with the beliefs of others is removed. In consequence, opportunities to understand and to develop the ability to empathize with others are diminished.

It is ironic that much postmodern thought encourages the same result: if there is no real truth about anything, what is the point of dialogue?

Postmodernity, although marked by increasing pluralism is providing two basic and competing ideologies as two sides of the same coin. On the one side is an inability to commit oneself to or believe in anything; on the other side of the coin a belief in the unquestionable truth of one specific world-view is encouraged. Much of postmodern thought, with its own certainty and its forceful rejection of modern, humanist and all other fixed world-views, manifests the fundamentalist habit of mind in a very secular way: it is *certain* that the truth cannot be known. The paradox is easy to spot. How can a belief in no absolute truths be so absolutely certain of anything?

Fundamentalist religiosity stands at the opposite end of spirituality to New Age eclecticism. Each is antagonistic to the other; they serve as examples of the sort of tensions that increasingly face society in the future.

Yet these opposing ideologies need not be allowed to set the agenda. As Leslie Newbiggin has pointed out, liberalism, at its best, carries an open mind which in humility is willing to learn. Conservatism, at its best, carries within it a moral courage and steadfastness which fails to give up on the truth. Can both liberalism and conservatism find a way forward together?

PART

16

Renaissance or Delusion?

NEW AGE THINKING

Shifting the Paradigm
Modern New Age Movements

Today, there is a lot of talk about a New Age dawning.

* Where does this idea come from?

* What is the New Age movement?

* Who is part of it?

* Which people are involved?

* Where are the places you can find it?

* What beliefs and philosophies underpin it?

The vision of a New Age has several sources. One source is astrology. According to astrological teaching, evolution goes through cycles. Roughly speaking, every 2,100 years, due to what is known as 'the precession of the equinoxes', the Earth appears to move backwards from one sign of the Zodiac to another. The age of Pisces has just ended and the Age of Aquarius is upon us. It is supposed to be an age of human harmony, mutual understanding and spiritual growth. Whether or not this view has any substance in fact, many people have adopted the Age of Aquarius as a metaphor for the New Age.

Another source is the idea of evolution. But instead of seeing evolution in the physical realm, there is a shift to evolution in the sphere of the psychological and spiritual. This is on a massive world scale. On this view, whole civilizations, just like individuals, go through profound changes which represent a shift from one evolutionary state to another. These changes are referred to as *paradigm shifts*. Marilyn Ferguson, in her book *The Aquarian Conspiracy* (1981), wrote:

> New perspectives give birth to new historic ages. Humankind has had many dramatic revolutions of understanding – great leaps, sudden liberation from old limits. We discovered the uses of fire and the wheel, language and writing. We found that the earth only seems flat, the sun only seems to circle the earth, matter only seems solid. We learned to communicate, fly, explore.

A paradigm is a framework of thought (from the Greek *paradigma*, 'pattern'). It is a scheme for understanding and explaining certain aspects of reality. The idea of a paradigm shift was introduced by Thomas Kuhn, a scientist, historian and philosopher. He wrote *The Structure of Scientific Revolutions* (1962), and in it the idea of the paradigm shift is seen to contain various elements:

* It is a new way of thinking about new problems.

* It can be a principle that was present all along but unknown to us.

* The new paradigm cannot be embraced unless you let go of the old.

* New paradigms are nearly always greeted with hostility (as, for example, those of Galileo, Copernicus, Pasteur...).

Kuhn makes the point that those who work with the old view are, out of habit, emotionally attached to it. The new paradigm demands such a change of perspective that scientists are rarely converted to the new.

What is it about this New Age that is supposed to be so different? New Age writers focus on different aspects of the movement, but there seems to be common thinking around core concerns:

New Age offers a holistic perspective on life: integrating body, mind and spirit.

Central to New Age thinking is the idea that human beings have many levels of consciousness. We tend to operate at the lower levels most of the time.

The key concern of New Age thought is that if our higher self could be awakened then we would achieve the goal of human life. We would be awakened and transformed.

New Agers therefore employ a variety of techniques and methods, ideas and activities to help them to expand their consciousness and transform their lives.

The history of New Age thought

New Age writers claim that their world-view has its roots deep in human history. Among these roots are the Hindu Vedas and Hermetic thought.

The Vedas are a collection of four Hindu sacred texts written between 1800 and 1200 BC. The word Veda means 'knowledge'. Taken all together, the Rig-Veda, the Sama-Veda, the Yajur-Veda and the Atharva-Veda include rituals, chants, spells, mantras and hymns.

Hermetic literature is a collection of magical doctrine, mainly Greek but including some Christian mysticism. There are references to pre-Christian deities, such as Thoth and Isis, and to ancient healing techniques. The central figure in Hermetic literature is Hermes Trismegistus (Greek for the Egyptian god Thoth) who was the scribe of the gods and who invented writing and the arts. Jung valued Hermetic writings and his work draws on the myths. Hermetic writings survived via the Gnostics and the Kabbalists (ancient Jewish magical and mystical writers whose work was finalized about AD1280 by Spanish Jew Moses ben Shemtob). They surfaced again in the Renaissance.

But certain individuals have also been important:

JAKOB BOEHME (sixteenth century) was a Protestant mystic who, at the age of twenty-five, had an experience 'like the resurrection of the dead'. He wrote *Aurora* which described the experience, but his home town of Gorlitz forbade him to write any more. He was an occultist as well as a Protestant, and his interests included alchemy, astrology and the study of symbolism in the Jewish Kabbalah. His work influenced later thinkers such as Hegel and Nietzsche.

EMMANUEL SWEDENBORG (seventeenth century) was born in Stockholm in 1688. He dedicated his life to science and astronomy. He put forward a hypothesis to account for the creation of the planets. Then, in his fifties, he suddenly became a mystic and a visionary. He publicly revealed that he was in communication with spirit beings and that his visionary experiences had convinced him of the truth that all things were ultimately contained within a single godhead. He claimed to have considerable psychic and clairvoyant powers. In 1788 a Swedenborgian Church was founded which is still active today.

WILLIAM BLAKE (eighteenth/nineteenth centuries) was a poet and painter. He lived from 1757 to 1827. In his works he created myths. These included a pantheon based on the four 'Zoas': Urizen, Luvah, Urthona and Tharmas, which are seen as reason, feeling, intuition and sense. Blake was a Christian but he interpreted Christian beliefs in an unorthodox way. His belief in humanity's fall was that it was an inner fall and that Satan who tempted Eve was equated with 'the Selfhood'. New Age thought identifies with this emphasis on the inner reality of belief rather than outer absolutes. Blake said: 'All deities reside in the human breast.' His work shows him as a man who experienced vast changes and varieties of consciousness, in line with New Age focus.

All of the above – Boehme, Swedenborg and Blake – influenced the Transcendentalists. This was a group of American academics including Ralph Waldo Emerson and Henry Thoreau. They formed themselves in 1836 to explore the Quaker and Puritan traditions of the church, the writings of Greek and German philosophers, and Eastern religions. Their philosophy focused on an inner search for meaning.

There are many other roots and influences which are identified by New Age writers. William James, Madame Blavatsky, Arthur Koestler and Rudolf Steiner are all seen as precursors to the present New Age movement. But one pioneer is Sir George Trevelyan. He founded the Wrekin Trust which promotes the ideas of healers, mystics and philosophers. Trevelyan captured the spirit of New Age when he wrote in 1984:

> We face a time of change. That no one can deny. It implies breakdown and breakup of much we know, but it also implies breakthrough... The huge hope for our time is that the ocean of power and divine intelligence has actually launched an operation for the cleansing of our planet. This seems to me implicit in the holistic world-view. Not only is the planet a living creature of which we humans are integrally part, but the macrocosm of the solar system is a Living Organic Oneness.

New Age practices

The New Age movement includes a range of ideas and activities.

HOMEOPATHY is an alternative therapy to established medical practice. It was developed by a German doctor, Samuel Hahnemann (1755-1843). Hahnemann thought that disease primarily resulted from an imbalance in the body. He introduced a treatment whereby minute dosages of different drugs – even deadly toxins – could be introduced into the body, thus inducing a reaction. By doing this he believed he was stimulating the body to call on its own substantial reserves to heal. Many believe the treatment to be effective, and homeopathy is now practised world-wide. It is very popular in New Age practice.

AROMATHERAPY is the art by which essential oils are extracted from pleasant-smelling plants and used in massage. Fruit, flowers, spices, herbs and perfumes are all used to bring improved health.

ACUPUNCTURE is a process during which thin needles are inserted at specific points in the body. Acupuncturists believe that the body contains a flow of subtle energy called ch'i, moving through fourteen different channels ('meridians') in the body. By inserting the needles at different points, the flow of energy can be channelled for healing. Western medicine, based on scientific principles, finds difficulty in accepting these Chinese ideas of ch'i because there has never been a satisfactory theory to support the practice.

Findhorn and Glastonbury

The New Age movement has many expressions from different perspectives, individuals, cultures and communities. In Great Britain, the Findhorn Community is one of the most successful New Age groups. It was started in 1962 by Peter and Eileen Caddy and Dorothy Maclean.

These three claimed to have spirit guidance. In a caravan park situated in Scotland they found that by communing with nature spirits (devas) they were able to grow huge, magnificent vegetables in very poor soil. Even weeds could not survive well in the soil, it was so devoid of nutrients. Their story spread and there are pictures of press reporters watching forty-pound cabbages growing in sand! The account of this can be read in *The Magic of Findhorn* (Paul Hawken, 1976).

David Spangler, in his book *The Rebirth of the Sacred* (1984), comments on the magic of Findhorn:

> The secret was a mystical relationship which the Caddys, and Dorothy McLean in particular, had established with the invisible, spiritual, formative forces within nature; through the relationship they were guided in how best to cultivate the garden, but they were also aided in how to develop their own human spirituality and the bonds of a loving, creative community.

Another New Age centre is Glastonbury. The legend of King Arthur is connected with the ancient Isle of Avalon. In the fifteenth century Sir Thomas Malory identified it with Glastonbury, where in 1191 monks had claimed to have found the coffins of Arthur and Guinevere. As the legend of King Arthur developed, its central point became the Quest for the Holy Grail, the cup used by Jesus Christ at the Last Supper. It is believed that the Holy Grail was carried from Palestine to Britain by Joseph of Arimathea, who provided the tomb for Jesus' burial, and was hidden near Glastonbury. The myth of the Holy Grail has influenced many spiritual and occultist groups. Glastonbury is a place of pilgrimage for many New Age people.

How to recognize the New Age

The New Age movement is notoriously difficult to define because it is so diverse. In his personal definition David Spangler has suggested four levels at which the image of the New Age may be met and explored:

> A COMMERCIAL LEVEL. This is superficial and includes reading New Age magazines, wearing New Age shoes or clothes.

> A GLAMOUR LEVEL. At this level individuals or groups are living out their own fantasies of adventure and power through occult or extra-terrestrial forms. The 'will and creativity of the individual is often surrendered to a powerful leader or a glamorous cause'.

353

NEW AGE AS AN IMAGE OF CHANGE. The idea here is of transformation or the paradigm shift. This image is the one most popular in New Age publications. The New Age is seen as a new set of values in social, economic and technological terms.

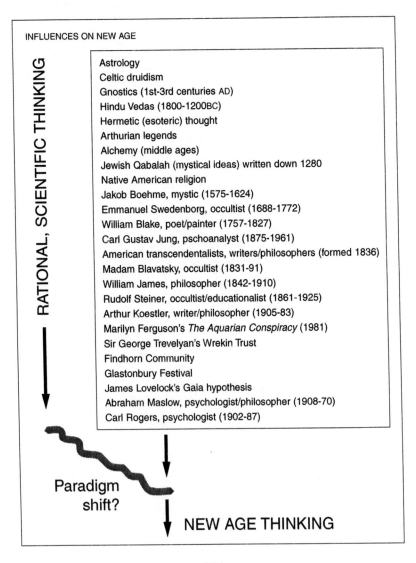

INFLUENCES ON NEW AGE

RATIONAL, SCIENTIFIC THINKING

Astrology
Celtic druidism
Gnostics (1st-3rd centuries AD)
Hindu Vedas (1800-1200BC)
Hermetic (esoteric) thought
Arthurian legends
Alchemy (middle ages)
Jewish Qabalah (mystical ideas) written down 1280
Native American religion
Jakob Boehme, mystic (1575-1624)
Emmanuel Swedenborg, occultist (1688-1772)
William Blake, poet/painter (1757-1827)
Carl Gustav Jung, pschoanalyst (1875-1961)
American transcendentalists, writers/philosophers (formed 1836)
Madam Blavatsky, occultist (1831-91)
William James, philosopher (1842-1910)
Rudolf Steiner, occultist/educationalist (1861-1925)
Arthur Koestler, writer/philosopher (1905-83)
Marilyn Ferguson's *The Aquarian Conspiracy* (1981)
Sir George Trevelyan's Wrekin Trust
Findhorn Community
Glastonbury Festival
James Lovelock's Gaia hypothesis
Abraham Maslow, psychologist/philosopher (1908-70)
Carl Rogers, psychologist (1902-87)

Paradigm shift?

NEW AGE THINKING

THE NEW AGE AS AN INCARNATION OF THE SACRED. For David Spangler this is really what it is all about. At this level the New Age is a spiritual event, the birth of a new consciousness, a new awareness and experience of life. In his words: 'This fourth level is concerned with identifying, naming and exploring the nature of the sacred experience that lies at the heart of that culture. This is not just a religious search, for the experience of the sacred is not only religious. It is also intellectual, artistic, emotional and physical... For me this issue of "renaming the sacred" is most deeply what the New Age is all about... To rename the sacred is to have a different view of the universe. It is to re-expand those boundaries we have placed around God, even to redefine the nature of divinity... It is to look at the objects, people, and events in our lives and to say "You are sacred. In you and with you I can find the sacramental passages that reconnect me to the wholeness of creation."'

This integration of the sacred and the material universe is captured in Buckminster Fuller's poem, in which he captures the sense of God as process:

> For God, to me, it seems
> is a verb
> not a noun,
> proper or improper;
> is the articulation
> not the art;
> is loving,
> not the abstraction of love.
> Yes, God is a verb,
> the most active, connoting the vast harmonic
> reordering the universe
> from unleashed chaos of energy.

And what do New Agers believe? Although very diverse, New Age thinking about God, the universe and reality centres around certain key concepts.

They believe that the individual contains God and the universe within him or herself. They also hold that everything in existence has a spiritual component. And they have a deep faith that the fundamental essence of the universe is unity.

These beliefs link New Age thinking with various older religious and spiritual movements, some of them pagan, some more philosophical.

ANIMISM: the ancient belief that all of nature is alive with spirits or divinities which inhabit mountains, trees, streams.

GNOSTICISM: the name applied to a number of sects which started in the early years of Christianity. The Christian church rejected Gnosticism as heresy. Gnostics were engaged in a search for hidden spiritual knowledge, through astrology or by concentrating on the so-called secret doctrines of Jesus. This knowledge was what saved a person, not faith in Christ or moral conduct. They were dualists in separating spirit (good) and matter (evil).

THEOSOPHY: a more recent influence literally meaning 'God-wisdom', from the Greek *theos* and *sophia*. The name suggests a mystical knowledge of the divine. The Theosophical Society was founded in 1875 by Madame Blavatsky and Colonel Olcott. Its aims included the study of comparative religion to establish a universal ethic and the development of the latent powers of the human soul. The doctrines of the society include a mixture of esoteric Buddhism and Hindu mysticism.

The Me-Cult
New Age Psychology

I LOVE ME. I am not conceited. I'm just a good friend to myself. And I like to do whatever makes me feel good... We live by a certain philosophy. We try to make our dreams come true today, instead of waiting for tomorrow. But before you can do good things for yourself, you have to know yourself... You need self-knowledge, before you can have self-satisfaction. Think about it.

So wrote a contributor to the New York Times in 1975. Sir Julian Huxley had said, in 1961:

The emergent religion of the near future could be a good thing... Instead of worshipping supernatural rulers, it will sanctify the higher manifestations of human nature, in art and love, in intellectual comprehension and aspiring adoration...

New Age thinking looks at what is the potential of being human. It explores possibilities of the physical, psychological and spiritual nature of humankind. It has therefore been referred to as 'the new humanism'. Marilyn Ferguson, in her influential *The Aquarian Conspiracy* (1981) wrote:

Carl Rogers described the Emerging Man: Lewis Mumford, the New Person, the age that would 'make the Renaissance look like a still-birth'...

Educator John Holt called for 'a radically new kind of human being'. The only possibility for our time, said Joseph Campbell, the mythologist, is 'the free association of men and women of like spirit... not a handful but a thousand heroes, ten thousand heroes, who will create a future image of what humankind can be'.

Humanism is a view of life that centres on the potential and achievements of humanity. Modern humanism rejects traditional belief in a personal God and elevates belief in human nature. Humanistic psychology is concerned with theories of the self. It stands in contrast to the determinism of the behaviourists and the Freudians because it is strongly optimistic about the power of men and women to change both themselves and society. Humanistic psychology has been called person-centred, holistic, and self-actualizing. It is also a psychology of personality, sometimes referred to as personalism. Some writers have stressed the religious nature of self-theory. Paul Vitz wrote:

> Psychology has become a religion, in particular a form of secular humanism based on worship of the self.

Self-theory

In the 1960s and 70s self-theory became very popular, especially in America. It appeared in several forms.

BESTSELLING BOOKS. In 1964 Eric Berne's *Games People Play* sold over three million copies. His self-theory is called transactional analysis. This approach to therapy is to encourage people to become autonomous. He emphasizes spontaneity, direct intimacy with others and heightened awareness of reality. Thomas Harris' 1968 *I'm O.K. – You're O.K.* was another best-selling transactional analysis book, looking at the relationship between the three ego states: Parent, Adult and Child. Other writers focused on business success and winning in the game of life. The slogan read 'You Were Born to Win'.

EST stands for Erhard Seminar Training, founded by Werner Erhard in 1971. It is now a multi-million-dollar business and offers intensive seminars. The teaching resembles the personal beliefs and the personality of its founder. The main goal is to enable people to transform their ability to experience living. The key emphasis is on the word 'experience', and this experience is of the self.

SELFISM AND SEX is one of the major ways of being open to all experience. Self-theory advocates openness to many sexual encounters. Various books have been enormously successful, such as *Open Marriage* and *Beginner's Guide to Group Sex*.

THE ESALEN INSTITUTE was founded in 1962 by Michael Murphy and Richard Price, based in Big Sur, California. Esalen has been the centre of the human potential movement, and during the 60s and 70s was a research centre for new ideas and for personal growth techniques. Carl Rogers, Abraham Maslow, Fritz Perls, Aldous Huxley and others have all been involved. Today there is a community at Esalen which numbers about 100 people and continues to be extremely popular in providing workshops, conferences and seminars on human potential.

Abraham Maslow

Born in 1908 in New York, Maslow was the son of a Russian Jewish immigrant. He taught psychology at Brooklyn College and Brandeis. Maslow's major work was on peak experiences and self-actualization. His work has been extremely influential in the human potential movement. Unlike many psychologists of his day he refused to study neurosis and human malfunctioning. Instead he was fascinated by what he called 'self-actualized' people: extremely healthy, fulfilled, successful individuals.

In his book *Toward a Psychology of Being* (1968), he wrote that all human beings have a hierarchy of basic needs beginning with the 'lower' needs of food, drink, sleep, shelter and clothing and ascending to a sense of belonging, friendship and self-esteem to even higher 'needs' of personal fulfilment, an integrated system of values and an aesthetic dimension to life. He listed the characteristics of the 'healthy' person who moves in the direction of self-actualization: 'ongoing actualization of potentials, capacities and talents, as fulfilment of mission (or call, fate, destiny, or vocation) as a fuller knowledge of, and acceptance of, the person's own intrinsic nature.' Such characteristics include increased spontaneity, a superior perception of reality, resistance to cultural conditioning and greatly increased awareness.

The increased awareness occurs in moments of peak experience such as falling in love, experiencing the intense beauty of music or being inspired.

During times of peak experience great strides can be taken towards self-actualization, although very few attain it.

Maslow has a dynamic view of personal growth and his work is a response to the question 'Why do some grow and others not?' His view of human nature is not Freudian and pessimistic, neither is it extremely optimistic like more radical thinkers in the human-growth school. He recognizes that human beings have blocks towards growth but he also believes that growth can be powerfully generated through 'single experiences such as tragedies, deaths, traumata, conversions and sudden insights, which force change on the life-outlook of the person'.

Carl Rogers

One of the best-known humanistic psychologists was Carl Rogers. Rogers was born in America in 1902 at a time when the rights of the individual to choose were all-important. He was brought up in a religious family whose beliefs kept them apart from the attitudes and habits of their neighbours. One of his mother's favourite Bible verses was 'Come out from among them and be ye separate'.

Rogers writes of himself that he was 'socially incompetent' as a teenager. In 1919 he went to the University of Wisconsin to study agriculture. It was there he met with humanist ideas within the liberal wing of Protestantism, and he grew away from his parents' views. He gave up studying agriculture and began to read history in order to equip himself for a life of 'religious work'. It was during this period that he wrote an essay on Luther which ended with a saying that was to become a lifelong belief: 'Man's ultimate reliance is upon his own experience.' He continued his studies and eventually discovered psychology. On qualifying as a psychologist he worked in the Child Study Department of the Society for the Prevention of Cruelty to Children. It was here that he began to move away from the directive approach of his training, where the psychologist took control of the interviews.

Rogers pioneered what is now known as non-directive, client-centred and person-centred therapy. He learned 'to rely upon the client for the direction of movement in the process of counselling'. His publications include *Counselling and Psychotherapy* (1942), an introduction to non-directive counselling in which therapy is seen as a movement towards personal autonomy. In *On Becoming a Person* (1961), Rogers sees the relationship created between counsellor and client, parent and child, teacher and student as the key to personal growth. He wrote:

> In my early professional years I was asking the question, How can I treat or cure or change this person? Now I would phrase the question in this way: How can I provide a relationship which this person may use for his own personal growth?

Important to Rogers' views is the idea of unconditional positive regard and empathetic understanding which the therapist needs to communicate to the client. By accepting someone for the person they are and trusting their personal capacity to change, a relationship develops between therapist and client which encourages and promotes change.

Criticisms of Self-theory

The best-selling pop psychologists, self-theorists and humanistic pychologists have been criticized on several accounts by different thinkers in biology, science, philosophy and Christian faith.

'Selfism' is rejected as a throwback to more rationalistic, optimistic and superficial interpretations of mind common in the eighteenth and nineteenth centuries. Some argue that it fails to acknowledge Freud's achievements which include the acknowledgement of unconscious irrational elements in human nature such as sadism and destructiveness.

Is human nature all that good? The popularizers who have sold millions of books assume the goodness of the self, but are they right? Is my idea of 'me' valid? Are there perhaps different and conflicting layers of the self?

The basic question is, what is the 'real' or 'true' self? How do you recognize the potential of the self? Is the self really a product of society? Or a biological product?

Selfism is a kind of substitute religion which trivializes life by claiming that suffering is without real meaning. Suffering is seen more as a man-made error which can be avoided if the environment can be controlled or the self can be actualized.

What do you think? Is the self a powerful source for change? Does it give meaning to life? Is it real or a delusion?

Tomorrow's World
A Bird's-eye View

How far have we really progressed as human beings? How do we think of ourselves? Where have we got to in what we believe or do not believe about God? What is humanity?

This book has traced the developing ideas of the centuries.

* With Copernicus, Kepler and Galileo, humanity is no longer the centre of the universe. What matters is matter.

* With Descartes mind is more certain than matter. We think therefore we are.

* With Newton mind is subject to the laws of motion and gravity. Human beings are mechanistic – purposeless lumps of matter moving in time and space.

* With Determinism comes the view that humanity is now certain. Evolution of every physical system is controlled by rigorous laws. Objective observation rules out subjective experience as being insignificant in determining reality.

* With New Age thinking comes renewed interest in the personal, the subjective and the self: a view of humanity as spiritual beings.

These beliefs and philosophies have been studied in theory but they affect the way life is lived. Take your own life in school, work or your neighbourhood as an example. What philosophy is your school or university giving you? How is it affecting your life?

In Britain philosophy is not included in the National Curriculum. That very fact says something about how we value certain forms of thinking. Other European countries, such as France, count it as very important. In Norway, six months' philosophy is compulsory to all new university students.

So what is the philosophy of education in a school that does not have philosophy on the timetable? Think for a minute, and apply some philosophical thinking to your own education. Here are a few lines of thought:

In your firm or school – is a person a mind? A machine? Is humanity all knowledge? All experience?

How are things organized? The structure is not haphazard, it has an underlying philosophy. So what philosophical message is being communicated about people and life? In your school or college, what subjects are actively promoted to the exclusion of others? Where are the most staff, the best resources? According to these priorities, what is a human being? What does a person need to become educated? Lots of mind exercise? Lots of body development? Lots of religious/spiritual education?

Who says what's important? Why? What are the assumptions of our academic culture?

The hidden curriculum

In every school there is a curriculum. Some educationalists would say that in every school there is also a hidden curriculum – not so much the content of what is taught but much more the process of what is actually going on. So, for example:

* When a school insists on a uniform, what is being taught?

* When it is forbidden to call a teacher by their first name, what is being taught?

* By sitting individually in desks, what is being taught?

* When most lessons are led by teachers and pupils say very little, what is being taught?

* When students are not consulted about their written school reports, what is being said?

How we are taught to think is as important as what we are taught to think. The very way you learn transmits a particular philosophy about you and your world. The study of philosophy in this book does not escape these implicit beliefs and values. Claude Levi-Strauss in his *A World on the Wane* (1961) described the intellectual patterns transmitted to him in his own French education:

> It was then that I began to learn how any problem, whether grave or trivial, can be resolved. The method never varies. First you establish the traditional 'two views' of the question. You then put forward a commonsense justification of the one, only to refute it by the other. Finally you send them both packing by the use of a third interpretation, in which both the others are shown to be equally unsatisfactory. Certain verbal manoeuvres enable you to line up the traditional 'antitheses' as complementary aspects of a single reality: form and substance, content and container, appearance and reality, essence and existence, continuity and discontinuity and so on. Before long the exercise becomes the merest verbalizing, reflection gives place to a kind of superior punning... Five years at the Sorbonne taught me little but this form of mental gymnastics.

What direction do you want to go in as a human being? How does your school or college reflect this? What patterns of thought and behaviour are being transmitted in your educational culture? What is the point of education?

Education shapes us. The history of educational theory is marked by two polar views, with variations in between:

* Education is formation from without (a 'traditional' view).

* Education is formation from within (a 'progressive' view).

Education from without is based on the view that education is a process of overcoming what is natural and substituting in its place external standards, moral training, and methods of instruction. The main purpose is to prepare the young person for the responsibilities of adult citizenship in society and for success in 'life'. The main subject matter looks to the past and is transmitted from outside, in textbooks and the teacher is the agent through which knowledge and skills are communicated to the student.

'Progressive' education sees the above model as one of imposition from above and from outside. John Dewey (1938) described 'progressive education':

To imposition from above is opposed expression and cultivation of individuality; to external discipline is opposed free activity; to learning from texts and teachers, learning through experience... to static aims and materials is opposed acquaintance with a changing world.

Change and progress

Some educationalists would say that a philosophy of change is the most useful basis for the education of the modern Western world.

Century by century the world moves on to change. Alvin Toffler's *Future Shock* (1970) argued that most change has taken place in the recent past:

> The overwhelming majority of all the material goods we use in daily life today have been developed within the present generation's lifetime.

But with all this change, has humanity progressed? How far have we got with the big questions of life? Do we know the purpose of our lives, the meaning of our existence? Can we distinguish between reality and unreality? Do we understand what things can be known and what things cannot?

We are hundreds of philosophical years on from Heraclitus, Plato and Aristotle. We have travelled through the Age of Renaissance, the Age of Reason and Enlightenment and we are now in the Age of Aquarius. In the light of all this thought and progress and knowledge, do people today lead better, more purposeful, integrated, productive, fruitful, satisfying human lives? Or is the modern world with all its change in a state of mental and spiritual decline? How far has our knowledge really progressed?

Let certain questions remain in our minds:

* Are we in charge of our universe? Has science shown us a reliable way of knowing what is real?

* Are we in tune with our universe? Is New Age to give us hope for a holistic view of reality?

* Do our senses offer us a sure way of knowing what is real? Has empiricism offered us a way forward?

* Is truth what works? Has Pragmatism given us a practical solution to the question of what is true?

* Is the use of the mind and reason the only way to determine reality? Does Rationalism provide a true way of knowing?

* Do human beings have all the potential they need in themselves to make sense of and live out reality? Is Humanism the religion of the future?

Or is the source of all truth and reality in a higher realm of meaning? Is the truth in God?

And just suppose it is. Given our education and our cultural assumptions, can we still think about God? Is God an open or a closed option?

Appendix
For further thinking

Chapter 1: Knowledge and Reason

1. What is philosophy?

2. What was the major philosophical problem for the early Greek (pre-Socratic) philosophers? Whose views do you most value and why?

3. If you have interested friends, arrange your own trial of Socrates. You need a prosecutor, defender and a jury. The charge is: 'Socrates is an evil-doer and a curious person, searching into things under the earth and above the heavens; and making the worse appear the better cause, and teaching all this to others.' Is he guilty?

Chapter 2: Theories of Knowledge

1. How do Plato and Aristotle differ in their philosophy?

2. How has Plato's Theory of Forms influenced the development of Christianity? Is this good?

3. What is meant by Metaphysics? Has the study of Metaphysics any importance in our world today? Choose one of the following viewpoints to defend: 'The study of Metaphysics is of real importance in the twentieth century.' 'The study of Metaphysics is outdated and unnecessary in our society today.' List all your reasons for supporting the preferred view.

Chapter 3: Faith and Reason

1. What is faith? Give examples from either your own life or the life of others you have read about.

2. Why did the early Church Fathers harmonize Greek philosophy with Christian faith? Do you think they did the right thing?

3. Why is Augustine of Hippo the greatest of all the early Church Fathers? Choose two different stages in the development of Augustine's thinking (preferably quite far apart) and write/record or act a conversation between the younger and the older Augustine on the question of the 'search for truth.'

Chapter 4: The Nature of the Soul

1. Do you think our Education System follows Aristotle or does not follow Aristotle in its views on the intellect?

2. How might a conversation develop between Plato and Aristotle concerning Immortality?

3. Draw a heraldic shield, and divide it into four parts. In each section draw a picture/symbol which represents a part of yourself, that is, your identity, your beliefs, for example, or your values or your hopes for the future. Discuss your shield with a friend. A year ago, would you have drawn something different? Do you think the shield will be the same in a year's time? Are there some things that are constant?

Chapter 5: Mind and Body Divided

1. What issues might a religious person who was also a rationalist encounter in their belief about God?

2. How important is your mind to you? What place does it have in your overall thinking about yourself?

3. With a friend, choose one of the following three exercises: Discuss whether in today's world the medical profession has any assumptions

regarding the mind/body division. Or else complete this exercise in self-awareness: Get into pairs. Person A has a clean sheet of paper and a pen and is ready to write. Person B is going to be the speaker. Person A asks the question 'Who are you?' Person B replies 'I am......' The response can be anything that comes into your mind, such as 'I am a son/daughter', 'I am a romantic'. Person A writes down the answer and then repeats the question again, and says 'Yes, but who are you?'

The exercise continues for between five and ten minutes. When you have finished, look at the responses and see how they developed. Reverse roles. Or else, write your own letter to Descartes questioning his views.

Chapter 6: What Price the Soul?

1. How would a materialist (physicalist) view life after death?

2. A discussion on animal experiments: Do you think these are justified for scientific/psychological progress?

3. Do you agree with Skinner's view that people are completely controlled by their environment?

Chapter 7: From Plato to Bertrand Russell

1. Can anything be certain? If it can, prove it. If it cannot, why not?

2. How would you either defend the ontological argument or criticize it?

3. Explain what is meant by a 'contingent' thing and a 'necessary' thing.

Chapter 8: The Five Ways

1. 'This dumb ox will fill the world with his bellowing.' How did Aquinas do this?

2. Choose one of Aquinas' five proofs of God and argue it further with someone who opposes you. Record your discussion. Were you consistent with Aquinas? What objections were raised? Were these valid?

Chapter 9: The Argument from Religious Experience

1. Have you, or any of your friends, had any religious experiences? Have you read of people who claim to have them? Collect as much information as you can. What reasons do people have for saying an experience is religious?

2. If religion is nothing but feeling and experience what intellectual problems does this bring? Conversely, is it possible to have religion without any feeling or experience?

3. How would Martin Buber's views affect the way a person lived their life?

Chapter 10: Knowing through the Mind

1. Do our senses always deceive us? Is everything an illusion? Discuss.

2. How convincing is Descartes' certainty that 'I think, therefore I am'? In groups of two select one person to defend Descartes' view and the other to oppose it. List your arguments and see if they can be improved by discussion with others.

3. Are our minds and bodies separate entities? Who might disagree with this view, and why?

Chapter 11: Knowing through our Senses

1. Locke wrote, 'All ideas come from sensation or reflection.' What problems does this pose for a Rationalist?

2. Imagine a discussion between either Descartes and John Locke on the subject of God, or John Locke and a scientist on the subject of scientific knowledge. Write down a conversation that would reflect both views.

3. If you took seriously Bishop Berkeley's view that only the contents of our experience can be said to exist, what effect would this have on the way you live your life and the way you think?

Chapter 12: The Limits of Knowing

1. Is thinking, or reason, merely a habit?

2. Hume said that we cannot assume one event causes another. If this is so, which group, which individuals, and what beliefs would it most affect? Why?

3. Do you believe that there is no self? If there is no personal self which exists, if inside people there are only collections of different perceptions in flux, how might this view affect how you see views on marriage, for example, or views on morality and moral responsibility, or Christian belief in the afterlife, or psychological theory and practice?

Chapter 13: Faith: the Highest Way of Living

1. Is Existentialism relevant in our society today? If so – how?

2. Write a sermon based on Kierkegaard's philosophy. What questions would you put to him about the sermon you have written?

3. Does faith begin where thinking leaves off?

Chapter 14: The Nature of Being

1. Write (or speak) a conversation between Heidegger and Kierkegaard on the issue of death and extinction. Which view do you support (or neither?) and why?

2. What, according to Heidegger, is the nature of Authentic and Inauthentic Being?

3. Would Heidegger's philosophy have any relevance to your school or community today?

Chapter 15: Free to Choose

1. Sartre believed that human beings were completely free to choose their own values and lifestyle. Write or discuss criticism of this from:
a) a Christian perspective; b) a determinist view; c) your own view.

2. Do you think Sartre's philosophy is ultimately positive or negative?

3. What is 'bad faith?' Can it be avoided?

Chapter 16: God as Psychological Projection

1. Do you think Feuerbach's views contribute to religious faith? If so – how? If not – why not?

2. Feuerbach said that 'What man wishes to be, he makes his God'. In your own experience and your knowledge of history – is there evidence for this view?

3. What arguments might a Christian believer put forward against Feuerbach's belief in God as a projection of the mind?

Chapter 17: The Unconscious Mind

1. Discuss Freud's belief that buried traumas and repressed emotional shocks can cause physical and mental problems later on in life. What is the prevailing view of the group/class? Do you agree with Freud?

2. Are dreams 'the royal road to a knowledge of the unconscious activities of the mind?' As a group pool your own experiences of dreams. Are there any dreams which have helped you, or given you an insight into your self?

3. What questions would you like to ask Freud?

Chapter 18: The Collective Unconscious

1. What is Jung's theory of Archetypes? Can you think of other examples in history, myth literature or religion that exist universally, across different cultures?

2. Who are a) the 'extraverts' and the 'introverts'; b) the 'feeling' and 'thinking' types in your class/group/family/school? In everyday life what misunderstandings might occur between these different types? Are there ways these could be avoided?

Chapter 19: The Republic

1. Is justice a universal value or can different kinds of justice exist in different societies? Is God's justice different from human justice? If so, how?

2. Would you like to live in Plato's republic? What are its good and bad points?

3. Can you recognize any of Plato's ideas in operation today?

Chapter 20: The Ultimate Political Pragmatist

1. 'All's fair in love and war.' How far can you go along with that statement?

2. How do you think Machiavelli would have approached the question of God's judgment if he had had to write about it?

3. Is a moral basis to politics possible?

Chapter 21: Class Conflict

1. Do you think society forms your ideas? If so, how?

2. What political changes do you think are necessary to bring about a better society? Write your own Manifesto and justify your criteria.

3. Marx said that if someone lives happily in a small house, but someone else comes and builds a larger house next door, the first person will want a larger house too. Even when we have enough, society teaches us to want more. What do you think? Is it possible to imagine a society where everyone has enough?

Chapter 22: The Rise of Humanism

1. What sort of Renaissance do you think we need today? In groups, design a futuristic programme of change for society. What past values, beliefs and skills would you include?

2. In what way did Erasmus combine theology and humanism? Do you think he was successful?

3. What problems and what possibilities arise when human reason is seen as the way to determine truth?

Chapter 23: Beyond Good and Evil

1. What objections might a Christian raise to Nietzsche's idea of a Will to Power?

2. Do you agree with the view that we make rather than discover values? How do you know the difference between the two?

3. Is the school or organization in which you work Dionysian or Apollonian or both?

Chapter 24: Humanism in the Modern World

1. In your view, has humanity progressed?

2. Is Utilitarianism fair?

Chapter 25: Christology through the Ages

1. Does Christian faith depend on Jesus being 'God with us'?

2. Divide your group into two. One group are Arians (Jesus was human alone) the other group are Apollinarians (Jesus' flesh is human but his mind is divine). With your knowledge of the gospels or with the gospels open in front of you, argue against each other for the position you have been given.

3. Why is the incarnation so important to Christians?

Chapter 26: The Kingdom of God

1. What do the gospel accounts show the kingdom of God to be?

2. What do you think Jesus meant by saying, 'Unless a person is born of water and the spirit he cannot enter the kingdom of God?'

3. What would the kingdom of God be like on earth?

Chapter 27: Revelation and Response

1. Would you bet on Pascal's wager?

2. What does Bonhoeffer mean by a religionless Christianity? Do you think his criticisms of the church are valid?

3. In our present Western society with its post-Enlightenment world-view (see Chapter 34) would it be possible for us to believe in a God who communicates through revelation?

Chapter 28: The Struggle for Understanding

1. What different views are held by Christians about the status of the Bible? Which do you most agree with and why? Which do you least agree with?

2. If the Bible had been edited by Gnostics what differences might there be in its content and beliefs?

3. How did the early church agree on which scriptures should become canon? Do you think their criteria were sufficient? Would you have added anything?

Chapter 29: The Reformation

1. What did Luther mean by 'justification by faith'?

2. What differences do you imagine there are in the life of a believer when he or she puts more importance on the teaching of the Bible than on the authority of the church government?

3. Why do you think Luther's beliefs spread so rapidly?

Chapter 30: Interpreting the Bible Today

1. What would be some of the differences between a Conservative and Liberal reading of the resurrection of Jesus Christ from the dead?

2. Imagine you are a scientist who holds conservative views about the Bible. What issues would you have to confront?

3. Does God speak through the Bible? Do you, or does anyone you know, believe that God reveals himself through it? Find out as much as you can about how revelation influences faith.

Chapter 31: Creation and Evolution

1. Do you believe that human beings are made by God, or are we a result of a random natural process? How might your views on this influence the way you live your life?

2. Some Christians see no conflict between science and religion. How do they manage to reconcile these two perspectives? Do you think reconciliation is possible?

3. What do you think about Process Theology? How might a conservative or a liberal Christian criticize Process thought?

Chapter 32: The Meaning of Modern Science

1. What is Einstein's theory of relativity? What is quantum theory? Why do the two not fit together?

2. Describe Einstein's beliefs about God and religious feeling. What part did these play in his scientific investigations?

3. You need at least five people for this exercise. Each person chooses to be one of: Einstein; Bultmann; Barth; Torrance; a conservative Christian. Your topic of conversation is 'God'.

Chapter 33: Miracles in a Scientific World

1. Do you think it is possible to have an event which is religiously true but not historically true? Why? Why not?

2. List Hume's arguments against the occurrence of miracles in order of strongest to weakest, explaining why you have given each its position.

3. If there are miracles, what is their purpose? Do you know of any modern-day events which have been seen as miraculous? If God does work miracles, how can we tell the genuine from the counterfeit?

Chapter 34: The Enlightenment

1. Do you think that reason should always reign supreme? If not, why not (consider faith and love for example)?

2. What makes a person moral? How far do you agree and disagree with Kantian ethics?

3. 'It is absolutely necessary to be convinced of God's existence; it is not equally necessary to demonstrate it.' What did Kant mean by this? Discuss the strengths and weaknesses of the statement.

Chapter 35: Language Games

1. Taking Wittgenstein's *Tractatus* as a guide, can one still talk of metaphysics and ontology? If so, why? If not, why not?

2. How would you explain the difference between logical positivism and Wittgenstein's Tractarian philosophy to someone who knew nothing of either?

3. The concept of the language game plays a major role within the philosophy of the *Philosophical Investigations*. How might this concept affect religious claims to truth?

Chapter 36: Pluralism

1. What in your view are the advantages and disadvantages of pluralism?

2. If you could choose, would you live at any other period of time other than the present day? What would be the reasons for this choice?

3. How might a committed Christian or Muslim respond to the pressure of pluralization? How would you go about creating a plausibility structure for religion in today's society?

Chapter 37: The Quest for the Transcendent

1. *The Times* reported that 83% of people interviewed believed in the paranormal. What is the percentage in your group? If a survey were done today, do you anticipate the figures would be as high or lower? Why?

2. Arrange a dialogue between a rationalist and an empiricist on the subject of whether the world of the paranormal exists.

3. What reasons and beliefs influence the Christian church in its response to the paranormal?

Chapter 38: The Devil and All His Works

1. How popular is belief in the devil today? How many people in your group hold the view that the devil actually exists? Are there others in the community who would agree with this? Find out and ask why these beliefs are held.

2. What are the main objections to belief in the devil? Which of these do you find most convincing and why? Which do you think are weak and why?

3. Dualism is the belief that there are two separate and equal forces (God and the devil) eternally in opposition to each other. What problems does this view present for Christians?

Chapter 39: The Problem of Evil and Suffering

1. Human suffering can cause some people to disbelieve in God. For others it is the occasion for faith in God. What factors might influence these different responses?

2. Why is the problem of evil a serious problem for Christian thought?

3. What non-religious responses to the problem of evil and suffering do you find most convincing and why?

Chapter 40: The Maleness of Reason

1. What do you think creates our concept of male and female – biology or culture? Discuss this as a group.

2. What religious factors have influenced how women are viewed in the history of the church? Choose one of these and criticize it from a feminist perspective.

3. If there was a Feminist government what do you think would change in our society? What would be the advantages and disadvantages?

Chapter 41: Patriarchy and Women

1. Is there evidence in your experience/community that male and female are both stereotyped to have certain roles and functions?

2. In this exercise you are asked to change positions. If you are a man, take the part of a woman and if you are a woman imagine for a moment that you are a man. In your new 'position' write a letter to the opposite sex setting out your views on Feminism. Read these out in the group and discuss the exercise. What was it like, taking another position? Did you learn anything about yourself?

3. Which women do you admire most? What are your reasons for this?

Chapter 42: Male and Female in the Bible

1. If God is feminine, what might the implications be for the Christian church, and for theology and belief?

2. What are the religious reasons for rejecting the view that God is feminine? Which of these is most convincing? Least convincing? Why?

Chapter 43: Moral Relativism

1. Does the end always justify the means?

2. Do your values and beliefs have cash value? Do they make a difference to how you live your life and solve your problems?

3. In answer to the question 'What is good?' what would a pragmatist answer? And what would a rationalist answer?

Chapter 44: Postmodernity

1. The Enlightenment sees scientific truth as more secure than religious truth. Can this be defended in the light of postmodern thought?

2. Can the analysis of the postmodern in this chapter, and the discussion of philosophy throughout this book, be sustained? Or does it face ultimate deconstruction too? Where does deconstruction stop? Should it?

3. What possibilities for life are there in the light of liberation to the postmodern moment heralded by Foucault? Is such a liberation itself an oppression which forbids other ways of living, believing and being?

Chapter 45: Fundamentalism

1. How can religions such as Islam, Christianity and Judaism maintain their own cohesion and sense of identity in the face of the opposing pulls of postmodern thought and fundamentalism?

2. How do you see yourself on the fundamentalism/postmodernity divide? Where are you most comfortable and why?

3. If both fundamentalism and postmodernism are rejected as ways of understanding and being in the world, what other possibilities for life are left?

Chapter 46: Shifting the Paradigm

1. What is a paradigm shift? What examples are there for this sort of change in social history? Do you think we are in the midst of a paradigm shift in the 1990s? Discuss this in your group.

2. Is change good? If you think it is, give three reasons. If you have mixed views describe your ambivalence.

3. What experience do you or your friends have of the New Age movement? Collect your knowledge together and identify what beliefs and assumptions underlie it.

Chapter 47: The Me-Cult

1. One of the major ways of being open to all experience is to advocate openness to many sexual encounters. What problems might this view present to religious people or to non-religious people?

2. Abraham Maslow established a 'hierarchy of human needs' which have to be met in order to be a self-actualized person. Apply Maslow's thinking to your group. If his views were taken seriously, how would your group change to accommodate them?

3. Is human nature good? Debate this in your group.

Chapter 48: Tomorrow's World

1. Do you think knowledge has progressed? How? How not?

2. As a group design a picture of what you think tomorrow's world will be like? What do you think will be the predominating ideas, beliefs and values?

3. What is the philosophy in your school or college?

Glossary

Anthropology: study of the nature of human being.

Aphorism: a short pithy saying expressing a general truth or maxim.

Apocalyptic: a type of literature concerned with the end of time.

a priori: a Latin phrase referring to thought or knowledge which is derived from a concept or principle independently of experience.

a posteriori: thought or knowledge based on experience.

Archetypes: universal symbols considered by Jung to be present in human consciousness, surfacing in religion, art and dreams.

Autonomy: the belief that human beings can be self-directing and independent.

Agnosticism: the belief that it is impossible to establish whether or not God exists.

Atheism: the belief that God does not exist.

Cartesian: referring to the philosophy of René Descartes (1596-1650). It is often associated with dualism and the separation of reality into *objective* and *subjective*.

Categorical imperative, the: Kant's universal law that one should do only what would be good if everyone did it.

Christology: the study of the person of Jesus.

Cultural-linguistic: an approach which sees religion and other human activities as best explained by a system of meaning with its own set of rules to be learnt. They in turn provide a way of living and being in the world.

Deconstruction: a method of describing and analysing reality which aims to show the arbitrariness, manipulation and biases in all forms of human organization and ways of understanding the world. Its aim is to open up the creative possibilities in understanding things.

Différance: This is a word Derrida created as a play on the meaning of the two French words 'différence' (the French word for difference) and 'differer' (the French word for defer). In doing this Derrida's 'différance' combines both meanings. So, différance, in pointing to the difference of things, calls for meaning to be held in perpetual question. By sharing the difference you always defer the meaning.

Dispensationalism: a theological movement which divided history into several epochs before and after the coming of Christ, and emphasized premillennial prophecy.

Deism: the idea that God created reality and then withdrew from further participation in it.

Determinism: the understanding of cause and effect in such a way that all historical events are inevitable, and there is no such thing as choice.

Dualism: any view which sees only two fundamental entities or types of entity, such as good/evil, mind/body.

Empiricism: the idea that nothing can be known without using the five human senses.

Enlightenment: eighteenth-century movement inspired by the physical sciences, often anti-religious.

Epistemology: the branch of *metaphysics* concerned with the nature and limits of human knowledge.

Eschatology: to do with the end of the world.

Feminism: a movement promoting the rights and dignity of women in society.

Existentialism: a philosophy concerned with the individual and the problems of human existence.

Fideism: the idea that faith in God is the central and irreducible basis of all philosophical and theological thinking.

Hermeneutics: the study of interpretation and meaning.

Humanism: a sixteenth-century movement which sought inspiration in the ancient civilizations of Greece and Rome. Also a nineteenth-century and modern movement which understands life without reference to God. Modern humanism seeks to promote respect for all human beings and confidence in the human ability to progress.

Infallibility: claim that the subject cannot be in error, applied by some Christians to the Bible, and by others to the Pope.

Materialism: the idea that reality is only physical, not spiritual.

Metaphysics: the search beyond the world of the senses to discover why the world is as it is.

Monism: the view that everything that is is part of a united whole.

Natural theology: the attempt to deduce the existence of God from the way the world is.

Objectivity: the belief that knowledge can be gained in a neutral way uncoloured by human wishes or interpretation.

Oedipus complex: Freud's idea that at a repressed level, from early childhood, boys are attracted to their mothers and see their fathers as sexual rivals.

Ontology: the study of the nature of being. The 'ontological argument' tries to prove the existence of God as the greatest conceivable being.

Pantheism: the belief that the universe is identical with God.

Paradigm: a framework of thought for understanding and explaining certain aspects of reality.

Platonism: the idea that ideal forms lie behind the physical reality which we can see.

Pluralism: the belief that no one system of values should have priority over another.

Postmodernism: the intellectual and philosophical side of Postmodernity (*see* Postmodernity).

Postmodernity: the cultural and social phenomena meaning that no global explanation of conduct or meaning is credible in an age in which rationality is so problematic.

Poststructuralism: a critique of the different ways we use language to give meanings by opening them up to question in a way which does not allow meaning to find any settled rootedness in reality.

Pragmatism: the principle that the value of one's actions should be based on their ability to achieve practical success.

Presupposition: any idea which we take for granted as true without questioning it.

Projection: psychological term meaning a fantasy in someone's mind which is applied to a person or object irrespective of what is really the case.

Psyche the Greek word for 'soul' – and also for 'butterfly'. Jung used this term to describe the psychological part of a human being.

Rationalism: the appeal to reason rather than experience as the source of all knowledge.

Reductionism: an approach which seeks to reduce complex structures to their simpler constituents in order to gain a more fundamental view of reality.

Reformation, the: sixteenth-century reaction against church failings led by Luther and Calvin which resulted in a split between Roman Catholic and Protestant church denominations.

Renaissance, the: fourteenth- and fifteenth-century rediscovery of classical culture leading to developments in the arts and sciences.

Scepticism: a view which doubts any claims to knowledge and certainty.

Sophists: professional Greek philosophers at the time of Plato.

Structuralism: an approach to the study of language and the social sciences seeking to uncover underlying structures and organizing principles within language and society.

Subjectivity: the idea that all knowledge and decisions can be based on personal opinions and beliefs.

Tautology: saying the same thing twice over in different words, for example 'she whispered in a quiet voice'.

Utilitarianism: the philosophy which aims for the greatest good of the greatest number of people.

Index

A

B

C

L

M

N

O

P

Discover the discipline that produces ideas

Life's Ultimate Questions

RONALD H. NASH

This introduction to philosophy gives you a breadth and depth of perspective unmatched by any other text of its kind. Reformed Theological Seminary professor Ronald H. Nash teaches the essentials of philosophy using three distinct approaches: topical, historical, and worldview/conceptual systems.

Part One of *Life's Ultimate Questions* begins by answering the question "What is a worldview?" and then explores the "six most influential worldviews in the history of thought": naturalism, and the worldviews of Plato, Aristotle, Plotinus, Augustine, and Aquinas. Part Two deals with important topics in philosophy, including the law of noncontradiction, possible worlds, epistemology, and the mind-body problem.

Hardcover: 0-310-22364-4

Find Life's Ultimate Questions
at your favorite Christian bookstore

ZondervanPublishingHouse
Grand Rapids, Michigan 49530
http://www.zondervan.com
A Division of HarperCollins*Publishers*

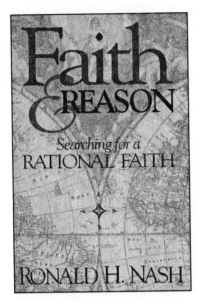

Defend your faith on the battlefield of ideas

Worldviews in Conflict

RONALD H. NASH

If you want to hold to your faith on the battlefield of competing ideas, you're going to need the right intellectual training. Make Ronald H. Nash, Professor of Philosophy and Theology at Reformed Theological Seminary, your instructor.

With the objective of teaching you to defend your mind as well as your heart, Nash outlines the Christian worldview—the way believers in Jesus Christ view God, themselves, and the world—and holds it up against the tests of reason, logic, and experience. Then he makes a case for its soundness by comparing it with worldviews like naturalism and the New Age movement. This gives you the training you need to know your beliefs and stand firm in them.

Softcover: 0-310-57771-3

More Counterpoints:

The **Counterpoints** series provides a forum for comparison and critique of different views—both Christian and non-Christian—on important theological issues.

Are Miraculous Gifts for Today?: Four Views
Wayne Grudem, General Editor
Softcover: 0-310-20155-1

Four Views on Hell
William V. Crockett, Clark Pinnock, and John F. Walvoord
Softcover: 0-310-21268-5

Five Views on Sanctification
Melvin E. Dieter, General Editor
Softcover: 0-310-21269-3

Five Views on Law and Gospel
Greg Bahnsen, General Editor
Softcover: 0-310-21271-5

Four Views on Salvation in a Pluralistic World
John Hick, Dennis L. Okholm, Timothy R. Phillips, and Clark Pinnock
Softcover: 0-310-21276-6

Three Views on the Rapture
Dr. Gleason Archer, Dr. Paul Feinberg, and Richard R. Reiter
Softcover: 0-310-21298-7

Four Views on the Book of Revelation
C. Marvin Pate, General Editor
Softcover: 0-310-21080-1

Three Views on the Millennium and Beyond
Darrell L. Bock, General Editor
Softcover: 0-310-20143-8

Three Views on Creation and Evolution
J. P. Moreland and John Mark Reynolds, General Editors
Softcover: 0-310-22017-3

Find Counterpoints *at your favorite Christian bookstore*

ZondervanPublishingHouse
Grand Rapids, Michigan 49530
http://www.zondervan.com

A Division of HarperCollins*Publishers*